IMPROVING THE ODDS FOR AMERICA'S CHILDREN

Improving the Odds for America's Children

Future Directions in Policy and Practice

KATHLEEN MCCARTNEY

HIROKAZU YOSHIKAWA

LAURIE B. FORCIER

Editors

Harvard Education Press

Cambridge, Massachusetts

Library of Congress Control Number 2013953416

Paperback ISBN 978-1-61250-689-0
Library Edition ISBN 978-1-61250-690-6

Published by Harvard Education Press,
an imprint of the Harvard Education Publishing Group

Harvard Education Press
8 Story Street
Cambridge, MA 02138

Cover Design: Ciano Design
Cover Photo: Steve Liss, courtesy of the Children's Defense Fund

The typefaces used in this book are Chapparal Pro for text and Franklin Gothic for display.

This book is dedicated to Marian Wright Edelman,
for inspiring us to use research as a tool
to advance practice, policy, and social justice
for all children in America.

Contents

Foreword

There are many reasons why I chose to serve in Congress forty years ago, with the Vietnam War winding down and the Watergate scandal coming to a close. None was more important to me, though, and, in my opinion, to our country, than the health and well-being of our children. That remains true today.

I learned from my father, a powerful state senator, and from observing national lawmakers like Hubert Humphrey, Ted Kennedy, George McGovern, and Walter Mondale that public policy can be a force for good in the lives of children, and I was determined to add to their great work.

Over the course of these last four decades, we can certainly point to real improvements in the lives of poor and middle-class children and their families, especially with regard to increased access to affordable, quality health care; the assertion of rights of *all* children, including children with disabilities, to a free public education; and a reduction in teen smoking, for example. But not one of us who cares about the well-being of all of our children can say we are satisfied.

To the contrary, we have hard work to do still to end hunger and poverty among children, to fulfill the promise of equal educational opportunity for all children, to better protect children from gun violence and sexual abuse, and to ensure that working parents who need quality child care can find and afford it.

Fighting for the rights of all children is a long-term challenge. It takes stamina. And it takes strong leadership. The greatest Speaker of the House of Representatives during my career, and perhaps in American history, Representative Nancy Pelosi, set a powerful example for all of us when, on receiving the gavel for the first time in January 2007, she invited children in the House chamber to join her on the rostrum. During her years as Speaker she could often be heard listing her top three priorities in Congress. "The children, the children, the children," she would say emphatically.

Our country needs to heed her simple yet compelling command.

When I arrived in Washington in January 1975, the alarm had already been rung over the plight of poor children in America. Marian Wright Edelman's Children's Defense Fund (CDF), not even two years old, was hard at work battling for official Washington's attention to the pressing priority of ensuring that all children—black, white, Hispanic, Native American, Asian, rich, and poor—had the opportunity to grow up healthy, safe, and well-educated, and to lead productive lives. Edelman and her talented staff had sounded the clarion call that in America it was, and remains, an unqualified disgrace for millions of children to live in poverty.

In 1974, CDF published its landmark report *Children Out of School in America,* documenting the enormous barriers our most vulnerable children face in attending school and persisting through to graduation. Congress responded by immediately passing several important pieces of legislation, such as the Education for All Handicapped Children Act, now known as IDEA. But many other problems identified then remain problems today. These are the issues that are so well discussed in the critically important volume that follows.

In 1983, together with several colleagues and in close consultation with CDF and other like-minded organizations and individuals, I convinced Speaker Thomas "Tip" O'Neill to found a committee in Congress devoted solely to children and their families. The Select Committee on Children, Youth, and Families, which I chaired for ten years, was formed in reaction to one of the greatest assaults on poor and middle-class families in America since the Great Depression: the election of President Ronald Reagan.

President Reagan and his allies in Congress and the private sector were determined to wipe out the social safety net that had been carefully constructed over the years by Franklin Delano Roosevelt and Lyndon Johnson. With his trademark slogan that "government is not the solution to our problem, government *is* the problem," he proceeded to dismantle services that were documented to have helped protect the poor and the once-great American middle class.

The Select Committee and its allies responded to the attack on the safety net with a new defense for public policies that benefit children and families. We held hearing after hearing in Washington and across the country and issued countless detailed reports. We documented how much taxpayers would save by investing in quality child care rather than cutting subsidies for it. Experts weighed in on the cognitive, social, and economic benefits of ensuring quality and comprehensive prenatal care. We made the case that neglecting children and families results in higher public costs for treating obesity; physical and psychological abuse; teen pregnancy; higher incarceration rates; alcohol, drug, and tobacco addiction; hunger; depression; and lost productivity. We enlisted an army of researchers, scientists, doctors, psychologists, psychiatrists, law enforcement officials, and social workers to show that America's failure to invest in its children was not only morally bankrupt but fiscally bankrupt as well. The evidence clearly demonstrated that it costs taxpayers more to ignore children and their families than it does to help them.

The result? On many issues from the 1970s through the early 2000s, we forged a bipartisan consensus, one that is sadly lacking today. We won bipartisan support to restore some of the Reagan-era cuts to the Women, Infants, and Children supplemental feeding program, for example, because we showed that it saved taxpayers three dollars for every one tax dollar invested. The Head Start early education program was similarly proven to save money in the long run, and it, too, won bipartisan support. The Elementary and Secondary Education Act, including Title I funding for low-income students and the requirement that schools ensure that all children, including subgroups of children, advance, was passed with bipartisan support, as was the Individuals with Disabilities Act. There was bipartisan support for a law to reform the decrepit foster care system and another to help reduce domestic violence. The Earned Income Tax Credit and the Child Tax Credit began with bipartisan support and have helped to keep millions of families out of poverty. Congress enacted or reauthorized many other policies during my time in Congress that have helped children directly or helped working families and the poor, some with bipartisan support and some, like the Affordable Care Act, enacted despite stiff opposition from the more radical brand of Republicanism that holds sway in Congress today.

Children's advocates always knew how hard the fight would be to challenge the most powerful and well-connected interests in our country: defense contractors, oil and gas corporations, and Wall Street firms. That was as true then as it is today, as we see repeated efforts in Congress in recent years to take resources away from poor and middle-class children and families, like food stamps and tax credits and education funding and access to affordable health care, and give even more to the wealthy and powerful. Bipartisanship has taken a severe beating in recent years, as has the willingness of Congress to enact or support policies driven by evidence-based research that help children and families and our country as a whole.

This imbalance of power in Washington directly contributed to a sharp rise in income inequality, which remains the greatest scourge that our nation still tolerates; it threatens our status as a world economic leader, as a leader in innovation, and as a model in democracy and decency, and it threatens the immediate and long-term health and well-being of our children. Left unchanged, the debilitating impacts of our skewed budget priorities will be felt for generations, as the middle class shrinks further, the ranks of the poor grow, and the concentration of wealth in the hands of the few swells ever larger.

We know too much about what works to let it be this way.

Every nation makes choices about its priorities. We have done much for our children over the past half-century. But despite the wins, there have been too many losses and missed opportunities. The well-being of our children is the foundation on which all else follows. We know so much more today about the developmental and educational needs of children, and it is our responsibility to ensure that our public policies reflect this knowledge.

We would be wise to heed the roadmap laid out in the following chapters that advances some of the best research and thinking to date on how to achieve the goals that Marian Wright Edelman, Speaker Pelosi, and so many others have spent decades fighting for: to ensure that all of America's children have the opportunity to be raised in a healthy, safe, and education-ally rewarding society and that taxpayers be protected by investing early in their lives.

—*Congressman George Miller*

Introduction

KATHLEEN McCARTNEY, HIROKAZO YOSHIKAWA,
AND LAURIE B. FORCIER

Forty years ago, in 1973, Marian Wright Edelman and her colleagues founded the Children's Defense Fund (CDF), embarking on a mission to ensure that every child, regardless of the circumstances of their birth, would have "a Healthy Start, a Head Start, a Fair Start, a Safe Start, and a Moral Start in life."[1] The opening lines of their first publication, *Children Out of School in America*, demonstrated compellingly that the millions of voiceless, voteless, vulnerable children in our country had a fearless new champion, one who would never shy away from speaking truth to power: "Americans think of themselves as a child-loving people. This is a myth. Idolizing youth is not the same as placing societal priority on ensuring that all children get enough food, clothing, health care, education and other services that will enable them to develop and function fully in American society. As a nation we have failed to provide every child a chance to a decent life."[2]

In this landmark report, the first of hundreds Edelman and her colleagues would go on to produce, CDF staff reported on their painstaking fieldwork on children not attending school—those who were being left behind. Their research revealed that an astonishing two million children comprised this group and identified demographic characteristics of these excluded American children—non-English-speaking children, children who experience early pregnancy, children from low-income backgrounds who could not afford transportation and other fees, ethnic-minority children suspended or expelled for "disruptive behavior," and, most importantly, and the largest group, children with disabilities. Following the release of *Children Out of School*, CDF staff acted. They built a bipartisan coalition comprised not just of members of Congress but of children and parent groups, teacher and educator groups, and doctor and lawyer groups, all of which were aligned in their support of the 1975 Education for All Handicapped Children Act. Once that historic legislation was passed, CDF acted again, working with states and communities to make sure the law, which ensures that all children with disabilities have the right to a free, appropriate public education in America, was implemented. Through the years, CDF has replicated this successful model—careful research, public education and dissemination, coalition building, policy development, and policy implementation support—many times over. In so doing, it has driven the enactment of laws and policies that have helped millions of children escape poverty and receive needed services, such as health care, nutrition, Head Start, Early Head Start, quality child care, education, family support, adoption and guardianship assistance, protections for children in the child welfare and juvenile justice systems, and protection from gun violence.

Concurrent with the launch of the Children's Defense Fund, the *Harvard Educational Review* (*HER*) published a two-volume special issue on the rights of children in the fall of 1973 and winter of 1974. The special issue included an opening statement by Senator Walter Mondale (D-MN), a wide-ranging interview with Marian Wright Edelman in which she laid out the top priorities of her new organization, and an article on children under the law written by CDF staff attorney Hillary Rodham. Edelman has described the *HER* special issue as a "crucial launch pad" for her new initiative and the Harvard Graduate School of Education as an important player in CDF's successes over the years. Now, with CDF entering its fifth decade of research and advocacy for children, it seems only fitting that a new volume, published by Harvard Education Press, usher in the next stage of CDF's important work.

Since its inception, the guiding philosophy of CDF has been that "children do not come in pieces"; children need comprehensive, integrated supports and services from birth through adulthood. With that in mind, and in consultation with Edelman, the editors of this volume have organized this book around seven policy issues in which the Children's Defense Fund has been particularly influential and that remain central to American child policy today:

- Prenatal and infant health and development
- Early childhood care and education

- School reform
- The achievement gap
- Vulnerable children
- Juvenile justice
- Child poverty

Importantly, we have not envisioned this as a retrospective of CDF's work, although we intend for this volume to be commemorative and celebratory. Instead, we asked each contributing author to produce short, forward-looking thought pieces, contextualized historically, that both diagnose current obstacles to progress and suggest key ideas for the next forty years. To ensure a full picture of each topic, we solicited two articles for each policy issue, one from a practice or policy-oriented perspective and a second from a research perspective. Practitioners, policy makers, and researchers alike wrote enthusiastic acceptance notes in response to our invitation, taking extra care to tell us about the importance of CDF and Marian Wright Edelman to their own work, using words like "inspirational," "personal hero," and "honored."

Echoing Mondale's forthright opening statement in *HER*'s special issue on children, Congressman George Miller (D-CA) has generously contributed a foreword to this volume. He started his career four decades ago, and so is in many ways a contemporary of CDF. As one of Congress's staunchest allies for children, Miller, as a member of the Select Committee on Children, Youth, and Families, has also been an important partner to Edelman and her team by helping to usher through numerous important pieces of legislation, including the Individuals with Disabilities Education Act, expansion of the Earned Income Tax Credit and the Child Tax Credit, and reauthorization of the Elementary and Secondary Education Act, including Title I funding.

The first part of *Improving the Odds for America's Children* looks at prenatal and infant health and development. CDF has produced more than a hundred reports and briefs, created award-winning insurance enrollment drives, organized stroller brigades, and even run a mock presidential campaign for a fictional child with no health insurance in their advocacy for affordable, quality health care from the earliest stages of life. Under CDF's watch, Congress has acted eight times to expand Medicaid eligibility for children and pregnant women; established the Children's Health Insurance Program (CHIP), the Children's Mental Health Services Program, and a child vaccination program; and most recently, in 2010, passed the Patient Protection and Affordable Care Act, which established the Maternal, Infant, and Early Childhood Home Visiting Program and will provide access to health insurance to 32 million previously uninsured Americans and 95 percent of all children. Millions of children and families have already benefited from the progress that has been made, but as Sara Rosenbaum and Partow Zomorrodian note, there is much work to be done, particularly for the approximately 20 percent of U.S. children who live in poverty. Childhood poverty, even after passage of the landmark Children's Health Insurance Program legislation, and at the threshold of implementation of the Affordable Care Act, still means limited health care access and poor health indicators in infancy, childhood, and adulthood. They argue that one key way forward would be to create a single pathway to public health care insurance for children, one that does not tie child health to the availability of parental workplace coverage or documentation status. In his companion chapter, Jack P. Shonkoff shifts the lens from federal policy to adult-infant relationships. Building on what is known from neuroscience, molecular biology, genomics, and epigenetics about early brain development and the negative impact that high levels of adversity (or toxic stress) can have on lifelong learning, behavior, and physical and mental health, he recommends innovative two-generational approaches to building the executive function and self-regulation skills of parents and early care and education providers, and thereby children.

The book's second part takes on the area of early childhood care and education, where CDF research, public advocacy, and work with congressional allies was critical to the creation of the 1990 Act for Better Child Care, which established the Child Care and Development Block Grant, one of the first major pieces of legislation to support low-income working families. CDF has also advocated tirelessly for the expansion of the federal Head Start and Early Head Start programs through mechanisms such as their Be Careful What You Cut campaign. However, the demand for services continues to far outstrip supply. In her chapter, Joan Lombardi notes that the United States ranks poorly on international indicators such as child well-being and investments in early learning despite compelling evidence of the importance of early childhood experiences to children's long-term health, behavior, and learning as well as economic stability. Tracing the historical evolution of U.S. early child care and education policy from the 1960s to the present, she notes a gradual yet still nascent move toward a continuum of coordinated services and education for young children. She suggests that one way forward would be to establish a new funding mechanism to support a developmental pathway (including parental leave, home visiting, quality child care, and Early Head Start for the most vulnerable) for young children from the prenatal period through age eight. Hirokazu Yoshikawa and Kathleen McCartney also make recommendations related to parental leave and quality child care in their research-focused companion chapter, but they do so against the backdrop of the burgeoning global early childhood research literature. Proposing sustainable development (the integration of economic development, social inclusion, and environmental sustainability that will be central to the post-2015 global goals) as an aligning framework, they explore innovative models from other nations and suggest ways in which preschool in the United States can contribute to important societal goals such as economic growth and reduced disparities.

The area of school reform is the focus of part three. Some of the earliest CDF research revealed the appalling lottery of geography facing students in preK–12 public education. Today, despite years of CDF research, advocacy, and lobbying, public schooling options remain grossly unequal by family income. For example, only eleven states and the District of Columbia mandate by statute that school districts provide full-day kindergarten. In her chapter, Deborah Jewell-Sherman, former superintendent of Richmond (VA) City Schools, reminds us that, at its very core, schooling is about the child and that it is the responsibility of those who teach in our schools to educate children well, regardless of their background. She suggests that we embrace three key ideas to reform American schools over the next forty years: a new vision for the meaning of schooling, teaching and learning of the whole child, and innovation as a gateway to public school redesign. In their companion chapter, Jal Mehta and Robert B. Schwartz also note that the current preK–12 system has fallen far short of the great expectations we have placed on it. They frame the problem as systemic—we use a nineteenth-century school system and expect it to produce twenty-first-century results—and propose two ways we might begin building a different kind of system. They suggest recalibrating and recasting the current "college for all" mentality to a more nuanced, multipathway paradigm which recognizes that all careers will require some form of postsecondary education, though not all will require four-year college degrees. And they propose building a teaching profession that is highly skilled and self-perpetuating.

Part four offers perspectives on the achievement gap. Over the years, CDF has put a spotlight on programs that close achievement gaps, create paths to postsecondary education, and produce successful, productive lives, particularly those designed for poor children. CDF's Cradle to Prison Pipeline campaign, first launched in the mid-1990s, focuses attention on one consequence of the United States' persistent achievement gap: currently, one in three twelve-year-old black boys and one in six twelve-year-old Latino boys will be sent to prison sometime in their life. Poor schools with limited resources, inexperienced teachers, and zero-tolerance discipline policies that push children out of school are among the pipeline feeder systems CDF has been working to change for decades. Jerry D. Weast, former superintendent of Montgomery County (MD) Public Schools, relates in his chapter his district's efforts to close the gap through a process of continuous improvement. He argues that there is no "Big Idea" that will eliminate the achievement gap and transform education. Instead, he argues for a series of foundational changes that can be undertaken by any district, regardless of size and setting. In their companion chapter, Greg J. Duncan and Richard J. Murnane document how growing income inequality and expenditure gaps over the past forty years have been accompanied by a steady divergence in the achievement and schooling attainment of children living in low- and high-income families. Their recommendations for closing the achievement gap include the possibility of evidence-based income transfer programs to alleviate the pressures of poverty on the most vulnerable; school supports designed to improve teachers' ability to provide effective instruction for their students; and well-designed accountability systems.

Vulnerable children are the focus of the fifth part of this volume. With CDF's support, Congress has passed more than a dozen important bipartisan laws to protect abused and neglected children and to promote positive child outcomes over the past forty years. CDF also built a national coalition to support the development of children in the child welfare system or at risk of entering foster care. The resulting protections include more than a dozen laws improving adoption procedures, educational continuity, and family permanence. An important component of CDF's work with vulnerable children has been strengthening families, the key recommendation of Michael S. Wald in his chapter. He first makes the provocative suggestion that the purview of Child Protection Services (CPS) should be reined in and restricted to protection from imminent harm alone. Then he outlines what a robust parenting support system might look like for parents with infants and young children who need such support. In her companion chapter, Jane Waldfogel also makes important recommendations for changes to child protection services, but she takes a different tack. Her key idea is an expanded role for CPS, in which their differential response function is greatly enhanced to better serve both low- and high-risk families.

Part six tackles juvenile justice, a system in need of urgent reform, as the CDF has argued for decades. CDF was instrumental in the passage of the 1974 Juvenile Justice and Delinquency Prevention Act, and in 1976 it produced the landmark report *Children in Adult Jails*, which exposed the abuse and neglect children face in the adult prison system. Despite great progress, including the creation of early intervention and prevention programs, the closure of dozens of juvenile detention centers, and the education of the American public on the capacity of children to change, every day in America ten thousand children are in adult jails or prisons. In his chapter, Robert G. Schwartz sees a bright spot on the horizon when he points to increasing public recognition that adolescent development is a unique time of experimentation and risk taking, that youth need room to make mistakes, and that a punitive justice system should not be used for minor, normative misbehavior. His key recommendations include diversion from the juvenile justice system or institutional placement, smoother reentry for those who do enter the system, reduction in the use of the criminal justice system, increased expungement of records, a retreat from sexting laws and other new status offenses, and a serious restructuring of sentences of youth convicted as adults. In his companion chapter, Laurence Steinberg recommends that future juvenile justice policies and practices be aligned with a scientifically based understanding of adolescent development, and he suggests three strands of research to attain this goal: first, the study of developmental differences between adolescents and adults that have implications for differential treatment under criminal law; second, the study of the impact of variations in juvenile justice policy and practice on outcomes other than recidivism; and third, a cost-benefit analysis of juvenile justice policy alternatives.

The book's seventh part takes on the overarching issue of child poverty. From food stamps to the Child Tax Credit, from child support enforcement to the Earned Income Tax Credit, from nutrition for women and children to summer feeding programs, CDF has worked tirelessly with its partners to help lift millions of children and families out of poverty. It has also produced more than a hundred reports exposing the debilitating effects of child poverty and how it severely impairs child health and education. One of these reports, *Wasting America's Future: The Children's Defense Fund Report on the Cost of Child Poverty*, was written by Arloc Sherman, a contributing author in this volume. Along with colleagues Robert Greenstein and Sharon Parrott, Sherman presents provocative new trend data on children living in poverty. They suggest that the best way to alleviate child poverty is through a combination of policies designed to support family income, specifically policies focused on subsidized jobs, job training, child care, and housing assistance. In his companion chapter, Eric Dearing presents two key ideas for advancing the relevance of research on children growing up poor. First, he argues that in order for future research on child poverty in America to be policy relevant, it will need to be generalizable to the large and growing immigrant population. Second, a promising and pressing priority is the development and evaluation of comprehensive multipronged interventions designed to interrupt or alleviate pathways of stress within children's homes, schools, and neighborhoods.

In closing, CDF president, Marian Wright Edelman, in her inimitable voice, offers her personal insights about the current state of affairs for America's children and the new work of the Children's Defense Fund as it embarks on its fifth decade. She lays out a six-pillar strategy focused on ensuring that all children grow into successful, productive adults, and she calls on each and every one of us to join the Children's Defense Fund in mounting "the transforming nonviolent social justice movement for children our nation desperately needs."

We hope this volume will provide an integrative road map for the next wave of child and family policy and catalyze action. In the forty years since the founding of the Children's Defense Fund, child advocates have increasingly used a cost-benefit frame to convince policy makers—at the local, state, and federal levels—to do the right thing. There is ample economic evidence that it pays to invest in young children, and Edelman has argued that "the issue is not are we going to pay—it's are we going to pay now, up front, or are we going to pay a whole lot more later on." Yet, she has also been steadfast in arguing for the need to invest in children from a social justice perspective: "Investing in [children] is not a national luxury or a national choice. It's a national necessity. If the foundation of your house is crumbling, you don't say you can't afford to fix it while you're building astronomically expensive fences to protect it from outside enemies." It is time to integrate the economic, developmental, and social justice arguments for investing in children. We know what to do and why to do it—now it's time to get busy.

PRENATAL AND INFANT
HEALTH AND DEVELOPMENT

CHAPTER 1

Health Care for Children

Forty Years of Health Policy

SARA ROSENBAUM AND PARTOW ZOMORRODIAN

Child Health: A Policy Context

The health of children is one of the seminal measures of the health of a society. In 1970, on the eve of the launch of the Children's Defense Fund, the death rate for children under age one stood at 2,142.4 deaths per 100,000 U.S. residents. By 2010, the infant death rate had declined to 623.4 deaths per 100,000 residents, a 70 percent decline.[1] The rate of decline in deaths among children ages 1–16 was equally dramatic.[2] These numbers underscore that on the most fundamental indicator of child health—survival—the nation has made enormous strides over the past forty years. These strides in great measure reflect the far-reaching improvements in access to health care that occurred over this time period as U.S. health care policy for children has been transformed. Advanced health care technologies, with the capacity to overcome even profound health challenges, have been made accessible through public policy reforms to the nation's most vulnerable families and children. These advances have in turn translated into life chances for infants and children who might have otherwise died.

Yet, by measures that may be less dramatic than mortality but are of central importance in measuring the health of children, child health in the United States continues to show disturbing trends. These trends are a reflection of not simply the greater survival of children who otherwise might have died but of the deeper root cause of childhood poverty. Despite our enormous wealth, the United States registers a childhood poverty rate well above that of other nations, more than double the rate of Germany and four times that of Finland.[3] In 2011, over 21 percent of U.S. children lived in poverty. Poverty is especially prevalent in the South, where in 2011 the childhood poverty rate exceeded 23 percent.[4]

The multiple underpinnings of America's child poverty crisis are covered in depth in chapter 13 by Sherman, Greenstein, and Parrott. In chapter 14 Dearing describes the health threats associated with childhood poverty that elevate the risk of poor health not only during childhood but also later in life. These health threats range from heightened exposure to external threats such as environmental hazards, alcohol, and drugs to a greater risk for illnesses such as AIDS, bacterial meningitis, and ear infections. Health problems associated with childhood poverty in turn become risk factors that threaten to impair social achievement and emotional health.

The consequences of childhood poverty show up in numerous measures of child health. Despite the drop in infant mortality, infant low birth weight, driven heavily by prematurity, remains significantly elevated. In 1970, 7.93 percent of children were born at a low birth weight, a condition that affects both the chances of survival and the presence of lifelong physical, mental, and developmental function. By 2010, the infant low birth weight percentage had increased to 8.15 percent.[5] Prematurity rates are especially elevated in the South, where childhood poverty is also at its highest rate.[6] Late entry into prenatal care and inadequate care, both of which are measures associated with prematurity and low birth weight, persist among women, particularly those with certain risk factors such as young age, low income, and low educational attainment.[7] Marked disparities in infant health by race and national origin persist. The low birth weight rate for black infants (who face a significantly higher risk of childhood poverty) remains far elevated above that for white infants, with rates for Hispanic infants variable depending on the country of family origin.[8] These elevated measures, among certain populations, have helped propel the United States' infant mortality rate to last place among thirteen Organisation of Economic Co-operation and Development (OECD) nations, including countries with population wealth well below that of the United States, such as Poland and Hungary.[9]

Indicators of poor child health extend beyond infancy. Compared to children of other nations, American children experienced diminished health status.[10] This is a cause of deep concern not only because of the impact of poor health on children's physical, mental, and cognitive development but also because poor health and traumatic stress in childhood are now understood to be precursors for the later overt presence of poor health among adults. This is true in particular for adult health issues such as cardiovascular disease, unintended pregnancies, alcoholism, and depression, which are believed to have roots in childhood.[11] As is the case with measures of infant health, the children most at risk for poor health are also most likely to face the social risk of poverty and its consequences. Low income is associated with a host of health problems among children. This association can be seen in the case of childhood asthma, attention deficit hyperactivity disorder, frequent ear infections, untreated dental caries, and childhood obesity.[12] Some 4 million children and adolescents experience one or more forms of mental disorders, with half of all cases of lifetime disorders beginning by age fourteen.[13] Low-income children experience a rate of mental illness double that of their higher-income counterparts.[14]

Just as poverty takes its toll on children's health, it carries important implications for access to health care, which in the United States depends heavily on the availability of adequate and affordable health insurance coverage. In 1984, 66.4 percent of all children eighteen years of age and younger received private health insurance through their parents' workplace coverage. Private health insurance through employment is associated with jobs that carry both higher wages and better benefits. By 2011, the proportion of children with workplace coverage had declined to 49.9 percent. Among children under age six, coverage declined from 62.1 percent in 1984 to 44.3 percent in 2011.[15] In 2012, nearly one in ten American children was completely uninsured.[16] The proportion of children without health insurance coverage remains far higher in certain states.[17]

Being uninsured is strongly associated with reduced access to health care among children. Other factors affect access to care as well, such as residence in impoverished communities. Uninsured children are far less likely to have a usual source of health care, and poor children are less likely to be fully immunized against preventable disease.[18]

Policy Reforms Achieved

Over the past four decades, reforms in child health policy have come in several distinct waves. The first wave addressed the health care needs of the nation's poorest children. The second wave focused on children living near the federal poverty level. The final and most recent wave, established under the Affordable Care Act (ACA), has been the establishment of a national system of health insurance that enables nearly all children to obtain afford-able health insurance coverage regardless of life circumstances. In each case, efforts to improve coverage of children were accompanied by incen-tives to extend coverage to parents as well. This is an indicator of the degree to which the health and well-being of children is closely aligned with that of their families.

The First Wave: Medicaid Reforms for the Poorest Children

Following a failed effort by the Carter administration to persuade Congress to extend Medicaid to pregnant women and children with family incomes up to a fixed percentage of the federal poverty level, the United States expe-rienced what at the time was the deepest recession since the Great Depres-sion.[19] The toll taken by the economic downturn of the early 1980s set the stage for what became the first of a series of bipartisan agreements among a Republican president (initially Ronald Reagan, then George H. W. Bush) and Republican and Democratic congressional leaders to transform Med-icaid coverage of children. These coverage reforms for pregnant women, infants, and children were achieved incrementally through a series of laws enacted between 1984 and 1990 that were made possible by two develop-ments of enormous political consequence: support for the expansion by political leaders opposed to abortion (in particular Illinois Republican con-gressman Henry Hyde) and support from the nation's governors (led by Richard Riley of South Carolina).

Although incremental in nature, by 1990 the Medicaid reforms led to two seminal transformations. The first development focused on eligibility for Medicaid coverage; the second addressed the issue of the quality and scope of coverage.

In the case of eligibility for coverage, the 1984–1990 period witnessed the expansion of mandatory Medicaid coverage of all low-income pregnant women as well as all low-income children born after September 30, 1983, and under age eighteen.[20] These reforms effectively severed Medicaid's historic family composition and income ties to cash welfare programs in the case of pregnant women and children, enabling these two populations to gain access to coverage on the basis of financial circumstances alone. These mandatory coverage reforms were accompanied by eligibility options extending beyond the mandatory minimums in order to open the program to children with near-poverty and moderate family incomes. Beginning in the mid-1980s and extending into the welfare reform era of the mid-1990s, other modifications were also enacted in order to effectively move the program away from its cash welfare assistance roots and into the status of a freestanding public health insurance program. These reforms consisted of extended Medicaid coverage for families leaving cash welfare assistance, state options to extend Medicaid to low-income working parents ineligible for cash welfare, automatic enrollment of newborns into Medicaid at the time of birth and without interruption of coverage during the first year of life, and a system of "outstationed" Medicaid enrollment that effectively repositioned the point of entry into Medicaid into community-based social and health care settings and outside of welfare offices. These reforms effectively presaged the broad eligibility reforms for low-income adults ages eighteen to sixty-four contained in the Patient Protection and Affordable Care Act of 2010.

In the case of the scope and quality of coverage, Congress revisited the Early and Periodic Screening, Diagnosis and Treatment (EPSDT) benefit, added as a required Medicaid benefit in 1967 as part of a major child health initiative undertaken by the Johnson administration. EPSDT was the product of studies documenting the health threats facing children in the nascent Head Start program as well as the seriously compromised health status of low-income military draftees. Unlike the original Medicaid coverage provisions enacted in 1965, EPSDT was intended to be preventive, to ensure that the health care system would take affirmative steps to identify and "ameliorate" health conditions affecting low-income children before long-term implications set in. Implemented over several presidential administrations in the face of state resistance over the affirmative terms of states' obligation to actually find and treat children, EPSDT was and remains unique in relation to other forms of public and private health insurance coverage.

The EPSDT benefit's original components consisted of periodic health exams, developmental assessments, treatment of vision, dental and hearing needs, and other treatments that states covered under their Medicaid plans. As implemented under federal rules, it gave states the option of providing diagnostic and treatment services for children at levels more generous than those available for adults. While some states did so, most did not.[21] This was the status quo until 1989.

In 1989, in response to widespread evidence of inadequate health care coverage for children with serious physical and mental health conditions, Congress included in the annual budget legislation a dramatic expansion of the EPSDT benefit. This expansion left in place all of the original EPSDT benefits and added two additional reforms. The first was "as needed" health exams to supplement the "periodic" screening schedules established by states in order to ensure that children could receive a full exam whenever health problems were suspected. The second reform was a new requirement directing states to cover all treatments falling within Medicaid's numerous classes of covered benefits that were medically necessary services to ameliorate physical and mental conditions in children under age twenty-one. This requirement applied regardless of whether such services were covered for adults under a state's Medicaid plan. In other words, the 1989 amendments overcame the state-imposed limitations on coverage (such as monthly or annual restrictions on mental health treatment or physical therapy) that apply to adults. To this day, the EPSDT benefit, as revised by Congress in 1989, represents a singular standard of pediatric coverage; it has never been replicated in either public or private health insurance.[22]

The Second Wave: The Children's Health Insurance Program

In 1997, Congress enacted the State Children's Health Insurance Program, renamed the Children's Health Insurance Program (CHIP in 2009. The goal of CHIP, whose benefit features were a harbinger of the ACA's coverage expansion strategy, was to incentivize states to further expand coverage for children by establishing an approach to coverage that eliminates Medicaid's entitlement structure and utilizes a narrower commercial market "benchmark" approach to benefit design that differs fundamentally from the highly defined and broad scope of coverage to which children are entitled under EPSDT. In effect, CHIP encouraged further state expansion by enabling states to move away from Medicaid's eligibility and coverage guarantees and toward an approach that ties children's coverage to commercial market norms while also potentially capping the number of additional children served, a form of flexibility barred under Medicaid.

Unlike Medicaid's legal entitlement to coverage, CHIP allocates a defined amount of funds to states to be used to extend "child health assistance" to "targeted low income" children. States have the choice to use their funds to either establish separate CHIP programs or expand Medicaid. Under CHIP, states are entitled to their defined allotment; eligible children, however, are not entitled to coverage. In states that elect to use their CHIP allotments to establish separate programs, coverage may be denied if the need exceeds budgeted funding levels, a phenomenon that has occurred over the years.[23] In separately administered programs, "child health assistance" purchased with CHIP typically takes the form of premium and cost-sharing subsidies designed to make private health insurance affordable for families. In short, where separately administered, CHIP functions as a form of premium support for commercial coverage, within far more relaxed federal coverage standards.

As noted, states have the option of using their CHIP funds to expand Medicaid, to establish entirely separate programs, or to create hybrids that combine Medicaid expansion with separate CHIP programs, such as expanding Medicaid to cover all children with family incomes under 150 percent of the federal poverty line and establishing separate premium support programs for children with family incomes between 150 percent and 250 percent of the federal poverty line. CHIP effectively has served to bridge Medicaid and private insurance, extending a defined amount of government assistance to support a market solution to coverage. Although the premium subsidies in the Affordable Care Act operate as an open-ended entitlement, the ACA's market reforms effectively use a restructured commercial insurance market to expand coverage to the uninsured.

CHIP is modest compared to Medicaid. In fiscal year 2012, 36.3 million children were enrolled in Medicaid, while 8.1 million children were enrolled in CHIP, a figure that represents all three approaches to CHIP coverage design.[24] The ACA reclassified all children under eighteen with family incomes under 133 percent of the federal poverty level as entitled to Medicaid, meaning that the children whose coverage is explicitly tied to CHIP financing has declined in relation to total Medicaid/CHIP enrollment.

The Final Step: The Patient Protection and Affordable Care Act

The Affordable Care Act is monumental legislation whose multiple legal reforms have fundamental implications for how the American health system operates, not only in terms of coverage but also in how health care is organized, delivered, and financed. The ACA achieves its goals through four principal reforms. First, it reforms private health insurance to guarantee access to coverage regardless of health status. Second, the ACA creates a Health Insurance Marketplace that offers coverage through qualified health plans as well as premium subsidies and cost-sharing assistance for low- and moderate-income individuals and families with incomes between 138 and 400 percent of the federal poverty line. (In states that opt out of the ACA's Medicaid expansion for adults, premium subsidies begin at 100 percent of poverty). Third, the ACA requires that all citizens and legal U.S. residents who can afford to do so secure health insurance coverage for their families and children. Fourth, the ACA extends Medicaid coverage to all adults ages eighteen to sixty-five with incomes below 138 percent of the federal poverty line, while also establishing the same mandatory 138 percent threshold for children under eighteen.

The ACA's reforms were intended to result in near-universal coverage. However, the 2012 decision by the U.S. Supreme Court in *NFIB v. Sebelius* effectively rendered the Medicaid adult expansion optional. By December 2013, twenty-five states and the District of Columbia had adopted the Medicaid adult expansion, with the remaining states opting out of the expansion, leaving millions of their poorest adults (with incomes below 100 percent of federal poverty) without coverage. The decision did not affect the reconfigured coverage rules for children under eighteen; but in the non-expansion states, not only are millions of adults (many of them parents of minor children whose low incomes nonetheless exceed their state's traditional Medicaid adult eligibility standard) left uncovered, but the loss of coverage confronts adolescents who reach age eighteen.

Obstacles to Progress

With the enactment of the Affordable Care Act, the nation has set itself on a course (although with a long and politically and practically challenging implementation period) of near-universal health insurance coverage, the basic prerequisite of access to health care. A number of challenges loom large, however.

Political Resistance to the Affordable Care Act

It is safe to say that in the history of social welfare change in the United States there has been no equal to the political resistance to the Affordable Care Act. The origins of this resistance are many: the fierce political battle that led to the ACA's enactment; the act's sheer complexity; and the fact that in the face of widespread political resistance by so many states, the act's success depends in large measure on a functional federal-state partnership over the regulation of insurance, the operation of the new Marketplace, and the alignment of new Marketplace coverage with the existing Medicaid and CHIP programs in order to ensure smooth transitions as family incomes fluctuate. As late as October 2013, when open enrollment began, public opinion polling continued to show that Americans remained unaware of the law and what it meant for them. If anything, the political fever that engulfed the ACA rose as a result of the administration's flawed roll-out of the law, although the successes registered by states that implemented the ACA on their own underscore its long-term potential. How implementation recovers from its rocky start is key in the short term. In the long term, the question remains whether the ACA will be able to take hold not just as a program but as the pathway to a new normal in American society in which nearly all people have access to affordable health insurance.

The Exclusion of Children and Adults Who Lack Legal U.S. Status

Despite its enormous advances, the ACA excludes children and adults who are neither U.S. citizens nor legally present in the United States. The number of unauthorized immigrants under eighteen has been estimated at 1 million, and over 4 million more children reside with an unauthorized parent or relative.[25] These children may not receive adequate health care because their caretakers fear sanctions and deportation.

The Problem of Broader Coverage and Better Access to High-Quality Health Care

Access to insurance coverage is the essential first step in reforming the health care system, but it is only the first step. The real work lies in ensuring that broader access to health care financing translates into the right care in the right place at the right time, regardless of whether the issue is timely preventive immunizations for infants and toddlers or high-quality community-based health care for children with serious physical or mental conditions and disabilities, who will require ongoing care coupled with enhanced educational and social services.

The ACA offers incentives for reforming health care itself and improving its integration with other educational and social services that are vital to promoting the health of children. The act establishes new options for both public and private health insurers to test innovations such as health homes and using payment reforms tied to measurable quality improvement. The act also continues efforts begun under the American Recovery and Reinvestment Act to encourage health care providers to invest in and make "meaningful use" of health information technology systems that can put better information into the hands of health care providers and enable communication across systems of care. In addition, the act invests in the expansion of community health centers offering primary health care in medically underserved urban and rural communities in order to promote more timely access to primary health care.

The ACA preserves Medicaid's expansive EPSDT benefit for the poorest children while setting important plan performance standards for children whose coverage is secured through qualified health plans sold in the new Marketplace. All such plans, as well as all plans sold to individuals and small groups outside of the Marketplace, will be required to cover preventive benefits without cost sharing. In the case of children, the Obama administration has defined the scope of preventive coverage to include comprehensive health and developmental exams for children as a routine matter. How health plans use this new coverage to leverage stronger performance among pediatric health plan network providers remains to be seen.

At the same time, important limitations continue under the act. Children in families whose incomes fluctuate may experience breaks in coverage as even slight shifts in income can cause families to move back and forth between Medicaid and Exchange subsidies. The act does not guarantee a minimum annual enrollment period, nor does it require that all health plans and their provider networks participate in both the Medicaid and Exchange Marketplace in order to minimize disruption in care and plan membership. Furthermore, beyond an expansive definition of preventive pediatric care, Health and Human Services secretary Kathleen Sebelius has not used her authority under the act to establish a standard of coverage for children under qualified health plans that is as broad, within covered classes of benefits, as that available to the poorest children through EPSDT. This lack of aggressive federal effort to ensure a broad scope of coverage significantly limits the degree to which plans will be incentivized to develop innovative care systems for children with high medical needs, since so much of what they need may well be excluded from coverage policies to begin with.

Finally, in the modern world of networked health insurance coverage—insurance plans that tie coverage to the receipt of care through a provider network—the potential exists for inadequate access to care for children who reside in medically underserved communities. The problem of medical underservice, resulting from the overall shortage of pediatric specialists in the United States, affects millions of children and intensifies an already serious situation facing children with special needs, regardless of place of residence or family residence.[26] Early anecdotal evidence suggests that health insurers offering qualified health plans through the Health Insurance Marketplace (known formally in the legislation itself as "Exchanges") may place strict limits on the size of their provider networks in an effort to hold down use of care as a basic cost-control measure.[27]

Drawing Stronger Links Between Health Care and Investments in Community Health

Certainly health care makes a profound difference in the health of children. But depressed measures of child health in the United States stem from the health risks that children face. Addressing these risks means combining health care interventions with other strategies for alleviating the social conditions—especially poverty and its consequences—that threaten children's well being. Effective interventions to improve the health of children stretch well beyond health care. They necessitate a reengineering of the educational and social services and supports available to American families that can better equip families to function effectively in a changing global marketplace. The poorest of today's younger American families are simply not able to avoid the health risks that confront their children. Furthermore, it is extremely difficult to form healthy families absent adequate educational opportunities, jobs with good wages, appropriate housing, community supports, and other interventions essential to a healthy society. The ACA is the most important breakthrough in the U.S. social welfare system in decades, and while it can revolutionize health care, it cannot singlehandedly produce healthy children.

Three Ideas for the Next Forty Years

Creating a Single Health Insurance Pathway for Children

The ACA sets the stage for the near-universal coverage of children. However, the act excludes unauthorized residents, to the health detriment of a million children and millions more parents. Furthermore, by preserving a fragmented approach to coverage, the act increases the risk of coverage disruptions as family incomes and living arrangements change over time. Since modern forms of insurance coverage are intimately bound up with care itself, and with the advent of insurance plans that operate by means of provider networks, the potential for a break in coverage that might also lead to discontinuity of care becomes that much more likely.

With the discussion of continuation funding for CHIP set for debate in 2015, the question arises as to whether, in the case of children, the fractured approach to coverage might not be replaced with one that simply enrolls all children in Marketplace coverage in the absence of employer-sponsored plans. This approach would effectively eliminate the pediatric component of Medicaid as well as CHIP, replacing both with a universal, single pathway to public health insurance coverage for children that could operate on a continuous basis, thereby reducing the potential for cross-market churn.

Beyond the question of whether to merge CHIP funding into the premium subsidy system available through the Health Insurance Marketplace lies the question of whether children's coverage should be more completely rationalized through the creation of a single, unified system of health care financing that covers children from birth through adulthood (with an outer limit age of twenty-two) and that enables all families to simply enroll their children one time and maintain continuous coverage regardless of changes in family circumstances. This approach to pediatric financing would effectively merge Medicaid, CHIP, and premium subsidies with a modest employer contribution into a single national pool that would underwrite pediatric health plans that offer comprehensive coverage to all children regardless of family characteristics, place of residence, or other factors unrelated to the need for health care. In this regard, the issue for children in the next forty years is identical to the one that faced the federal government at the time of the creation of Medicare: how to ensure stable and continuous coverage that transcends matters of place and wealth.

Reaching such a point does not compel creation of a government-administered program. The government's role in such a model would be to act as the financial sponsor of coverage, collecting employer and family contributions and adding public financing to the pool to enable its reach across the entire child population. The plans in which families enroll their children could, like CHIP plans, be administered by private insurers on a national basis, permitting all families access to benefits for their children on a direct basis. This approach would also overcome the steady erosion over the past forty years in employer-sponsored coverage of dependents. With a single-point-of-entry system of coverage for children and the elimination of the need to move among sources of health care financing as family circumstances change, this type of approach could stabilize the threshold question of financing while shifting the focus to quality improvement and broader integration of health care into other systems crucial to child health, in particular, the establishment of clear relationships between health care services and education reforms.

Enriching the Scope and Level of Health Insurance Coverage for Children

In imagining what a unified approach to child health financing might look like, the question becomes what coverage principles should guide such a reform. As noted, the ACA actually authorized the Health and Human Services secretary to establish comprehensive standards of pediatric coverage akin to the breadth of coverage and high cost-sharing protections found in EPSDT. But this authority has not been exercised, and, as a result, the enormous breakthrough in health care financing established by the EPSDT benefit has never been replicated. Indeed, both CHIP and the ACA's essential health benefit coverage standard applicable to qualified health plans move away from this model by permitting significant limitations on the scope and depth of coverage and the use of considerable cost-sharing requirements for children whose health needs go beyond the merely preventive. The EPSDT benefit offers a framework for a pediatric coverage plan that addresses physical, mental, and developmental conditions from the broadest possible plane. What is needed is a definition of pediatric coverage that is free of the arbitrary treatment limits and high cost-sharing that will continue to characterize coverage for adults despite the ACA's wide-ranging insurance reforms.

A Broader and Richer Vision of Quality Health Care and a Workforce Trained to Meet the Challenge

A bolder approach to pediatric health care financing could be coupled with an expansion of investments into the creation of new primary care access points in medically underserved communities, expanded investment in pediatric residency and health professions training programs, and investment in an expanded effort to develop quality standards that focus on the developmental needs of children, including children with special health care needs. Existing quality standards for pediatric care tend to focus on indicators that are vital to measuring the quality of primary health care but fail to capture system performance for children with serious and chronic physical and mental health conditions. Furthermore, measures of quality tend to focus on the technical proficiency of clinical care, rather than the responsiveness of the health care system to the larger world in which children live.

Developing mechanisms to measure quality is particularly important for children with special health care needs. Although relatively small in number, these children represent some of the most complex cases in health care. The quality of clinical treatment and management techniques and interventions is vital, but equally vital is understanding how effectively the health care system addresses the health needs that flow from the types of risks that far too many children experience today. Developing this type of measurement capability is of enormous importance not only for child health but as a matter of long-term health as well. In this regard, performance measures need to be expanded and retooled in order to measure how well health care systems respond to health problems that emerge in the real-world settings in which children are found. The question of whether a health plan serving children is able to effectively respond to the health effects of learning disabilities uncovered through school is as important as measuring how well the plan performs when the issue is a heart problem present at birth.

Testing the quality of health care where children are concerned requires measurements that move outside the immediacy of the clinical care setting and consider the efficiency and quality of care in addressing health problems uncovered through school, child care, and simply living in community environments that create elevated health risks.

CHAPTER 2

A Healthy Start Before and After Birth

Applying the Biology of Adversity to Build the Capabilities of Caregivers

JACK P. SHONKOFF

Historical Perspective

Extensive research in child development over the past forty years tells us that the foundations of learning and behavior are influenced by the environment of relationships in which young children live. Over the past two decades, this fundamental concept has been enriched by converging evidence from neuroscience, molecular biology, genomics, and epigenetics that is advancing our understanding of how early experiences are literally built into our bodies and how early influences not only affect the evolving architecture of the maturing brain but also have other physiological impacts that can influence a lifetime of physical and mental health. The implications of this growing knowledge base for policy making, program development, and child rearing are compelling and clear. The early childhood years represent a time of both remarkable potential and considerable vulnerability. As such, there is an urgent need to strengthen the capabilities of parents and other caregivers to be able to provide safe, stable, and health-promoting environments beginning prenatally and continuing throughout the infant and toddler period.

Above and beyond the insights provided by basic research in child development and its underlying neurobiology, half a century of program evaluation research has generated extensive data to support the conclusion that we have the ability to produce favorable impacts on a range of long-term outcomes for young children who face the burdens of significant economic and social disadvantage.[1] One prominent example of a program for young children living in poverty was the Abecedarian Project, a 1970s center-based program that delivered year-round, full-time services to young children from early infancy until age five.[2] Staff members were highly trained; child care settings featured high adult–child ratios; and the structured curriculum emphasized language, cognitive, social, and emotional development. A small, randomized controlled trial reported numerous positive impacts in academic performance and behavior from infancy through adulthood.[3] According to economic evaluations, the benefits of the program outstripped the costs.[4]

Building on the Abecedarian model, the Infant Health and Development Program (IHDP) was implemented in the 1980s to provide comprehensive services (including pediatric care, home visiting, and center-based child care) for children through age three who had been born prematurely with low birth weight in order to bolster their physical, cognitive, and socioemotional development. A large national, multisite, randomized controlled trial found that infants in the intervention group demonstrated gains in IQ and vocabulary and fewer behavioral problems, although the benefits decreased over time and the short-term gains were smaller and not sustained in children with the lowest birth weights.[5]

When viewed through a historical lens, these and other flagship demonstration projects provide an important "proof of concept" for the potential benefits of early childhood intervention for vulnerable infants and toddlers. However, their value as evidence for the effectiveness of current services is limited, in part because there has been no significant replication or scaling-up of these program models with sufficient fidelity or comparably trained staff. Moreover, the relatively modest magnitude of the original program effects, particularly for IHDP, underscores the need for more work to be done.

Finally, it is important to acknowledge forty years of dramatic reductions in infant mortality in the United States—from 26.0 deaths per 1,000 live births in 1960 to 6.2 per 1,000 in 2010—while highlighting the significant challenges that remain.[6] For example, notwithstanding important gains, the pace of progress in the United States has been slower than that of other industrialized nations. Moreover, the rate of newborns with low birth weight has continued to increase, and disparities linked to race/ethnicity remain prominent for both mortality and low birth weight. Increasing evidence points to the importance of looking beyond the medical care system and focusing greater attention on broader economic and social influences on lifelong health, such as the proximal environments in which children are born and raised and where their parents "live, learn, work, and play."[7]

Progress in Research

Although the basic concepts from developmental psychology that inform early childhood programs have stood up well over the past four decades, recent advances in the biological sciences offer an unprecedented opportunity to stimulate fresh thinking by illuminating some of the underlying causal mechanisms that explain differences in the developmental trajectories of young children. In order to explain these key scientific concepts to a general audience, extensive and growing evidence from neuroscience, molecular biology, genomics, and epigenetics has been synthesized and translated into a "core story" of development by the National Scientific Council on the Developing Child.[8] Accepted research findings include the following:

- The architecture of the developing brain is constructed through an ongoing process that begins before birth and continues into adulthood.
- Genes provide the basic blueprint for development but environmental influences affect how neural circuits are built in a bottom-up sequence.
- Ongoing reciprocal interactions among genetic predispositions and early experiences affect developmental trajectories.
- Cognitive, emotional, and social capacities are inextricably intertwined.
- Significant adversity can disrupt neural circuits and other maturing biological systems in ways that undermine lifelong learning, behavior, and physical and mental health.
- Brain plasticity (or flexibility) and the ability to change behavior decrease over time.

Extensive scientific evidence about the interaction between genes and environment clearly illuminates why adult-infant relationships are so crucial to healthy development. Stated simply, genes determine when specific brain circuits are created, and experiences shape how they are formed. This developmental process depends on appropriate sensory input (e.g., through hearing and vision) and responsive engagement to build the sturdy circuitry that constitutes healthy brain architecture. Young children naturally reach out for interaction—through such behaviors as babbling, facial expressions, and words—and adults respond with responsive vocalizing, gesturing, and short sentences. This serve-and-return process continues back and forth, like a game of tennis or volleyball. These interactions begin in the family but often also involve other adults who play important roles in young children's lives.[9]

When a supportive and responsive environment facilitates well-being during the infant–toddler period, it builds a strong foundation for all the development and health that follow. However, beginning during pregnancy and continuing throughout the early years, significant adversity can produce deleterious effects on brain architecture and function that are associated with later difficulties in stress responsiveness, learning, and behavior as well as with alterations in physical health and accelerated aging. Put simply, the brain is the body's primary control center. As such, it influences both physiological and behavioral responses to threat as well as the development of coping skills in the face of adversity.[10]

When we are threatened, multiple stress systems are activated for a fight or flight response, which stimulates increases in blood pressure, heart rate, blood sugar, inflammatory chemicals, and stress hormones that are essential for survival. When a young child's stress response is activated within an environment of supportive relationships, adults help him or her develop adaptive coping skills that promote the development of healthy stress management capacities and bring these physiological elevations back to baseline levels. However, if the stress response is strong, frequent, or long lasting, and buffering relationships with adults are unavailable, toxic stress can result, and these persistent physiological activations can lead to disruptions in brain architecture and other biological systems that have lifelong repercussions.[11] Examples of such disruptions include persistent elevations of cortisol that can affect developing circuits in the prefrontal cortex of the brain and increased inflammation that can accelerate atherosclerosis.

Science tells us that the healthy development of children begins with the health of their mothers before they become pregnant, and that the active ingredient of environmental influence after birth is the impact of children's relationships with the important people in their lives. When interactions within the family are burdened by adversity associated with any combination of economic hardship, limited parent education, and/or discrimination associated with minority group status, the levels of daily stress experienced by all family members are typically quite high. When stress response systems are overactivated early in life, they are programmed to adapt to an environment that is expected to remain adverse. As a result, the threshold for activation is lower, and the hair-trigger nature of the stress response often results in greater risk for aggressive behavior in childhood as well as stress-related chronic illnesses decades later, such as hypertension, coronary heart disease, diabetes, and stroke. That is why the capacity to protect or buffer young children from the physiological disruptions of toxic stress is essential in conditions characterized by significant adversity.

Obstacles to Progress

Despite dramatic scientific advances in our understanding of how early experiences get built into the body and how adversity produces biological disruptions that can literally reshape brain architecture and influence a lifetime of development and health, public awareness of this knowledge is still incomplete. The extent to which many policy makers and civic leaders do not yet fully understand the significance of this rapidly growing knowledge base is compounded by a political culture that views the prenatal period and infant–toddler years as domains of exclusive personal or family responsibility rather than an opportunity for strategic, public investment that would benefit all of society.

Perhaps the most significant consequence of this dominant individual responsibility frame for the early childhood years is the failure to understand (or resistance to believe) the widespread benefits that could be achieved by science-based actions that strengthen the capabilities of families and communities to enhance the current well-being and future life prospects of vulnerable, young children. That absence of a broad-based belief in the possibilities of significant beneficial impact has been a major contributor to the persistent gap between what we know (from science) and what we do in our policies and practices. The disproportionate support for investment in preK for four-year-olds versus targeted interventions for infants experiencing significant adversity is a striking example of policy failing to heed the powerful message from neuroscience about critical/sensitive periods, toxic stress, and decreasing brain plasticity over time. Significant limitations on maternity or paternity leave policies, with particular concern about the lack of paid leave for low-income families, reflect failure to take seriously the overwhelming evidence of the critical importance of parent-infant attachment and the growing economic evidence that poverty in early childhood is more detrimental to child development than poverty at older ages. Inadequate public oversight of the safety and quality of child care settings is yet another obstacle to knowledge-based public policy. President Obama's call in his 2013 State of the Union address for a historic federal investment in the early care and education of infants and young children, including universal preschool education, represents an important step forward. Increasing numbers of governors and state legislative leaders who are supporting expanded investments in an array of early childhood initiatives illustrate additional examples of shifting public concern about the foundational years of human capital development in a changing economic environment.

Finally, it is essential that we confront those members of the early childhood policy and practice community who claim that we know exactly how to eliminate disparities in educational achievement and health outcomes—and that all we need is the money to do it. Without minimizing the positive effects of many evidence-based interventions, even the best don't fully reverse the consequences of poverty and social exclusion, and the most disadvantaged young children are typically not reached at all by conventional services. Within that context, the current revolution in biology suggests that children who experience toxic stress may benefit less from early childhood programs because of disruptions in their developing brain circuitry that undermine their ability to reap what the programs have to offer. The design and testing of new, science-informed interventions that reduce or mitigate the biological impairments associated with toxic stress must therefore be a compelling priority for early childhood policy and practice.

Key Ideas for the Next Forty Years: Improving Child Outcomes Through Greater Attention to the Capabilities and Needs of Their Caregivers

When significant adversity in the lives of young children overwhelms the capacity of early childhood service providers to respond effectively, the positive impacts of an otherwise effective intervention will be limited. In such circumstances, the biology of adversity supports the hypothesis that the magnitude and sustainability of program impacts on the most vulnerable could be increased by balancing the provision of enriched learning opportunities with increased investment in strategies to provide greater protective buffering from the biological consequences of toxic stress.[12] This proposition points toward a critical need for innovative approaches to strengthen the capacity of both parents and early childhood program staff to reduce sources of excessive adversity as well as to build effective coping skills in young children who experience high levels of stress.

Central to the task of addressing this challenge is the need for enhanced theories of change that draw on advances in both the biological and behavioral sciences, build on current best practices, and catalyze creative thinking. To this end, research on the biology of adversity has led developmentalists to formulate more robust theories of change to launch a new era in two-generation programs for children and families experiencing the burdens of significant economic and social disadvantage. With that goal in mind, a unified framework grounded in a common, interdisciplinary science that extends from conception to adulthood could help us move beyond the simple co-location or coordination of child-focused and adult-focused services and begin to address the transactional impacts of risk and protective factors on the developmental trajectories of both children and the adults who care for them.

Mobilizing science to drive successful innovation requires a highly disciplined commitment to the development of precise strategies that target specific causal mechanisms to produce breakthrough gains on key outcomes. With that goal in mind, a core of caregiver and community capacities are emerging as highly promising domains of influence on the development of young children that are amenable to change through focused intervention.[13] Three components of a potentially integrated model stand out as particularly ripe for fresh thinking.

Building the Executive Function and Self-Regulation Skills of Parents and Providers of Early Care and Education

The full spectrum of these evolving competencies includes the ability to focus and sustain attention, set goals and make plans, follow rules, solve problems, monitor actions, shift course, defer gratification, and control impulses. These skills enable adults across the socioeconomic spectrum to care for themselves and their children, run households, seek and maintain jobs, and achieve financial and social stability. Executive function skills are built over time within the context of close relationships with individuals who have well-developed abilities in these areas. However, for those adults who grew up without access to such models—or who experienced childhood adversities such as maltreatment, parental mental health problems or substance abuse, chronic violence at home or in the community, or deep poverty—the poor development of these skills makes it more likely that their households will be chaotic and their responsiveness inconsistent. The location of the neural circuitry for these capacities in the prefrontal cortex (which remains relatively malleable well into young adulthood) provides a promising focus for the design of a new, fully integrated model of intervention for vulnerable children and their parents as well as a basis for informing the content of professional development programs for early childhood personnel in community-based programs.

Strengthening Caregiver Mental Health

Beyond the need for well-developed skills in planning, monitoring, and self-regulation, successful parenting and effective staff performance in an early childhood program cannot be separated from the importance of adult mental health. For example, maternal difficulties with depression and/or anxiety are correlated with a range of poor outcomes in the cognitive, behavioral, and psychological development of their children.[14] Recent studies that have found high rates of depression among personnel in early care and education programs are equally worrisome.[15] These findings underscore the importance of greater attention to the needs of mothers and early childhood program staff whose unaddressed mental health problems can undermine the well-being of the young children who rely on their daily care.

Enhancing Family Economic Stability

Beyond the importance of parenting skills, there is extensive research about the extent to which economic security plays a significant role in an adult's capacity to provide the kind of stable, consistent, and stimulating environment in which a young child will thrive. Parents with limited education who are burdened by the stresses of poverty are more likely to experience a mind-set of chronic crisis that triggers poor self-regulatory behavior and diminished impulse control in contrast to the more future-oriented perspective associated with educational achievement and economic security that promotes the "luxury" of reflective planning and delayed gratification. There is also growing evidence that family poverty is particularly threatening to healthy development in the early childhood years.[16] A potential explanation for this finding is that parents who have a stable source of income are better able to provide sound nutrition, higher-quality child care, and a plethora of material benefits that enhance their children's early learning and are better able to promote engagement in growth-promoting interactions on a more consistent and predictable basis.

These foundational domains—the executive functioning, self-regulation skills, and mental health of adult caregivers and the economic stability of the family unit in which young children live—present a promising focus for fresh thinking in the quest for more effective interventions to reduce intergenerational disadvantage. To this end, the following three hypotheses are worthy of future exploration.[17]

Hypothesis 1: Protecting children from the impacts of toxic stress requires capacity building, not simply the provision of information and support, for the adults who care for them. Improving the life prospects of young children who experience significant adversity depends on the availability of adults who can help them develop effective coping skills that bring their overly activated stress response systems back to baseline. Caregivers who are able to provide that buffering protection must themselves have sound mental health and well-developed skills in problem solving, planning, monitoring, impulse control, and self-regulation. Poor executive functioning and high levels of depression in low-income mothers who experienced significant adversity in their own childhoods make these domains critically important targets for focused intervention.[18] Staff members in early care and education programs who had disadvantaged childhoods that contributed to their own limited education and low income are also constrained in their ability to promote these critical skills in young children. Given the magnitude of these burdens on adult caregivers, it is reasonable to speculate that simply providing parents with information and advice about child development is not sufficient—and that this may explain why the impacts of such interventions are typically modest, particularly for those families who are the most disadvantaged. Evidence that these skills can be strengthened through focused coaching, training, and practice underscores the compelling need to design and test new intervention approaches for both parents and early childhood staff whose underdeveloped capabilities are not being addressed sufficiently by existing programs.[19] The fact that elite athletes rely on coaching and practice to strengthen exceptional skills offers a nonstigmatizing frame for implementing these strategies with vulnerable adults.

Hypothesis 2: Interventions that improve the caregiving environment by strengthening executive function skills and promoting mental health in vulnerable parents will also enhance their employability, thereby providing a synergistic strategy for augmenting child outcomes by strengthening the economic and social stability of the family. The disconnection between services focused on the developmental needs of vulnerable young children and programs focused on remedial education, workforce preparation, financial literacy, and asset building for adults living in poverty has been the subject of criticism for decades. Although most complaints have focused largely on turf battles and the inefficiencies of fragmented service delivery, advances in the developmental sciences now offer a compelling new strategy for reducing the intergenerational transmission of poverty through a truly integrated focus on a core set of adult capabilities that are essential for success in both the home and the workplace. These competencies can be strengthened through focused training during any stage of development, from infancy through young adulthood.[20] Moreover, without minimizing the importance of sensitive periods in early brain development, the extended plasticity of the prefrontal cortex provides a strong rationale for targeted skill building for both parents and service providers.[21] The extent to which these skills are foundational to both parenting and economic self-sufficiency provides an exciting new opportunity to advance an integrated approach to child and family services based on substantive content rather than improved communication.

Hypothesis 3: Community-based initiatives and broad-based systems approaches are likely to be more effective in promoting the healthy development of children if they focus explicitly on strengthening neighborhood-level resources and capacities that can prevent, reduce, or mitigate the adverse impacts of toxic stress on families. Decades of place-based initiatives designed to address a variety of social and economic challenges have been fueled by broad concepts such as building social capital, strengthening self-efficacy, and eliminating structural inequities.[22] Advances in the developmental sciences now offer an opportunity to augment impacts on school readiness and lifelong health by directing community-level efforts toward the reduction of specific sources of toxic stress in young children. Examples could include targeted efforts to increase access to effective treatment for maternal depression and expand the availability of safe places for parents to congregate and build social capital.[23]

Concluding Thoughts

The science of learning and the biology of adversity tell us that healthy development requires the availability of responsive adults to provide young children with growth-promoting experiences and support in facilitating their mastery of the adaptive capacities needed to manage stress. Stated simply, child well-being unfolds within an environment of relationships that promotes competence and builds resilience.

This science suggests that significantly greater impacts on the life prospects of vulnerable young children could be achieved by strengthening the capabilities of the adults who care for them, rather than focusing primarily on the provision of parenting advice for mothers and enriched learning experiences from others. Extensive evidence also indicates that improving the economic stability of families living in poverty is likely to have an added positive effect on the healthy development of their young children. In short, if we want to augment the ability of policies and programs to transform the lives of vulnerable infants and toddlers, we have to figure out how to transform the lives of their adult caregivers.

The implications of this proposition for the way we think about two-generation approaches to poverty alleviation are potentially game changing. It compels us to think beyond the simple co-location or coordination of separate child-focused and adult-focused programs. It recognizes the importance of engaging parents and program staff in activities that focus on building skills, not just transmitting information. It requires the motivation and ability to see beyond the traditional rallying cry to break down the walls that separate deeply entrenched silos and to build the foundation needed to support a new unified structure for intergenerational policy and practice that rests on a common science base. Breakthrough impacts for vulnerable young children are more likely to be achieved by two-generation programs that focus on strengthening the common foundational capabilities needed by any parent to create a supportive and stimulating home environment, succeed in a job that provides economic stability, and function as a contributing member of a healthy community.

Dramatic advances in science are waiting to be used to catalyze the design and testing of new ideas. Incremental progress is important, but the need for breakthrough impacts is compelling. Full funding for what we know how to do should not be the goal. Current best practices must be viewed as a starting point, not a destination.

EARLY CHILDHOOD CARE
AND EDUCATION

CHAPTER 3

A Great Beginning

Ensuring Early Opportunities for America's Young Children

JOAN LOMBARDI

In 2014, some 4 million babies will be born in the United States, on average approximately 11,000 babies a day.[1] This group of children, the high school graduating class of 2032, will be the most diverse group ever, adding to the richness of the country. There are almost 20 million children under the age of five in the United States, making up more than a quarter of the population of children under eighteen.[2] While many children are flourishing, more and more of our youngest children are growing up without access to the kind of early opportunities that promote healthy development and contribute to the economic strength of a country. The time to address this growing inequality is long overdue.

This chapter calls for a new and unprecedented set of investments in young children, an early learning challenge for the nation. Building on past efforts, new research, and growing momentum and interest in the early years of childhood, it calls for partnerships among federal, state, and local communities and between public and private entities to provide a new pathway of early opportunities for children, particularly those most vulnerable from the prenatal period through age eight.

Young Children in the United States: From Inequality to Opportunity

Despite all the potential that children bring into the world the day they are born, there is inequality from the start. In the United States, almost half of the young children grow up in low-income families; one child out of every four lives in families below the federal poverty threshold.[3] While the majority of children live with two parents, more than a quarter live with a single parent.[4] The United States ranks twenty-sixth among twenty-nine of the world's advanced economies on measures of child well-being (see figure 3.1).[5]

The income gap in academic achievement starts early. An analysis of data from the Early Childhood Longitudinal Study Birth Cohort found that disparities in child outcomes are evident at nine months and grow larger by twenty-four months. These disparities between infants and toddlers from low-income families and their more affluent peers exist across cognitive, social, behavioral, and health outcomes.[6] Young prekindergarten children living in poverty are much less likely to have cognitive and early literacy readiness skills than are children living above the poverty threshold.[7] The achievement gap continues into the elementary grades and beyond.

When reviewing a dozen large national studies conducted between 1960 and 2010, Sean Reardon found that the rich-poor gap in test scores is about 40 percent larger now than it was thirty years ago. At the same time, the rich now outperform the middle class by as much as the middle class outperform the poor.[8]

When it comes to investments in early childhood, we are facing a paradox. There is growing interest in the early years and mounting evidence of the importance of early childhood experiences to long-term health, behavior, and learning. Yet, at the same time, investments in many states remain stagnant and federal budget cuts undermine the very children who could benefit the most. The United States spends less on preprimary education than the average spent by OECD countries.[9]

Public policies affecting young children and families seem stuck in a time warp. While there is much talk about modernizing the nation's ailing infrastructure, its bridges and roads, there has been much less attention paid to modernizing our human infrastructure to respond to the needs of families in the twenty-first century.

The United States is at a turning point. To be competitive in a global economy, our businesses need employees who are well prepared. Twenty-first-century jobs demand teamwork, technology, and communication skills. The United States needs a labor force of problem solvers; it needs workers who are creative, persistent, and have critical thinking skills. The foundation for these skills begins in the early years. We need a bold new

FIGURE 3.1   A comparative overview of child well-being in rich countries

		Overall well-being	Dimension 1	Dimension 2	Dimension 3	Dimension 4	Dimension 5
		Average rank (all 5 divisions)	Material well-being (rank)	Health and safety (rank)	Education (rank)	Behaviors and risks (rank)	Housing and environment (rank)
1	Netherlands	2.4	1	5	1	1	4
2	Norway	4.6	3	7	6	4	3
3	Iceland	5.0	4	1	10	3	7
4	Finland	5.4	2	3	4	12	6
5	Sweden	6.2	5	2	11	5	8
6	Germany	9.0	11	12	3	6	13
7	Luxembourg	9.2	6	4	22	9	5
8	Switzerland	9.6	9	11	16	11	1
9	Belgium	11.1	13	13	2	14	14
10	Ireland	11.6	17	15	17	7	2
11	Denmark	11.8	12	23	7	2	15
12	Slovenia	12.0	8	6	5	21	20
13	France	12.8	10	10	15	13	16
14	Czech Republic	15.2	16	8	12	22	18
15	Portugal	15.6	21	14	18	8	17
16	United Kingdom	15.8	14	16	24	15	10
17	Canada	16.6	15	27	14	16	11
18	Austria	17.0	7	26	23	17	12
19	Spain	17.6	24	9	26	20	9
20	Hungary	18.4	18	20	8	24	22
21	Poland	18.8	22	18	9	29	26
22	Italy	19.2	23	17	25	10	21
23	Estonia	20.8	19	22	13	26	24
24	Slovakia	20.8	25	21	21	18	19
25	Greece	23.4	20	19	28	25	25
26	United States	24.8	26	25	27	23	23
27	Lithuania	25.2	27	24	19	29	27
28	Latvia	26.4	28	28	20	29	29
29	Romania	28.6	29	29	29	27	29

plan to ensure that all children across the country have access to enriched early opportunities. It is only in recent years that hope for change has appeared on the horizon.

Early Childhood Policies, 1965–2013: The Evolution of a Revolution

When Head Start emerged in 1965, it was a revolutionary idea: an integrated program to address the health, education, and family support needs of the most vulnerable children in America. Although federal and state early childhood policies have evolved over the years to include child care, home visiting, Early Head Start, early intervention, and state-funded preschool, taken together they still fall far short of meeting the needs of young children and families.

Multiple Tracks, Cyclical Funding: 1965–1990

The history of early childhood policies in the United States has been characterized by a split between care and education and cycles of investments followed by years of flat funding or budget cuts. Programs grew on different tracks. Some were seen as benefiting the child, others as benefiting working families; some were designed for the very poor, others were more universal.[10]

Before 1965, services for young children were mainly delivered in private nursery schools. Head Start emerged in response to both poverty and as a way to "equalize" education. In the late 1970s, research studies such as the *Lasting Effects of Preschool* documented the medium-term benefits of early childhood programs.[11] By the mid 1980s these early research findings encouraged some states to invest in state prekindergarten programs.

At the same time, on a separate track, the role of child care for working parents was debated. While the 1971 Comprehensive Child Development Act would have brought these separate pieces closer together, President Richard Nixon's veto of it shattered the opportunity to build a more unified system of early childhood development for years to come.[12] It was not until twenty years later that the Child Care and Development Block Grant (CCDBG), one of the first major pieces of legislation to support low-income working families, was enacted. Unfortunately, despite the word *development* in its name, the educational and developmental needs of children were not a priority. Funds set aside for quality were limited and standards were very minimal, continuing the split between care and education.

Science, Systems, and the States: 1990–2008

As the 1980s came to a close, early childhood gained new momentum as President George H. W. Bush and the nation's governors announced the National Education Goals.[13] The first goal—that by 2000 all children in America would be ready to learn—was supported by both political parties, putting early childhood on the agenda as a serious education issue. State preK programs, particularly for four-year-olds, continued to grow.

By the mid 1990s, interest in the emerging science of early brain development gained popular attention, with increased media coverage and the first White House Conference on Early Childhood. During the Clinton administration, this interest led to the establishment of Early Head Start for pregnant women and children under age three. However, lack of resources remained a serious issue. The percentage of eligible children served by Early Head Start remained in the single digits. And while child care funding increased as a part of welfare reform in 1996, the entitlement to child care was lost and quality remained strained.

As we approached the end of the decade and moved into the twenty-first century, two trends emerged: a movement to create a more coordinated system across early childhood programs and a new focus on continuity throughout the early years. The George W. Bush administration encouraged states to develop standards and professional development plans across programs. The Maternal and Child Health Bureau provided grants to states to create early childhood systems. Similarly, a group of private foundations launched the BUILD Initiative to help states develop a more systemic approach to early childhood. And the 2007 Head Start Act encouraged the coordination and establishment of Early Childhood State Advisory Councils in every state.

While this movement to coordinate across programs was taking place, private foundations invested in a range of age 0–8 activities to promote a continuum of services. While some focused on ages 0–5, others focused on expanding preK or promoting better alignment from preK to grade 3.

Early Childhood and the Life Course: 2008-2013

It was against this backdrop of early childhood system reform, growing interest in the science of early childhood, and an emerging life-course approach that Barack Obama became president. From the early days of his administration, a strong commitment to early childhood emerged. In 2009, the inclusion of $5 billion for early childhood as part of the American Recovery and Reinvestment Act provided much-needed resources after almost a decade of flat funding.[14] These funds helped expand Early Head Start, make critical quality improvements in child care and Head Start, and provide needed resources for early intervention. They also sent an important message: providing resources for early childhood is an essential investment in the economy of a nation. Unfortunately, much of this funding was not sustained into later years.

Building on earlier collaborative action in some of the states, important new steps were taken at the federal level to promote better coordination across agencies and to move toward more continuity across ages 0–8. For the first time, a high-level position on early childhood development was established in the U.S. Department of Health and Human Services, with a formal link to other agencies, including the U.S. Department of Education. Also for the first time, a senior adviser on Early Learning to the secretary of education was appointed and an Interagency Policy Board was launched between the two departments.[15]

But progress in early childhood policy went beyond structure. As part of the Affordable Care Act, in 2010 the new evidence-based Maternal, Infant and Early Childhood Home Visiting Program created a nationwide system of home visiting in high-risk communities across the country. Just one year later the Early Learning Challenge provided incentive grants to states to promote systems reform with a goal of ensuring that low-income children receive high-quality services. The initial rounds of funding provided one-time grants to fourteen states.[16]

In January 2013, President Obama announced a historic early childhood plan that built on the progress made during his first term. The proposal called for a $75 billion investment in State Preschool and a $15 billion investment in home visiting over the next ten years, both to be paid for with a $.94 per pack federal tax on cigarettes. In addition, the proposed fiscal year 2014 budget included an increase of $1.4 billion for Early Head Start/Child Care Partnerships and additional resources for Head Start and CCDBG with a focus on quality.[17]

Something was changing. With federal and state leadership, a new focus on the science of early childhood development, and new champions from the private sector, early childhood issues began to move to the top of the domestic agenda.

A Great Beginning: Creating a Pathway to Success Prenatal–8

A new framework is emerging that calls for increased investments and more alignment in policies focused on children as they grow and develop. Research is documenting the fact that a single year of preschool alone is not enough. In order to avoid fade-out and to continue the gains, high-quality supports throughout the early years are needed, particular for at-risk children. More than seventy-five years ago, the United States made a solemn commitment to ensure that older Americans were provided some level of protection and support, lifting millions out of poverty and providing for core services. The next generation deserves the same investment to provide an equal start for all children.

Policies should align to support a developmental pathway for young children from the prenatal period through age 8. Parents of children under three should have more and better options: paid leave, home visiting, quality child care, and Early Head Start for the most vulnerable. When children turn three, they should have access to two years of quality preschool delivered by a network of providers, with comprehensive services for the most vulnerable. As children enter school, they should be greeted by redesigned primary grades with specially trained teachers, enriched curriculums, engaged families, full-day services, and partnerships with community-based organizations. The success of this proposal will be judged not only by the number of children served but also by improved health, learning, and behavioral outcomes for children at birth and at ages 3, 5 ,and 8. Communities should come together to track outcomes, build networks of supports for parents and other caregivers, and promote voluntary action in support of families with young children.

Providing Better Options for Families with Children Ages 0-3

Parents of very young children in the United States need time, family support, and quality child care, yet they face very limited options at a time when their children are at their most vulnerable.

Prenatal care. The health and well-being of both mother and child begins with a healthy pregnancy and delivery. The health of the mother before pregnancy and the extent and quality of prenatal care during pregnancy are important factors in healthy child development. Pregnant women who receive no prenatal care, or whose care begins only in the last trimester of pregnancy, are more likely to have babies with health problems. The United States needs to step up efforts to ensure that all women have quality prenatal care from the first trimester, that the full range of needed services are covered, and that special outreach efforts are made to reach women in low-income communities. In addition, evidence-based teen pregnancy prevention programs should be expanded.

Paid parental leave. All industrialized countries *except* the United States provide paid leave during the period surrounding childbirth.[18] While the Family and Medical Leave Act provides twelve weeks of unpaid leave, only slightly more than half of all employees are eligible.[19] We can do much better than this for newborn children. The United States should move to expand Family and Medical Leave by ensuring all parents at least six months of paid leave for mothers or fathers on the birth or adoption of a child.

Over the years, a number of options have been put forward to finance paid parental and medical leave: building on Social Security, establishing a family leave insurance fund, increasing general revenue or general revenue in combination with a payroll tax, or providing incentives for state action to provide paid leave. Public funding is critical to ensure access to low-income parents and to diffuse costs for small business owners. Although federal policy would be the preferred option, states should move forward to create paid leave policies, expanding on efforts that have been developed in states such as California and New Jersey.

Parenting support. In several countries around the world, a home visit by a nurse or paraprofessional is offered to all families with newborns, especially first-time parents. Yet this important service is often out of the reach of even the most vulnerable American families. According to a survey of state home visiting programs, in 2010 no state had either sufficient funding or infrastructure to reach all of its highest-risk families.[20] Despite new federal and state resources, serious gaps remain.

As the debate around federal early childhood policy continues to move forward, an increasing focus should be put on supporting the emotional well-being of parents in light of what we know about the impact of mental health on the early development of children. When children are born, all families should be offered a minimum number of visits to provide initial support and to screen for further needs. While low-income families could perhaps benefit the most from home visiting, families across the economic spectrum have children with special needs or face maternal depression and need additional services. Those families at risk should receive more intensive evidence-based home visiting services and social networks of support through the expansion of the Maternal, Infant and Early Childhood Home Visiting Program. In this way, the United States would have a universal platform for early screening as well as offer more intensive services for those most in need.

Quality infant toddler care. Few issues are more daunting for parents than finding quality affordable care for their babies and toddlers. According to the latest report from the U.S. Census Bureau, child care costs overall have gone up over the past twenty-six years.[21] The Child Care and Development Fund (CCDF), the largest source of child care assistance for low-income working families, still reaches only about one in six eligible children.[22] The United States needs an aggressive plan to build the quality and supply of infant toddler care across the country.

Of the estimated 1.6 million children served by CCDF, nearly a third of the children are under age three.[23] Low reimbursement rates, high co-payments, and an inadequate supply of quality affordable care plague the system. The Child Care and Development Fund should be redesigned to give priority to the provision of quality care for families with infants and toddlers. Resources should be expanded to ensure that all families with incomes below the state median income are provided access to quality care, and new efforts should be launched to attract and retain a qualified workforce.

Rather than relying primarily on vouchers, the funding should include a better balance of grants made directly to programs to build the number of quality options as well as portable assistance to families. Infant and toddler programs could be "chartered," or certified to become a preferred provider that meets quality standards and be eligible to receive additional funding. Each state would have to take steps to establish standards, ones modeled after Early Head Start. Quality improvement grants would be provided to child care programs as well as to community-based organizations that network and support family child care providers and reach out to family, friends, and neighbor care. The focus would be on education, health, family support, and continuity of care.

A younger Head Start. Since its inception in 1965, Head Start has established deep roots in communities and provided services for some of the most vulnerable children in the country. Recent efforts by the Obama administration have begun to improve quality and eliminate those agencies that are not performing to standards. The road ahead for Head Start leads in two directions: younger children and expanded partnerships. First, as universal access to preschool becomes more a reality, federal Head Start funds should serve more pregnant women and young children through age three; thus, the "new" Head Start is an earlier Head Start.

A new set of partnerships should be established to encourage quality Head Start agencies to become hubs of comprehensive services for children ages 0–5 in low-income neighborhoods. While Head Start programs could continue to serve preschool children directly through various funding streams, additional federal funds could be provided to promote Head Start partnerships with local preschools and community-based child care providers serving children in poverty to ensure comprehensive services in a range of early leaning settings. At the same time, Head Start should continue to work closely with child welfare agencies and organizations serving homeless children and immigrant families. In this way, Head Start would build on one of its greatest assets: serving as a trusted ombudsman and voice for the poorest and most vulnerable young children in the country.

Ensuring Universal Access to Preschool

According to *the State of Preschool 2012* report from the National Institute of Early Education Research, only 41 percent of four-year-olds and 14 percent of three-year-olds are served in publicly funded preschool programs, including Head Start, state-funded prekindergarten, and special education.[24] At the same time, cuts in funding in recent years have caused enrollment to stagnate and have threatened programs' quality. This is the wrong direction. All children in the United States should have access to high-quality preschool for at least two years before they enter school.

Funding and a diverse delivery system. Given that the growth in preschool funding has stalled over the past few years, federal funding should be provided throughout the next decade as an incentive to states to encourage additional investments. Over time, however, funding for preschool may become part of the education funding in states and communities, with federal funds focused on ensuring quality comprehensive services for the poorest. However, keeping with the tradition in early childhood, resources should be provided to a diverse delivery system, with funding to a network of providers in the community, including child care, Head Start, and schools. Integrating preschool funding into community-based child care settings is one way to ensure both quality standards and supports for working families.

Ensuring quality. The promise of preschool can be met only if we provide high-quality services. If we look at the research from successful preschool programs—from Boston to Oklahoma to New Jersey—we see highly qualified teachers, mentoring, and specially designed curricula.[25] Coaching and mentoring for teachers should be intensive and frequent enough to promote improvements in classroom practice, positive relationships between children and teachers, and supportive instructional environments. Moreover, many early childhood programs have long traditions of engaging families and respecting the language and culture of the home. As the population of young children becomes more diverse, and preschool becomes more widespread, we need to ensure that these core elements, including family support, remain a central part of quality, comprehensive services.

Reforming Education from the Bottom Up: Developing a New Vision for K–3

More than twenty-five years ago, the National Association of State Boards of Education commissioned the Task Force on Early Childhood Education. The task force heard concerns about increased testing of young children, large kindergarten classrooms, high teacher turnover in early childhood programs, and other issues that we hear echoed today. Their landmark report, *Right from the Start,* provided a vision for more focused and developmentally appropriate attention around early childhood and schools.[26]

Calling for the establishment of Early Childhood Units in elementary schools, the report recommended new pedagogy and focused work for enhanced services for children and families, including curriculum reform, programs that involve parents and respond to comprehensive needs of children and families, and programs that draw on the resources and expertise across the community. Given the importance of continuity of service, it is time to dust off the idea of creating early childhood units in schools; these units could be specially designed to improve the quality of programs for children in the early grades and reignite closer partnerships with the community. Rather than aligning down from school to preschool, the goal would be to reform from the bottom up, bringing some of the principles from the 0–5 community into the primary grades and encouraging a more developmental and holistic perspective.

Curriculum reform and retraining. In recent years, preK–3 initiatives have emerged across the country, helping lead the way to better alignment between preschool and public schools. However, there is often more attention to the development of preK than K–3 reform. We need a new national dialogue about how best to meet the developmental needs of children in the primary grades and new resources to better prepare teachers to work with diverse students and engage families. For example, while social emotional development has become an integral part of early learning standards across the country, only a few states, like Illinois, have social emotional learning integrated into their standards for older children.[27] In addition, new efforts are needed to enrich the curriculum of the primary grades, integrating science, technology, civic education, and the arts into the teaching of basic math and literacy skills.

Community-school connections. Working parents want full-day/year-round programs, and, at the same time, they also want to make sure that their children have access to the traditional community-based activities so important to a well-rounded education. It is not enough to expand the school day without reconfiguring the type of services provided. To move forward and support partnerships between community-based providers and schools, funding for the federal 21st Century Community Learning Centers should be at least doubled and investments in community schools should be a priority of education reform.

Furthermore, schools serving a high percentage of low-income children need incentives to better integrate comprehensive services into their delivery system, creating new relationships with health, mental health, child welfare, and child support agencies, among others. In order to make this happen, federal, state, and local agencies must be better aligned.

Bringing It All Together in Communities

This proposal to establish a pathway of services prenatal through age eight calls for the funding of a network of early learning programs and improved K–3. Success will depend on how these services are aligned in communities. The very climate of a community can have an impact on child development. From coast to coast, from Palm Beach County, Florida, to Alameda County, California, communities are coming together to develop a continuum of care, to provide prenatal care, to ensure developmental screening, to track child development, and to build a system of support for families and other caregivers.

Building caring communities. In the years ahead, it will be important to "connect the dots" so that community system efforts feed into state efforts and that these, in turn, help inform federal policy. Community-wide early childhood councils or child and family councils are important for planning, data collection, and coordination and can help ensure connections across programs. Several community planning initiatives have emerged as part of statewide efforts (such as Smart Start in North Carolina or First Things First in Arizona); others have emerged as part of a national initiative, such as Promise Neighborhoods; and still others are single community efforts emerging through local leadership. Federal and state funds should promote such community-wide system efforts across services for children ages 0–8.

Of course, the heart of the community remains in those volunteers who come together on behalf of children and families: the elderly, the faith-based communities, civic and service organizations. Creating more formal structures is meant to build on these longstanding traditions and values, not supplant them.

Supporting adults in children's lives. Young children learn through relationships with caring adults. While we build a pathway of community services for children ages 0–8, we have to take special steps to ensure that we are promoting a two-generation approach.[28] The ability to parent depends on many factors, among them mental health and past experiences, social supports, family economic stability, and an understanding of how children develop. At the same time, the work environment of teachers affects their ability to effectively interact with young children. Appropriate working conditions such as time to plan, sufficient materials, and adequate compensation impact the ability to recruit and retain staff as well as the quality of services. Historically, education has not recognized this full array of needs.

As part of supporting parents, every community could develop a Family Resource Network that connects family service agencies and provides more accessible and efficient information and support for parents across the community. Such a network could include agencies that provide home visiting; disability services; social networks of supports for families; child care resources and referrals; outreach to family, friend, and neighbor care; and linkages with supports needed by families, including postsecondary education, referrals for health care, housing, and employment services, and asset development and financial assistance. Such a network should have a focal point that is more than a telephone line. It should have some central location in the neighborhood that parents can identify with and a network of family advocates that can help parents access supports; it should also provide more intensive intervention in times of special need.

Yet, just as parents are supported, there needs to be a hub of support for the teachers and providers who care for young children in the community. Early Learning Alliances could be developed to bring providers together and support the early childhood workforce across programs. Such an infrastructure could employ mentors, provide a bank of substitutes, work with higher education institutions, provide scholarships and wage supplements, and improve the overall working conditions of teachers and caregivers of young children. This vision brings together several initiatives that have emerged across the country, including shared services sites, local quality-improvement and referral efforts, workforce registries, and other initiatives to support those adults who work with children.

A Great Beginning for Young Children, a Great Future for America

The time to increase investments in our youngest and most vulnerable children is long overdue. In order to fund new initiatives, we need to establish a new funding mechanism: An American Family Trust for Future Growth, a partnership among federal, state, and local governments with incentives for private-sector involvement. Financing could include a combination of taxes on consumer goods that adversely affect public health at the federal and state levels, an expansion of state and local education funding formulas to include early childhood services, the use of health funds for preventive early child development services, and incentives for public-private partnerships and other innovations. While the mechanisms and size of such a fund needs further discussion, the vision the fund would support is the establishment of a pathway for young children throughout the early years of life.

At the same time, we need to balance public and personal responsibility. Such a partnership would call on parents—fathers as well as mothers—to focus on their children above all else. We have to maintain high expectations for parents while we support efforts to help them stay engaged in the lives of their children creating strong and lasting bonds. This new partnership should encourage parents to talk and listen to their children, provide them healthy food, monitor and limit screen time, and set a good example for them every day.

The wealth of a nation can be measured by the success of its children. The United States has the potential to move a bold new agenda forward—to revolutionize education, to support its families right from the start, to ensure that all children are healthy and successful, and to become a stronger country. This is a long-term investment we need to start now.

CHAPTER 4

A Future for Preschool in the United States

Integrating Innovations from Global Perspectives

HIROKAZU YOSHIKAWA AND KATHLEEN McCARTNEY

Preschool education in the United States has a rich history, building on nineteenth-century efforts such as settlement house and kindergarten movements and twentieth-century policies such as the establishment of Head Start as part of national poverty reduction policy (see chapter 3 for a historical overview). The advent of Head Start as a preschool education program enriched by health, nutrition, and family support services was a groundbreaking precursor for integrated, multisector early childhood programs worldwide, including the Integrated Child Development Services (ICDS) program in India and many others.

The innovations in early childhood development (ECD) in the United States in the twentieth century were influenced by evidence suggesting the particular sensitivity of human development to environmental enrichment in the first years of life. The past two decades have seen a further explosion in our knowledge of the importance of ECD for societal development. The neurological, biological, psychological, developmental, and economic sciences have converged on the importance of the first years for lifelong health, learning, and behavior. Rigorous evaluations have shown that high-quality preschool education has achieved important life-course effects, with evidence of cost-effectiveness in both small- and at-scale programs, and across high-, middle-, and low-income countries.[1] Never before has it been so clear that quality early childhood development programs and policies have a critical role to play in the economic and social progress of nations.[2]

This chapter draws lessons from the global research literature to propose future directions for preschool education policies in the United States.

Building on the impressive accumulated evidence base on the importance of early childhood development, we consider the potential for the United States to learn from and adopt effective preschool practices that have been tested and proven elsewhere. In addition, we examine how advances in preschool education in the United States might align with important global goals of sustainable development. The 2012 Rio+20 summit and accompanying UN General Assembly resolution defined sustainable development as the integration of economic development, social inclusion, and environmental sustainability.[3] Sustainable development represents a more universal vision, integrating while also extending the more targeted focus on extreme poverty reduction put forward in the Millennium Development Goals.[4] The rationale for this integration, simply put, is that the world is on a dangerous and unsustainable course, and the urgency of this expansion is dictated by the rapidity with which the world's nations are falling short on economic development (slow rates of poverty reduction and rising income inequality), social inclusion (as measured by the extent of social marginalization and armed conflict), and progress in environmental sustainability. In the United States, we believe that alignment with these three areas of sustainable development goals would further strengthen the contribution of preschool to societal goals of economic growth and reduced disparities.

Preschool Education as Economic Development

The promise of early childhood education for economic development drove the founding of the Head Start program. Looking back, we can see the naïveté in President Johnson's promise that Head Start would single-handedly break the intergenerational cycle of poverty. Yet, evidence suggests that high-quality preschool education can indeed produce important life-course benefits, such as increased high school completion rates, earnings, and reduced teen pregnancy and crime.[5] These long-term benefits can occur despite short-term fade-out, or convergence of achievement test scores between children who received a preschool education and those who did not.[6]

The potential, however, of preschool education to contribute to the economic security of families could be much stronger. In particular, there is not strong evidence that three key components of family socioeconomic status—parent employment, income, and education—have been boosted in the short term during the preschool period. This is unfortunate, because there is very strong nonexperimental evidence that the impact of family income poverty has the strongest and most long-lasting effects on life-course health, learning, and behavior when experienced in early childhood and by disadvantaged children.[7] If preschool education could be supplemented with more intensive antipoverty efforts for families, the benefits not only for families' economic security but for children's life-course outcomes could be amplified considerably.

Clues for how to accomplish poverty reduction in combination with early childhood education come from the global movement toward social protection policies in early childhood. Two kinds of social protection policies that aim to improve the low and fluctuating incomes of low-income parents with young children are cash transfers and paid leave. Cash transfers have been implemented more often in low- and middle-income countries and are most often conditioned on behaviors that support health, such as immunization. However, recent efforts have begun to condition cash transfers on preschool education attendance.[8] In the United States, the primary conditional cash transfer program is the Earned Income Tax Credit, which rewards parental employment with additional income supplements delivered through the tax system for low-wage workers. Conditioning supplemental cash transfer to the poor on preschool attendance could be attempted as a way to not only strengthen poverty reduction in the United States but also to raise the levels of attendance for those in the lowest income ranges (enrollment among the lowest income quintile, for example, is twenty-five percentage points below that of the highest income quintile).[9] As state and federal policies move further toward expansion of preschool, especially for low- and lower-middle-income families, such an incentive-based policy could help ensure that quality preschool reaches those who may benefit the most.[10]

Parental leave is a second poverty reduction policy area in which the United States falls far short relative to other rich countries. Paid leave provides flexibility for early child care and economic and time flexibility for the extra care and attention on dimensions of health, nutrition, and learning that infants require. The U.S. policy for family leave is unpaid, short (three months), and inaccessible for nearly half of American working families. Of

173 countries included in a recent global overview of paid parental leave policies, 169 provided a public system for paid leave for parents with infants and young children. The only nations without such a system among the 173 are the United States, Liberia, Papua New Guinea, and Swaziland.[11]

Building two other dimensions of family socioeconomic status—parental employment and parental education—within preschool education requires a renewed and intensified vision for multigenerational learning. Participation in adult education activities among parents with young children, for example, was causally related to improved middle-childhood achievement in one recent study.[12] Recent efforts on this front include integrating quality preschool education, whether in Head Start or other preschool systems, with sectoral workforce development (e.g., targeting training in occupational sectors with good entry-level jobs and career ladders) and comprehensive adult education opportunities. For example, the Tulsa Community Action Program Head Start and Early Head Start convey the expectation for all entering Head Start parents to engage in weekly activities to build their own human capital or parenting skills. The program supports four strands of adult education activities, ranging from ESL classes tailored to specific work sectors to GED and college classes and job training for the strong health care sector in the Tulsa, Oklahoma, area.[13]

Preschool Education to Build Social Inclusion

The emphasis of the post-2015 global development goals on social inclusion can be realized through a greater emphasis on the most marginalized. In preschool education, this includes groups of children most likely to be excluded from this powerful learning opportunity. In the United States, low-income immigrant parents are some of the least likely to access early childhood education for their children. For example, low-income children from Latino immigrant backgrounds show lower rates of enrollment in preschool education than their counterparts from other immigrant or nonimmigrant backgrounds.[14] Although some of this might be attributed to differences in family preferences, studies show that the large majority of Latino parents would prefer to send their children to preschool by the time their children are four years old. Barriers to doing so include language issues, lack of information about the availability of preschool, and documentation status of parents (undocumented parents may be reluctant to provide the proof of employment and earnings to qualify for means-tested preschool programs).[15] Renewed outreach efforts and a pathway to citizenship for undocumented parents, who represent parents of 5.5 million children in the United States, must be a priority to achieve greater social inclusion in preschool.

Efforts in low- and middle-income countries to increase social inclusion include an emphasis on social capital, or the social ties that are key in building human capital. Early childhood programs in these countries, as well as some in the United States, emphasize social capital development through network and community building activities integrated with quality early childhood learning experiences. At the social network level, programs can strive to reduce isolation and increase collective efficacy (the capacity of adults in a community to increase the collective well-being of network and community members). Examples include the home-based preschool program in Cambodia, which brings networks of parents together in rural villages without preschool centers. The curriculum includes training for lead mothers, who bring village parents together in learning activities; development of play materials from locally available resources; and health and nutrition education. An emphasis on culturally grounded local learning activities and materials was retained as the program expanded beyond its pilot sites to multiple provinces in the country. An evaluation study found that children exposed to this program, relative to those who were not, showed more positive cognitive and social outcomes.[16] Other examples include the well-known Madres Comunitarias program in Colombia and the child care programs of the Self-Employed Women's Association in Gujarat, India.[17] The Madres Comunitarias program, a long-standing program to support low-income community mothers by providing group-based care in their homes, has become a vital social and political force in Colombia by advocating for children and low-income communities. This transition in some respects is similar to the power of Head Start to support an effective grassroots parent and staff organization. In the United States, efforts are emerging that place a central role for parents' social networks in early childhood poverty reduction (the Family Independence Initiative or Abriendo Puertas, for example).

Although child care and preschool programs are important sources of naturally occurring social capital, the most isolated parents or those suffering from mental health problems or chronic stress are the least likely to participate.[18] These parents may be the least likely to enroll their children in preschool programs, and once enrolled they may be the least likely to be engaged with the program. Family stresses can result in low child attendance, reducing the benefits that preschool can provide for learning and development. Some recent innovations have addressed parent mental health problems in at-scale systems. For example, a program in Pakistan in which community health workers were trained to provide evidence-based strategies based on brief cognitive-behavioral therapy techniques to mothers of young children with depression produced spectacular effects. These strategies were integrated into their daily work in such a way that the workers felt it was part of their mission and not a burden. The program was evaluated using a randomized controlled trial design. At a one-year follow-up, 59 percent of the control group met the criteria for major depression, compared to 27 percent of the experimental group—an enormous positive impact.[19] What made this program especially impressive is the relatively low levels of education of the workforce implementing the program (community health workers in the public health system in Pakistan). Another example in the United States is the Family Check-Up program, which adapted strategies from brief motivational interviewing, a proven approach from the substance use brief treatment field. Facilitators trained in this approach integrated it with a goal-setting intervention for parents of young children in Women, Infants, and Children (WIC) clinics with positive impacts, improving parenting skills and reducing children's problem behaviors.[20] These examples suggest that advances in recent decades in brief therapy for depression or brief treatment for substance use can be applied to professional development and training of community-based caregivers. Such innovations could be integrated into preschool education programs (such as through training of family service workers in Head Start). Such efforts might build on the recent advances in mental health consultation that have occurred in Head Start, home visiting, and other systems by expanding preventive services even further.[21]

At the community level, social capital efforts can build networks of organizations to share expertise and resources. Early childhood development as a sector spans disparate efforts across child care, early childhood education, health, poverty reduction, and social service organizations. Linking these into a network of high-quality services for children and families can be a challenge. For example, preschool programs and child care programs often have different sets of quality program standards, learning standards, and curricula. In any particular community children may experience a huge range of program quality as a result. Blended systems, such as state preK programs using Head Start funds and/or performance standards, have increased in recent years and can help make standards more consistent.

In Boston, the city's public preK system integrated evidence-based language and math curricula with weekly in-classroom coaching support for teachers, producing large benefits in children's reading and math skills in an impact evaluation. The Boston Public Schools program also substantially reduced racial/ethnic and class disparities in these school readiness skills.[22] Other community-based providers in the city with fewer resources struggled to provide quality services. For example, these providers often do not have the financial resources to hire bachelor's- and master's-level preschool teachers, as did the school district. The director of early childhood services for the city subsequently began providing the curriculum materials and coaching supports to community-based providers outside the public school system. One system provided its particular expertise through professional development supports to other organizations. In this way, disparities across organizations, systems, and children can potentially be reduced. Public and private systems can foster the goal of social inclusion at the organizational level through such efforts to build the collective capacity of multiple workforces in early childhood and level the city- or state-level playing field for young children in the process.

Preschool Education to Build Environmental Sustainability

Can preschool education address the third pillar of global development—environmental sustainability? The forthcoming sustainable development goals are be based on the thesis that the world is dangerously off course, with planetary boundaries being breached simultaneously on multiple fronts: climate, biodiversity, and depletion of renewable and nonrenewable natural resources.[23] Education systems can do much more than they currently do to support learning about these issues. More broadly, they can also encourage the civic, entrepreneurship, and moral dimensions of learning and development in their practices so that the next generation becomes a better steward of the planet than the current one.

There are a few examples of how education in the early years can help build sustainable communities. A recent report by the United Nations Educational, Scientific, and Cultural Organization (UNESCO) highlighted several innovative efforts. One, the Raglan Road Multi-Purpose Community Centre in Grahamstown, South Africa, represents a good example of how preschool can advance the goal of environmental sustainability.[24] This center is located in a high-poverty community with high levels of health problems, substance use, and child maltreatment and low levels of literacy among adults. It began as a preschool founded in 1990, and the current center still has preschool as its core, with more than 120 children attending each year. The preschool grew beyond classroom instruction to encompass a much wider set of community activities than are traditionally associated with preschool, with sustainable practices at the center of its mission. First, a food garden established on school premises helped enable a sustainable, nutritious, and healthy diet. The garden was used as a learning resource for children and provided "resource income" for community members who worked in exchange for a portion of the yield. Second, the preschool curriculum itself fostered awareness of more sustainable nutrition and community practices, with the intent for children to become natural advocates at home for both the practices and engagement with the center. Third, the program used indigenous knowledge to support children's health in more traditional ways and used locally available low-cost resources. Elders (often primary and secondary caregivers) were assisted by a schoolteacher to develop the skills to grow the plants in a new herbal garden and to make traditional medicines. For younger caregivers and parents, efforts to build human capital were introduced at the center: math, computer, and literacy classes for adults and out-of-school youth supported by skill programs on alcoholism and child abuse awareness. Although no impact evaluation has been conducted of the program, a process evaluation showed the integration of sustainable practices in both the content and implementation of the classroom curricula and the activities for teachers and parents.[25]

The challenges of scaling-up a program such as the Raglan Road center include the necessity for staff motivation and skills to stretch well beyond the traditional emphases of preschool education on classroom instruction. Comprehensive models of preschool education, such as Head Start in the United States or the Integrated Child Development Services program in India, have for decades aimed at contributing to poverty reduction and social inclusion, not just education. Head Start, for example, requires family support, social service, and mental health staff in every center through its Performance Standards. Adding environmental sustainability to this set of aims represents an important next challenge in early childhood education, yet one that builds naturally on established traditions of community action.

Transforming Preschool to Achieve Economic, Social, and Environmental Goals: Leadership, Training, and Innovation

Fifty years after Head Start's founding, preschool enrollment in the United States has fallen below that of not only most other rich countries but also some poorer countries. Just under 70 percent of four-year-olds were enrolled in any form of center-based care or preschool education in 2010, below the Organisation of Economic Co-operation and Development (OECD) average of 79 percent; 42 percent of four-year-olds were enrolled in publicly funded preschool (public preK, Head Start, or public special education preschool).[26] In contrast, Mexico achieved nearly 100 percent enrollment of four-year-olds in preschool by 2005, three years after a universal attendance law was passed.[27] And beyond enrollment, issues of quality are troubling, with only a minority of U.S. preschool classrooms rated as having excellent quality in recent large-scale studies.[28]

An expanded vision for preschool education emerges from attention to the three goals of economic development, social inclusion, and environmental sustainability. The vision is challenging. Teachers and staff do not typically support parents' economic well-being, education, and mental health in the intensive ways that the Pakistan program for maternal depression and the Tulsa program's two-generation program do. Preschool programs do not typically reach out to provide professional development to other preschool systems, such as the Boston Public Schools preK program has begun to do. Three kinds of supports are required to achieve this broader vision for preschool education and to implement it with a focus on quality at scale.

First, a new generation of leaders in preschool education must be equipped to generate solutions in economic development, social inclusion, and environmental sustainability. Innovations in K–12 leadership development worldwide have yet to be integrated at scale into preschool education. For example, a recent program in India developed a highly selective fellowship program not for teachers, as in Teach for America or Teach for India, but for coaches of principals. The Kaivalya Education Foundation (KEF) program for principal leadership development pairs each participating principal with a Gandhi Fellow, drawn in a competitive application process from the leading fifty universities in India.[29] The fellows complete a rigorous initial training period, including teaching at one of the schools they will work in as a coach and a "village immersion" phase, during which they live in the village or urban neighborhood and have no access to phone or Internet and are required to find their own housing. They then receive a two-year curriculum in coaching principals, visiting five schools each week to work with principals on issues of organizational, instructional, and family/community leadership. The principals receive their own curriculum provided by KEF staff and integrated with the coaching. An emphasis on poverty reduction, inclusion of marginalized groups (as defined by caste, gender, class, and language), and environmental sustainability is integrated in this program's curriculum as well as its leadership. This two-generation—the Gandhi Fellows, who are in their twenties, and the principals, who are generally in their forties or fifties and who have achieved their positions solely through seniority rather than merit—approach to leadership development aims to produce national leaders committed to improving the public sector in India. The program has tracked the increases in principal competencies through its program, through a measure developed in consultation with leading educational measurement scholars in India. In the United States, efforts to improve early childhood education through support for principals exist but generally are less intensive, do not include such frequent and on-site contact, and do not consciously develop a younger generation of leaders to innovate in the field.

Second, teacher training programs must be revamped to address these broader aims of preschool education. The field experiences in degree programs could be expanded to include exposure to the on-site coaching and observation supports that have proven successful in improving preschool quality in recent studies. Innovations in education such as the flipped lecture, where didactic aspects of instruction are accessible on line and instructional time is transformed for experiential learning, can support this expansion of practice opportunities. Field experiences could support direct work with families and communities to address the goals of economic development, two-generation approaches, social capital building, and environmental sustainability. The science base for these efforts could be integrated into training curricula as well, so that the intellectual basis for preschool education includes a stronger and broader rationale for its contribution to societal development.

Finally, preschool education stands to benefit from innovations from the field of entrepreneurship, which span economic, social, and environmental sectors. Social entrepreneurship has transformed the fields of economic development, community and social development, environmental sustainability, and K–12 education. Much of this injection of new ideas and innovation into education has bypassed early childhood education. One example is Teach for America, which has struggled to keep its fellows in preschool education due to the markedly lower salaries, prestige, and perceived innovation in the sector. The commitment of the world's most creative young educators to stay in the field of early childhood education and lead in its next generation of programming and policy is low relative to other fields in education.

Entrepreneurship training programs grow the collaborative, teamwork, program development, and management skills that constitute the building blocks of effective entrepreneurship. These emphases could be integrated into all aspects of training and professional development in preschool education so that the base for innovation in the sector is much broader than exists currently. Approaches such as venture capital and entrepreneurship training programs, of which relatively few examples target early childhood, could be greatly expanded.[30] Recent advances in communicating the importance and value of investment in early childhood development could serve as recruiting materials for a new generation of entrepreneurs and leaders in the field. Although there are signs that this is emerging, the scale and pace of change is still far too slow given the huge potential of early childhood education to transform human development among both adults and children.

Preschool for Sustainable Development

Early childhood education has come into its own as a major contributor to societal transformation and improvement. After decades of advocacy by organizations such as the Children's Defense Fund and with the emergence of a new wave of research across the biological and social sciences, learning and development for the youngest children have been rightly acknowledged as a priority by governments and nongovernmental organizations worldwide. Yet, the potential for preschool education to contribute to three dimensions of global development—economic development, social inclusion, and environmental sustainability—could be much stronger. The strategies in this chapter addressing these three goals extend the promise of preschool beyond its educational function. They show how innovations across the rich, middle-income, and low-income countries can be relevant and how the United States has much to learn from other countries around the world. They are examples of how preschool education in coming decades could make even more powerful contributions to both human and societal development.

SCHOOL REFORM

CHAPTER 5

The Past as Prologue to the Future

Envisioning School Reform for the Twenty-First Century

DEBORAH JEWELL-SHERMAN

My life-long ambition was to make a difference in the world as an educator, so I witnessed with curiosity and interest modern school reform from varied perspectives: as a youth, as a teacher and principal, and, most pointedly, as the superintendent of the Richmond (VA) Public Schools. My six-year tenure as superintendent commenced in 2002, the same year as the launch of the No Child Left Behind Act, and allowed me an upfront and personal view of the landscape during this pivotal time of change. As participant and observer I have recognized and valued the importance of public education as a lever that promises to promote social justice, enhance each citizen's quality of life, and strengthen our democracy. Yet, I'm equally aware that many school reform efforts have fallen woefully short of their lofty goals to the detriment of generations of learners.

In this chapter, I offer a summary of pivotal periods in school reform from the mid–twentieth century to the present and then identify some of the obstacles that have thwarted greater progress. I also offer three considerations for education leaders, researchers, and policy makers as they envision school reform for the twenty-first century.

Historical Perspective

An Equality School Reform Model

The catalyst for school reform changed frequently over the last half of the twentieth century. From the 1950s to the mid-1970s, reform efforts, fueled by liberal politicians, researchers, and practitioners, focused on bringing about equality in educational opportunities and funding through the dismantling of de jure and de facto segregation policies, legislation, and practice. Education policy driven by Supreme Court mandates, beginning with *Brown v. Board of Education* in 1954, demonstrated both the power of judicial decree and the recalcitrance of state and local governing bodies. It took unprecedented civil rights actions and federal legislation to provide the momentum for long-delayed efforts to dismantle legal segregation in America's schools.[1] The vestiges of segregation, however, remain, and with them vanish the hope of a technical legal solution to the persistent challenge of unequal and inadequate public education for too many of America's children, especially those in its urban core and rural outlands.

Perceptions in the late 1960s and the 1970s of a deteriorating public education system led to criticism of the sector and increased sponsorship of seminal studies. For example, two years after the signing of the 1964 Civil Rights Act, the Coleman study reported that the socioeconomic status of students and families—not schools, teachers, and fiscal resources—was the primary determinant of academic achievement.[2] Ironically, in 1973, as the newly formed Children's Defense Fund (CDF) focused on the needs of all children, the promises of President Johnson's Great Society were giving way to a belief by different, more conservative, reformers that the public education provided in the nation was woefully inadequate. And later in the decade, while the Carter administration was creating the Department of Education and scholars like Ron Edmonds were launching the Effective Schools Movement in 1979, the design of school reform was undergoing a dramatic shift.[3]

A Standards and Teacher Professionalism Model

The 1983 release of *A Nation at Risk* galvanized the public with its clarion call for significant school reform, including the adoption of more rigorous standards, increased professionalism of teaching, and greater educational accountability.[4] One result of the report was the unleashing of "corporate education reforms," the proposals and strategies of which have driven certain education policies at the federal and state levels ever since.[5]

In the late 1980s and early 1990s, the impetus for a second wave of school reform came from several sources, and its impact began to be felt and yield results.[6] For example, *A Nation Prepared: Teachers for the 21st Century* called for professional teaching standards, which later became National Board certification criteria for exemplary teachers.[7] Believing that a free-market approach to school reforms would improve public schooling, in 1987 Secretary of Education William Bennett, who supported both school vouchers and curriculum reform, called for heightened accountability at the school level. This sentiment was echoed by both business and legislative leaders, who signaled that educational improvements would need to be measured to justify increased funding.[8]

Corporate School Reform Model

Corporate school reform efforts were further promulgated in the 1990s and 2000s by legislation and philanthropic individuals, whose foundation largess frequently tipped the policies and programs enacted at the federal, state, and local levels to align with their ideological perspectives about the best strategies to improve public schooling across the nation.[9]

In January 2002, President George W. Bush signed the No Child Left Behind Act (NCLB).[10] Few could argue with the noble and worthy ambitions of the act; however, school districts and states struggled to reform their instructional and operational strategies to best meet the yearly benchmark targets. Labeling schools that showed growth but did not meet yearly benchmarks as "failing schools" contributed to a serious reduction in the public's confidence in its public schools and frequently demoralized the very teachers and administrators tasked with ensuring increased student achievement.

Since the onset of NCLB, many schools and districts have failed to make adequate yearly progress (AYP).[11] In the wake of NCLB, there was a proliferation of and support for charter schools and alternative means to certify teachers, central office administrators, and superintendents (e.g., Teach for America, The Broad Foundation). And in 2010 Secretary of Education Arne Duncan, citing the release by the National Governors Association Center for Best Practices and the Council of Chief State School Officers, promoted the adoption and implementation of the Common Core State Standards, which explicitly delineate what students should learn and be able to do and what teachers and parents can do to support them.[12] And incentives such as Race to the Top and the issuance of waivers for some of NCLB's accountability provisions are further administration efforts to increase funding and allow greater flexibility in meeting benchmarks.

During this critical juncture of school reform, communication among reformers has rarely been more acrimonious and positions been more fully entrenched. As the CDF moves into its fifth decade, the collaborative rethinking, recommitting, and redesigning of future school reform efforts must be one of our nation's highest priorities.

Diagnosis of Obstacles to Progress

Given the billions of dollars spent to improve public education in the nation, it is disheartening to recognize the limited progress. An exploration of three key issues—implementation, impact, and sustainability—provides insight into some of the challenges inherent in modern school reform.[13]

Implementation

The nonsynchronistic nature of school reform development presents untold challenges to those tasked with implementing new policies, programs, and practices. The promulgation of late twentieth- and early-twenty-first-century reforms has frequently resulted from a confluence of political ideologies and shifting combinations of problems, solutions, and decision makers. The precipitating causes for specific school reforms often are not aligned with other policies and practices being implemented within schools and communities. And too frequently when some measure of alignment between policy, implementation, funding, and practice is achieved, such coherence is dissipated by external events.[14] Nor do school reform measures and mandates occur in a vacuum. The ambitious NCLB timeline for the development of state standards, the administration of standardized assessments, and the actualizing of public school choice and supplemental services presented a bureaucratic nightmare at the state and local levels, resulting in a focus on logistical and procedural checklists to ensure compliance rather than on enhancing teacher capacity to improve students' learning.

Impact

NCLB signaled an urgent need for reform. I believe there is benefit derived from the use of rigorous standards in the formulation of curriculum and student and teacher expectations. In addition, when used for student growth and diagnostic purposes, for identifying teacher strengths and areas of needed capacity building, and as one measure for determining student achievement over time, standardized testing has a valid role to play in school reform. However, those tasked with sorting through the barrage of changes emanating from the federal and state governments often witnessed the devastation that accompanied some of the benefits of such school reform. The pace of change was rapid and comprehensive, leaving many teachers, administrators, and school communities feeling both battered and maligned. The reforms' impact was felt across the classroom, school, and district levels, and, as a district superintendent, I witnessed educators responding in three ways.

First, some educators accepted the notion that demography was destiny and that the external influences besetting students and communities were so great that it was beyond the capability of schools to ameliorate these challenges and appropriately educate their students. In these instances, failing student scores served to verify beliefs about their students' capabilities and in so doing freed educators from the responsibility of enhancing their own capabilities to better meet their content and pedagogical challenges and deficiencies. Without imbuing such teachers and administrators with a sense of their own efficacy, their own ability to "get smarter," and providing them with professional development and support, these kinds of educators will continue to adversely impact or have no positive effect on the achievement of the students under their watch.[15]

Second, some educators disputed vehemently the notion that demographic data points and zip codes would define their students' learning outcomes. Too frequently, however, these teachers and administrators had to rely on their own knowledge, skills, and assets to compensate for the lack of direction and support they received from building, district, and state officials. Succeeding often in spite of, not because of, the school reform mandates and administrative directives, these are our heroic educators. The saga of these heroes resonates with our American belief that we live in a meritocracy and that the best and the brightest will always be able to excel. Conversely, it affirms the belief held by some that those who aren't able to accomplish equal feats under the same set of circumstance are woefully inadequate and that improvement at scale is impossible. The truth of the matter is that those performing well in an environment of unfocused vision and mission, in a culture devoid of relational trust, and in learning communities lacking support and opportunities often become burned out because the pace and demands put on them by themselves and others are not sustainable. These are the valiant educators who too frequently leave the schools where they're most needed for schools and districts happy to have and support them.[16]

Last, some schools and districts embraced school reforms like NCLB, with its mixed messages and challenges, and, against the odds, made AYP. In these instances, their positive outcomes resulted in part from collaborations between state and district administrators; the establishment of belief systems that viewed their educators as having the capacity to get smarter; the professional development of teachers and administrators concomitant with the challenging expectations held for them; and the rewarding and recognition of success while using failure as an opportunity to rethink and improve.

Sustainability

Initially, NCLB was slated to target urban, heavily minority, and challenged school districts; however, with each passing year, the failure to educate subgroups of students within suburban and rural schools caused the criticism of NCLB to emanate from many more districts.[17] The push for reaching escalating benchmarks in the context of "no excuses" during the retrenchment of financial support caused great consternation in school districts across the nation

In the wake of such challenges and outcry, the Department of Education has provided waivers and other exemptions with an expectation that other state and district school reforms will ensue. However, I believe that it is imperative and nonnegotiable that the focus of NCLB remains on ensuring and being accountable for *all* children's success. Too many actors and stakeholders in the educational sector are engaged in an either-or struggle for the minds, hearts, and fiscal resources of our constituents, parental stakeholders, teachers, administrators, staff, and, most especially, our students. The energy spent on reform debates such as whether we should focus on existing schools or charters or on teacher-centered instruction or student-centered learning has yielded, at best, a hodge-podge of student results.

As the reauthorization of the Elementary and Secondary Education Act is once again contemplated, the pertinent question before us is whether the corporate reform model can deliver on the promise to educate well the poorest and most vulnerable of our nation's students.[18] National and individual school successes demonstrated in countries like Finland and by entities like Green Dot with Locke High School in California and the school transformations accomplished under turn-around principals across the nation offer a hopeful picture of what the future may hold for public schools and the reforms undertaken.[19] What we sustain and replicate cannot be a function of political and financial might or which individual or group has the bully pulpit and is riding a crest of public sentiment. It is imperative that scholars and researchers, in concert with front line teachers, district school administrators, and state leaders, validate reforms that evidence shows work well and are scalable and repudiate those that do not.

Three Key Ideas for the Next Forty Years

Embrace a New Vision for Public Education

John Dewey prophetically pronounced in 1899 that "what the best and wisest parent wants for his own child, that must the community want for all of its children."[20] Yet, there is no longer a common vision of what an educational experience should look like and produce—what our children should know; what information our children should be able to locate, identify, evaluate, and use; and what our children should become in the process and be able to demonstrate as adults and citizens of our nation.

At a time of such powerful and far-reaching changes, it is imperative that we reach consensus about the meaning of schooling. No longer can the debate be whether we focus on equity or on fostering high achievement. The new vision for public education must embody a simultaneous focus on both. And a place to begin is with an acceptance that the primary focus of our work is to educate well the children entrusted to our care. We have become disoriented and confused into believing that the primary mission of schooling is employment and job security for teachers, administrators, and support staff. I believe that if a clear connection cannot be made between the work anyone does in a school or district and the teaching and learning of children in classrooms, that position is extraneous and should be eliminated.

And those educators who don't believe and/or are unwilling to accept that their children can "get smarter" in the face of the right motivation, pedagogy, content, support, and care should be helped to make a different career decision quickly. Tenure and seniority rules can no longer be used to protect the ineffective, and so modifications must be made to more easily remove those educators who cannot develop their knowledge and pedagogy to meet the demands of twenty-first-century learners. However, for the majority of teachers, whether in unions or right-to-work states, the negative rhetoric so common in today's discourse on school reform is both disrespectful and unworthy. Rewards and supports must be a staple in the recruitment, onboarding, and continuous training of our nation's teaching force. Capacity-enhancing professional development, coupled with explicit and ongoing support, is a prerequisite for the learning and preparation society expects from our teachers and leaders. If we believe that our students can "get smarter," we must hold the same belief for our teachers and administrators. [21]

Also, in creating a new vision for public education, issues of race, gender, socioeconomic status, and primary language of origin are important and relevant and must be inexorably embedded in the debate about the design, implementation, impact, and sustainability of school reform.

Embrace the Teaching and Learning of the Whole Child

We have an obligation to help our students surmount the deleterious effects of past and present discrimination, such as the challenges of inadequate housing and the pressures on families of a legacy of poor educational and career opportunities. Therefore, this new vision of public schooling must address the needs of the whole child as he or she enters our schools. We also must accept that schools cannot and should not be expected to take on this crucial task alone. Enforcing a tough "no excuses" policy regarding student failure without providing supports for our most vulnerable students, such as those in poverty, in foster care, and in the juvenile justice system, is unconscionable and immoral. And it will not work. Political leaders and corporate entities have joined with parents and other stakeholders in demanding far more from their public schools than ensuring quality and effective teaching and learning. Therefore, today's school leaders must continuously join with the larger community and be willing to collaborate with service providers in the public, private, and not-for-profit sector to ensure that the teaching, learning, and care of the whole child is at the center of the educational enterprise.

S. Paul Reville, the former Massachusetts education secretary, has challenged reformers to think beyond the numbers and "admit that closing achievement gaps is not as simple as adopting a set of standards, accountability and instructional improvement strategies." He has said, "It is now clear that unless and until we make a more active effort to mitigate the impediments to learning that are commonly associated with poverty, we will still be faced with large numbers of children who are either unable to come to school or so distracted as not to be able to be attentive and supply effort when they get there."[22]

I, too, believe that there is a need for "wraparound services" that will allow schools and their partners to provide students with a healthy and fair platform for learning. CDF, along with other stakeholders and organizations committed to improving the lives, education, and outcomes of our nation's children, must convene and collaborate to reach consensus about what we want our children to know, do, and be. Such an effort would elevate the current partisan rhetoric to a level of vision, aspiration, and hope.

Embrace Innovation as Gateway to Public Schooling Redesign

It is with great frustration and dismay that I recall the obstacles placed in the way of true public school transformation by incoherent policies and procedures emanating from all levels of government, by the ineptitude and petty tyrannies manifest by too many school boards and other local governmental entities, by the lack of courageous and bold action when confronted with clear conflicts of interest, and the intractability of people, policies, and programs entrenched in bureaucratic silos. These impediments warrant swift and powerful change. For the reform of the educational enterprise, we will need to embrace "hybrid thinking for educational innovation" by "taking the best elements of what has been, integrate diverse sources of knowledge and talent, and create a break though that hasn't been imagined before and is driven by the promising 'edges of innovation.'"[23] This type of redesign is fraught with challenges, including our human "immunity to change."[24] The case will have to be made strongly that to ensure the high achievement of all learners, children will need to become globally competitive, will have to initiate and be at the center of much of their learning, and will have to learn in places outside of their current school buildings and, at times, beyond their traditional school day. There also will be a need for transparency in the development and decision-making processes of future school reforms so that possible models will appeal to the wider sector rather than an ideological or parochial base. School reform cannot continue to be "done unto" those who have the responsibility of teaching and leading. Discourse, especially in the age of social media, is messy, discordant, protracted, and what finally ensues is usually not anything any stakeholder group wanted. But it is how we will have to do the work.

A major anticipated obstacle to this type of innovation and change is funding. Thought leaders and entrepreneurs suggest that such large-scale innovation in education will happen at the nexus of "policy, research, capital, and practice."[25] I believe that with moderate investments, thoughtful redesign of the current school structure and organization can be both incentivized and implemented. Anthony Jewett of the Tides Foundation suggests that what is needed are flexible funding sources that are more suited to the cycle of entrepreneurship than are government and philanthropic dollars, and that "crowd-funding capital" may be a viable means to secure resources for innovation by educational entrepreneurs and innovators embarking on such projects as system-level redesigns of school structures and organizations.[26]

Clearly, future school reform design and implementation will not be easy. Something of such import, by its very nature, will be the subject of discord, controversy, heated emotions, and frequent jockeying for position and advantage. In spite of significant challenges, the work of school reform must continue and must deliver the results we seek for our current and future learners. For in 2013, forty years after the inception of the Children's Defense Fund, our nation continues to grapple with the predominant challenge of its day: ensuring quality educational opportunities and outcomes for all of its children.

Dr. Martin Luther King Jr. admonished all who struggle to bring about a more perfect union to remember, especially in the difficult times, that the arc of justice, though long, always veers toward righteousness. Certainly, the arc moving toward a just public education system for all of this nation's children has been both long and steep, and the school reforms behind it have yet to deliver on their promise. Yet, I still believe.

CHAPTER 6

Building a Twenty-First-Century School System

Creating a Teaching Profession and Multiple Student Pathways

JAL MEHTA AND ROBERT B. SCHWARTZ

The past twenty-five years of school reform in the United States have seen some progress but also revealed the limits of our current strategies to reach the ambitious goals we rightly seek. One of us (Schwartz) was a longtime champion of the standards movement; the other of us (Mehta) has written extensively on the limits of the test and accountability heavy approach that characterizes our current education system. But we both agree that the current system is unlikely to achieve what we seek.

Look at the evidence. First, the positive. The greatest progress has come in math, particular in elementary and middle schools, where scores for nine- and thirteen–year-olds have increased by twenty points over the past thirty years. Scores in reading have changed much less at all ages, and there has been little progress in high school scores in either subject.[1] Within this national story there is also substantial state variation; some states, like our own Massachusetts, have made considerable progress in boosting scores and closing achievement gaps, while others have stagnated. There have also been success stories among some traditional districts, such as Montgomery County (MD), Long Beach (CA), and Union City (NJ), which suggest the ways in which a coherent and sustained campaign for improvement can lead to positive outcomes. Among more "reform" actors, some charter networks have shown impressive results, including "no excuses" models like Aspire, Uncommon Schools, KIPP, and Achievement First, as well as more pedagogically progressive networks like High Tech High and Expeditionary Learning.

More qualitatively, there has been a positive shift in the broadening of the coalition thinking about and working seriously to improve schools.

Closing achievement gaps is now a goal for many mainstream politicians, both Democrats and Republicans, and one frequently hears that education is the "civil rights issue" of our generation. Sparked by the release of the Program for International Student Assessment (PISA), the past ten years has also seen the United States beginning to become part of a global conversation about education reform, which has opened up new vistas for how to think about whole-system improvement.

At the same time, it is clear that there have been significant limits to reforms to date. PISA results still place the United States squarely in the middle of the pack; the 2012 results rank us seventeenth in reading, twenty-first in science, and twenty-sixth in math. Much of the progress on the National Assessment of Educational Progress (NAEP) has been concentrated in the elementary and middle grades; results in high school NAEP are remarkably unchanged from decades ago (particularly in reading). Our schools are much better at helping schools achieve "basic skills" (two-thirds of students) than higher-order skills that require thinking and reasoning (one-third of students). National studies reveal that 70 percent of students are bored daily in high school.[2] Charter schools still house only about 5 percent of students, and, while there have been some successful networks, on average they have performed no better or worse than traditional publics. Despite the collective efforts and talent of many thousands of teachers, administrators, and policy makers, there is still a huge gap between our aspirations for schooling and what it is able to currently achieve.

Our belief, which is shared by many other observers across the spectrum, is that the essence of the problem is that the United States is trying to use a system that was created at the end of the nineteenth century to respond to the challenges of the twenty-first century. Of course, good education is good education, from Socrates to Cardinal Newman to the present; the changing of the centuries does nothing to change the qualities of good schooling. But education does sit within a system, and it is that system which is mal-adapted to our present realities.

Included in the building of a twenty-first-century system would be a revamping on many fronts. Some of these relate to what we currently see as the boundaries of the "school" system. Any modern system would heed James Heckman's and others' ideas that the effects of schooling are cumulative and thus would start with building a robust early childhood education system.[3] We also have, unfortunately, siloed our school system from other social services that support children and families, and a reconceived system would integrate those functions. Other changes would relate to the nature of schooling itself: all children need a developmentally appropriate, highly demanding curriculum and assessments to match; schooling can and should be more individualized, both to meet the challenges of different learners and to respect students' interests and choices as they get older; and technology needs to be much more intentionally integrated into modern schooling. The agenda here is a large one, and it will require a series of changes on many dimensions that would, cumulatively, gradually transform the system we have inherited from the end of the nineteenth century to one that we have designed for the beginning of the twenty-first.

In the remainder of this chapter, we want to highlight two major issues that are of particular interest to us and are critical to any vision of the future. The first is the need to clarify the mission of high schools and create a more diverse set of pathways through high school on to a postsecondary degree or certificate with currency in the labor market. At present, only about one in three young adults in their midtwenties earns a bachelor's degree, and yet states and school districts are increasingly making the college prep curriculum the default curriculum for all students. If we continue to behave as if the four-year college and university is the only socially acceptable destination for young people, not only are we unlikely to make progress in reducing our unacceptably high dropout rate, but we will perpetuate the current skills mismatch: millions of good "middle skills" jobs are going begging because of a shortage of people with appropriate technical training and skills. As one of us (Schwartz) has argued, we need to follow the lead of the strongest European and Asian education systems by bringing together educators and employers to create programs that integrate strong academic and technical education; span high school and the first two years of postsecondary education; provide internships and other forms of workplace learning that enable students to apply academic concepts in real-world settings; and lead to credentials in such high-growth, high-demand fields as information technology, advanced manufacturing, and health care.

The second is building a profession of teaching that can achieve that mission. It is hard to imagine how any of the other goals we have for schooling can be realized without a widely skilled teaching force. As one of us (Mehta) has argued, developing a consistent mechanism for training and credentialing teachers also is key for moving away from command-and-control bureaucracies where the emphasis is on monitoring and supervision from above. If we were able to certify quality on the front end, we could lessen the need for extensive testing and accountability on the back end. This would move us away from a vertical system based on compliance (the early-twentieth-century organizational structure) and toward the kind of horizontal system of social learning that ties together and networks front-line practitioners and that is characteristic of the most effective modern organizations.

We see these two issues as connected. The first is about clarifying the goals of the system and developing a realistic plan for what it is intended to achieve. The second is about greatly increasing the capacity of the system to enable it to reach those goals.

High Schools and Multiple Pathways

With the rise of the standards movement over the past twenty years, most Americans now understand that all students need to be given a solid foundation of core academic knowledge and skills to keep on learning, whatever their immediate post–high school destination. That understanding has in some states morphed into the view that all students need to be prepared to attend a four-year college or university, leading these states to adopt the college prep curriculum as the default curriculum for all students. The extreme version of this position can be seen in four of the largest urban districts in California—Los Angeles, San Diego, San Francisco, and Oakland—which have recently adopted the policy that all students *as a condition of graduation* must complete the curriculum requirements set for admission to the state's four-year public universities.

Historically, we have thought of high schools as having a three-part mission: preparation for citizenship, further learning, and careers. What these policies represent is the narrowing of the purpose of high school into a single mission: preparation for college (which for most people means a four-year college or university). Despite the current rhetoric about "college and career readiness," it's really only college that counts. The problem with this single-minded fixation on college is that it ignores the reality that only one young American in three actually attains a four-year college degree. We believe it is critically important to our country's future that we work to raise the percentage of college completers and commit to a set of strategies designed to radically increase the proportion of low-income and African American and Latino youth who attain a four-year degree. Today, if you are born into the top fifth of the income distribution, your chances of earning a college degree are nearly ten times greater than if you are born into the bottom fifth. If education is again going to become an engine of social and economic mobility, this shameful situation must be addressed.

But let's assume for argument's sake that over the next decade we can bring the proportion of young Americans earning a four-year degree up to 40 percent, which would enable us to reclaim our position of international leadership in university-level attainment, a goal articulated by President Obama. We outline some steps below that we think will move us toward that goal. But there remains a very large question: what is our national strategy for equipping the other 60 percent of young people with the skills and credentials they will need to take their place in our increasing challenging labor market? The United States remains an outlier among advanced economies in relying so heavily on its higher education institutions to support the transition from the end of compulsory education to working life and in neglecting to build a stronger set of career pathways where educators and employers work collaboratively to design and implement programs to equip young people with market-relevant skills and credentials.

Today, roughly 33 percent of Americans in their midtwenties have a four-year degree, 10 percent a two-year degree, and another 10 percent a one-year postsecondary certificate of value in the labor market. The state of Oregon has recently adopted an ambitious set of postsecondary attainment goals that it refers to as "40-40-20": 40 percent bachelor's degrees, 40 percent associate degrees or one-year occupational certificates, and 20 percent high school completion (i.e., virtually eliminating the dropout problem). We believe these goals accurately reflect the realities of the twenty-first-century labor market, for, as President Obama stated in his 2009 State of the Union address, nearly all young people will need some form of education or training beyond high school if they are going to enter a path to a middle-class wage.

We believe the Oregon goals make sense not just for that state but for the nation as a whole. What would it take to move us toward those goals, especially the two 40 percent goals? For the first 40 percent four-year degree goal, there are a variety of strategies we need to employ, especially if we want to change the profile of those attaining a bachelor's degree to more accurately reflect the nation's student demographics. These strategies need to be applied universally through the first nine or ten years of schooling so that all students understand from an early age that they need to be prepared for some form of education beyond high school. These strategies include:

- ensuring a rich, challenging untracked curriculum aligned with Common Core State Standards and taught by well-prepared teachers;
- establishing a college-going culture beginning in the early grades;
- early exposure through campus site visits to the world of higher education;
- in the high school years, engaging schools and community-based organizations to work with parents and students on the college application and financial aid process (including waivers of application fees).

These are strategies that good schools already have in place. The challenge is to make them the norm, especially in schools serving groups that have been historically underrepresented in higher education.

Perhaps the most important and promising breakthrough in recent years in increasing college-going rates among such groups of students has been the remarkable success of the Early College High School (ECHS) movement. ECHSs are schools that begin in grade 7 or 9 and that, in partnership with a local higher education institution, design and carry out an accelerated learning program to ensure that all students not only graduate from high school but are earning at least thirty college credits. There are now nearly 250 such schools serving more than 75,000 students, mostly low-income and from non-college-going families. Their results are extraordinary: roughly one quarter of students graduating high school with two years of college credit, half with at least one year. A recent study of ten ECHSs conducted by the American Institute of Research comparing ECHS students with students who applied but were not admitted by lottery indicated that on virtually all measures—high school graduation, college enrollment, college persistence and completion—ECHS students outperformed their matched peers.[4]

But getting started on college is one thing; persistence and completion is quite another, and here the success stories are fewer. One organization with a proven track record is the Posse Foundation, which for twenty-five years has been identifying young people whose potential for success in college may not be apparent through the traditional measures for assessing college readiness and then convincing its forty-six partner colleges and universities to take a chance on these students. The key to Posse's success is that the students enroll in these colleges in teams, with training and coaching in how to support one another in navigating the academic and social challenges of college life. Again, its success rates are extraordinary: a 90 percent college graduation rate for the nearly five thousand students it has enrolled since its founding. The big question posed by Posse, as by the ECHS movement, is not only whether these models can be expanded to serve more young people—they can, with expanded funding and political will—but whether the underlying principles that have made these models effective can be adapted more broadly by high schools and colleges. These initiatives demonstrate that it is possible to change the socioeconomic profile of those who seek and attain a college degree.

The Next 40 Percent

The good news about our prospects for reaching the first goal—40 percent of young people obtaining a four-year degree—is that there has not only been broad agreement within the education community around the college-going mission but lots of hard work to make it happen. Consequently, we are now beginning to see progress, as reflected in the jump from 30 percent to 33 percent in the last five years.

However, there has been no such focus within the education community on helping another 40 percent of young people acquire a postsecondary credential with value in the labor market. But this is beginning to change. For one thing, major national foundations like Lumina and Gates have begun to invest in programs and strategies to increase the numbers of people with

"Sub-Baccalaureate" degrees and credentials. For another, the Georgetown Center on Education and the Workforce has released an influential series of reports arguing that roughly 30 percent of the jobs projected over the next decade will be in the "middle skills" category, requiring some education or training beyond high school but not necessarily a four-year degree, and demonstrating that those with two-year technical degrees or one-year technical certificates are outearning increasing numbers of four-year degree holders.

In 2011, one of us (Schwartz) released a report with two Harvard Graduate School of Education colleagues, *Pathways to Prosperity*, that draws on the Georgetown data and other sources to make the case for building a stronger set of career pathways to sit alongside the dominant four-year college pathway.[5] That report stimulated enough interest in the field to enable the creation in 2012 of a Pathways to Prosperity Network of eight states committed to building such a career pathways system.

The best examples of the kind of pathways we are envisioning in the high schools are the career academies developed under the umbrella of the National Academy Foundation (NAF), and especially the academies developed in the Long Beach Unified School District under the banner of Linked Learning, a statewide initiative sponsored by the James Irvine Foundation and a well-staffed intermediary organization it created, ConnectEd California. Career academies are one of the few high school innovations that have been subjected to rigorous evaluation and found effective.[6]

Career academies are designed to blend rigorous academics with relevant career and technical education. Their goal is to use their career focus not only to expose students to some of the core elements associated with careers in their chosen area but also, through applied learning via internships and other forms of workplace learning, to help engage and motivate students to master core academic skills. The NAF academies operate in five career areas: finance, hospitality and tourism, engineering, information technology, and health care. The Linked Learning academies cover a broader range of fields, including law and justice, media, arts and humanities, and the environment. While both NAF and Linked Learning academies have active employer advisory committees, they see their academies primarily as a high school reform strategy and only secondarily as vehicles to help young people get launched on careers.

Our view is that if the goal is to help many more young people not only get through high school but go on to attain a postsecondary degree or credential with value in the labor market, career academies and other strong high school career-focused programs need to be more directly connected to postsecondary programs in the same career field. The Pathways to Prosperity Network brings together employers and educators from secondary and postsecondary institutions to design pathways that span grades 9–14, are aligned with regional labor market needs, and lead to a postsecondary degree or credential. Initially, the network participants are focused on three career areas with a strong STEM foundation and where there is high demand for people with "middle skills": health care, information technology, and advanced manufacturing. As the program expands, additional fields will be added. The single biggest challenge faced by NAF, Linked Learning, and the Pathways Network is to provide sufficient opportunities for internships or other forms of work-based learning to make this a central part of the program for all students. This will require convincing employers that it is in their long-term economic self-interest to invest in the development of the next generation workforce, a proposition that is well understood by employers in western Europe but harder to sell here.

In order to meet the second 40 percent goal, we would need over the next decade to double the percentage of young people acquiring an industry-relevant two-year degree or one-year certificate. The biggest obstacle to overcome in meeting this goal is the second-class status most Americans ascribe to anything associated with vocational education. This is in part a function of our history, where too often in our cities voc ed has been seen as a dumping ground for students who were deemed not able to do challenging academic work and where too often programs had weak or nonexistent connections to the labor market. One big lesson from the strongest European vocational systems is that their power and political legitimacy derive from the fact that they are mainstream systems serving a broad cross-section of students and preparing them for white-collar as well as blue-collar careers. This is one reason why the Pathways Network is focusing on the sectors it has chosen rather than the traditional trades that were the focus of old-style vocational programs. The cliché that has too long prevailed in the United States is that vocational education is a fine thing—for other people's children. By creating career pathways that link secondary and postsecondary institutions, are driven by employer demand in high-growth fields, and combine rigorous academics with relevant workplace training, the new vocational reformers hope to change public perception.

Creating the Capacity to Achieve the Mission: Building a Highly Skilled Teaching Profession

How are we going to achieve the above goals? A big part of the answer lies in increasing the capacity of our teaching force. Perhaps because of its decentralized origins, the United States does not have a strategy for the development of its teaching force. Bearing the legacy of its Progressive Era origins as an occupation for unmarried women, teaching has always been a mass profession with little systemic attention to who would teach, how they would be trained, what would count as competent practice, and how they would be evaluated. In recent years, there has been growing attention to the last of these pieces, with a growing policy commitment to ever more elaborate systems of teacher evaluation, but there has not been a commensurate commitment to building the needed structures that would support a consistently strong teaching profession.

Recent research on international systems that far outpace the United States on the PISA suggest that this is not how other countries organize their systems. PISA leaders draw their teachers from the top third of the academic performance distribution, compared to the bottom 60 percent in the United States. Training is also more extensive and more frequently paid for by the state. Extensive test-based accountability focused on individual teachers is much less in these countries; greater quality control in the selection and licensing process allows for more trust placed in practicing teachers. The consequence is that teaching is a much more desired occupation in these countries. In Finland, it is the most preferred occupation for fifteen-year-olds. This supply of people who want to get into teaching enables greater levels of selectivity in who can become a teacher, beginning the virtuous cycle anew.[7]

A revamped human capital strategy in the United States would seek to tackle each part of this pipeline. In the past year, the American Federation of Teachers (AFT), the National Education Association, and the Council of Chief State School Officers have voiced support for substantially increasing the requirements to become a licensed teacher. The most promising proposal has come from the AFT, which has supported the idea of a "bar" or "board" exam for teaching. In the version of this idea that we favor, it would not be a one-time paper-and-pencil test but, rather, akin to the medical boards, would be a phased set of milestones over several years that would demonstrate not only knowledge but evidence of actual teaching skill.

Such a system of exams should be paired with an approach to training that could also borrow from the teaching hospital model. Beginning teachers would be closely overseen by master teachers and be given greater responsibility as they demonstrate increasing levels of competency. The responsibility for teacher training should become more vertically integrated. Rather than the current approach of teacher preparation providers giving the initial training and then districts inducting teachers, we would suggest that a better model would put one set of providers in charge of the entire apprenticeship period, which would last the first three years. At the end of that time, teachers would take the final step of their "boards," which, if passed, would mark full-fledged entrance into the profession. Such an approach would provide a reasonable pathway to ensure that new members of the profession receive proper practical training and would assure the public that fully certified teachers could demonstrate a professional level of teaching skill.

These efforts should be coupled with a renewed effort to build a real knowledge base to guide teaching. Professions are marked in large part by the knowledge that guides their work. Education has a very individualistic approach to professionalism that emphasizes practitioner autonomy, as opposed to developing a shared technical core that would serve as the basis for good teaching practice. Part of the problem here is that it is not really anyone's responsibility to develop such knowledge: researchers write mainly for other researchers; good teachers have such knowledge but do not have mechanisms to share or vet it; commercial entities like textbook publishers do much to structure practice, but their incentives are generally to make what districts will buy. Knowledge is not a sexy topic, but the rate at which fields' progress is largely dependent on their mechanisms for generating a usable and improving knowledge base. It is long past the time that the educational field more seriously addresses this problem.

We suggest a joint effort that would involve a number of key stakeholders. Most critical is more consistently bridging the divide between researchers and practicing teachers, who need to work together.[8] Teachers provide practical knowledge and can identify what sorts of questions will yield relevant answers, and their involvement is critical for generating increasing take-up of new knowledge. Researchers have skill around designing studies and drawing causal inferences; they also have the needed time and incentives to write and try to make local knowledge more generally available. Since such an effort would initially run against all of the incentives and norms of both schools and education schools, we think the creation of new entities that are intentionally devoted to producing usable knowledge would be wise. We think that partnerships, like the one between Hunter College and three leading charter networks; schools running their own graduate schools of education, like High Tech High in California and Match in Boston; and teacher residency programs, like the Boston Teacher Residency, all show early signs of how the training and research functions could be integrated with an eye toward practice in a productive way.

If training, licensing, and knowledge production were improved, the last step would be for the profession to develop ongoing standards and accompanying mechanisms to guide daily practice. These mechanisms would be akin to hospital rounds in medicine and peer review in academia: they would provide an ongoing mechanism which seeks to ensure that daily practice is consistent with the standards of the field. They do not deskill the profession; no scripted curricula here. Rather, they do the opposite: they provide a set of concepts, language, and frameworks that allow professionals to talk and work in common but complex ways that enable sophisticated discussions among fellow travelers about how best to do the work.

The overall result of such a system is that it would create a unified profession from top to bottom. New teachers would be trained by master teachers and would thus see themselves as part of a common profession. The training would include, as is the case in Finland, an emphasis on investigating one's practice and contributing to knowledge; from the beginning, teachers would be part of the knowledge production process. Training would be run by the profession and would flow into schools organized around professional standards, which would reinforce what teachers had learned during their training. Some portion of each entering class would someday become master teachers, roles in which they would contribute knowledge and train new entrants, beginning the cycle anew.

Such a system would also enable teaching as a field to enhance its status and lessen the kind of invasive test-based accountability that in recent years has become such a striking feature of the American system. Teachers these days are beset by ever increasing demands from districts and states, teaching to tests they don't believe in, and, in the most extreme cases, having their names published in the newspaper showing how well they perform on value-added metrics. The alternative approach we suggest is much more likely to engender the kind of sustainable commitment needed to grow quality teaching, as well as to make the profession much more attractive to new entrants.

Finally, at the broadest level, this system would allow the field to move away from the hierarchical bureaucracy that it inherited and toward a much flatter, networked structure that is characteristic of modern learning organizations. The Progressive Era model emphasized a small number of supervisors making decisions for the many schools and teachers, which was consistent with then-cutting-edge business notions of centralized efficiency. But in the years since, it has become clear that the key to organizational success is to tap the knowledge and skill of frontline practitioners, because they are closer to the work and their sheer numbers yield a much wider variety of good ideas. This form also recognizes that much useful learning is peer-to-peer and creates ways to allow people in similar roles to learn from one another. We are beginning to see this kind of work in education through teacher lesson sharing Web sites and through networked improvement communities, in which schools work across contexts to solve common problems of practice together. We imagine that such approaches will only grow in the future.[9] We see such a shift as not only potentially greatly accelerating the rate of learning but as also creating an empowered class of practitioners that would make the field much more attractive to talented young people.

• • • • •

We advocate true reform for a system built at the end of the nineteenth century to address twenty-first-century challenges. As Paul Reville, the former secretary of education in Massachusetts, has emphasized, even the most educationally successful state in the nation is still a long way from closing gaps in achievement and maximizing the performance of our system.[10] To do so will require more fundamental redesign than we have thus far been willing to contemplate. We need to look to other sectors and other nations and be willing to reconsider our ends as well as our means. What we currently produce is the result of the system we have; if we want qualitatively better outcomes for all of our students, we will need to build a different kind of system.

THE ACHIEVEMENT GAP

CHAPTER 7

Confronting the Achievement Gap

A District-Level Perspective

JERRY D. WEAST

The uneven performance of our public schools has long been on the national radar. The Supreme Court *Brown v. Board of Education* decision of 1954 acknowledged the disparities of educational resources available in schools serving white and black students in the segregated South and mandated change. That decision was the precursor to more than two decades of civil rights actions undertaken with a goal to even the academic playing field for all children. The battle for school integration is no longer the focus of today's struggle to close the achievement gap, but the war has not been won these many years later.

Historical Perspective

When, in the 1950s, I attended public school in rural Kansas, the notion of an achievement gap—a disparity in academic performance among groups of students—was nonexistent. Such was the case then in much of the United States, a relatively homogeneous nation that was nearly 90 percent white, where little more than half the population lived in areas characterized as "urban" or "urbanized." But change was afoot, catalyzed by undeniable inequities fomenting unease and overdue outrage in Topeka, Kansas, in 1951, resulting in that landmark *Brown v. Board of Education* decision affirming that separate but equal schools are inherently unequal; in Little Rock, Arkansas, in 1957, where the governor obstructed the integration of Little Rock High School; and elsewhere in the country.[1]

Pervasive discrimination based largely on race motivated the civil rights movement that burgeoned in the mid–twentieth century. A focus of this broad movement was efforts to address the discrepancies in academic performance among students across racial groups and socioeconomic circumstances. In fact, it was the landmark civil rights legislation of 1964 that caused the federal government to commission in 1966 the document referred to as the Coleman Report—*Equality of Educational Opportunity*—perhaps the most important single piece of research on public education in our history.[2]

The report's findings are cited in education research to this day. Most agree with James Coleman's conclusions, confirmed in later research, that in-school factors are significant predictors of school achievement but less impactful overall than home and community influences. Importantly, Coleman found that American public education was inherently unequal across the country in part because of racial segregation—most notably in any area where "Negroes" comprised a significant proportion of the population. Furthermore, Coleman found that all students performed better when they attended schools in which the student body had a higher average socioeconomic status. Interestingly, in a finding that generated considerable debate at the time, Coleman found that school resources were not a primary component of student success; that, in general, the differences in resources among schools in the United States were less consequential than other factors and that it was more likely how those resources were applied that was relevant to student success at any given school.

Since 1966, remedies to reduce racial segregation in public schools have had some positive effect on academic achievement by black students. As the percentage of black students attending schools in which they comprised a majority declined, their performance on the National Assessment of Educational Progress (NAEP) improved relative to their white peers. However, legislative imperatives regarding segregation have diminished as courts have found that such segregation is due to individual decisions rather than to action by the school system. Schools have gradually resegregated since the 1980s, in part because our nation is now far more racially and ethnically diverse than it was in the mid–twentieth century. There has tended to be a parallel increase in the gap between white and black student performance on the NAEP, although the scores of black students have increased from the 1970s overall.[3]

Other measures of academic success have shown improvement. Recent assessments of progress since the 1983 report *A Nation at Risk*, which chronicled overall mediocrity in America's public schools, have noted increases in high school graduation rates and increased enrollment in rigorous high school courses (Advanced Placement, International Baccalaureate, and others) for all students, including black and Hispanic.[4] Despite these positive signs, the gap between white students and black and Hispanic students persists.

The achievement gap about which Coleman wrote has a broader connotation today. In contemporary parlance, it refers to the performance gaps between African American and Hispanic students and their non-Hispanic white peers and between students from low-income families and those who are more affluent. Achievement gaps also exist as a function of English-language proficiency, gender, and special education status. It is undeniable that an academic achievement gap exists and that closing it presents a Hobson's choice, only a single option: our national interest can accept no alternative but to close that gap in all its forms. If we fail to provide equitable access to opportunity through education, neither our citizens nor our nation will thrive. As Victor Hugo is popularly credited with saying long ago, he who opens a school door closes a prison.[5]

Confronting a persistent disparity in academic outcomes between white students and their nonwhite—now black and Hispanic—peers, and cognizant of the many factors that can affect student success, in this century the federal government again sought to devise a legislative mandate to confront the academic achievement gap. The No Child Left Behind Act of 2001 (NCLB) was the result. Its provisions, familiar to all who work in public education, require that all academic achievement gaps be eliminated by 2014. Perhaps its most useful component, and one that may survive the lengthy reauthorization process still under way, is the requirement that student performance data be disaggregated by race as well as for students receiving special education or English language learner (ELL) services, or support through the free and reduced-price meals program. This one requirement removed the national blinders and opened up the conversation on this difficult topic. Nevertheless, despite a decade of targeted interventions and the linkage of sanctions for schools where students fail to make adequate progress, the achievement gaps have not narrowed significantly.

That achievement gaps have not narrowed is a matter of even greater national consequence today than it was when Coleman wrote his report in 1966. The United States in 2014 is more racially diverse than at any other time in its history and has the highest rates of poverty overall (17.1 percent) and among children (23.1 percent) of any industrialized country.[6] In fact, the majority of Hispanic and black children live in poverty, according to a recently published report from the Foundation for Child Development, "Diverse Children."[7] The report lays out the scope of the educational challenge confronting the United States in sobering detail. Fourth grade proficiency rates on the 2011 NAEP, broken down by race and between households in which English was or was not the primary language, found fewer than half of all children, regardless of race or language status, were proficient in reading or math. Remarkably, children with immigrant parents "fared equally well, or better, than children in the corresponding groups with US-born parents on six indicators" of well-being, including having at least one securely employed parent and living in a two-parent family. However, black and Hispanic children were far more likely than their white and Asian peers to live in poverty.[8]

Greg Duncan and Richard Murnane, in their companion chapter in this volume, document the insidious impact of the widening income gap between well-off and poor that has occurred over the last forty years. They correlate indices of academic success more closely with income than with race, though, as we've observed, the poor are disproportionately black or Hispanic.

As one report noted, "We know skin color has no bearing on the ability to achieve," and "it is clear that educational achievement is associated with home, school, and societal factors, almost all having their roots in socioeconomic factors affecting this country."[9] Researchers from Coleman on have found that socioeconomic factors are the predominant obstacles to student success: low birth weight, hunger and poor nutrition, exposure to lead poisoning; correlated factors such as frequent moves, absent, unemployed, or poorly educated parents; no access to quality preK programs; too much television and too little exposure to books. All these contribute to dismal academic outcomes when children at last reach public school. At issue is how to address the needs of all the children who are lined up at the classroom door. Failing to do so imposes on the country the economic equivalent of a permanent national recession.[10]

Building Consensus in Montgomery County

When I became superintendent of schools in Montgomery County, Maryland, in 1999, I already had more than two decades of service as a school superintendent under my belt. Montgomery County Public Schools (MCPS), a well-regarded large district (the seventeenth largest in the country), adjacent to Washington, DC, was on the cusp of demographic change, and I was eager to confront the challenges that were on the horizon there. We began, two years before NCLB, by disaggregating student performance data by race/ethnicity and posting it in schools for all to see. It's hard to say who was the more surprised or chagrined by the findings—staff or parents. In fact, the gap between black and Hispanic students' academic achievement and that of white and Asian students was similar to those gaps nationally. When not disaggregated, the disparity was masked by the high scores of the white and Asian students in this historically affluent county. Transparency is the first step to building a consensus around the need to change. NCLB got that right, and it's clear to me that transparency was and is the right way forward in Montgomery County.

In Montgomery County, the conspicuously well-off live but a stone's throw from the very poor. The very poor are increasing in number and as a proportion of student enrollment in the public schools each year. I had ideas about how to address the discomfort and discontent that were unleashed when we posted the disaggregated student data in school corridors. Those ideas (and others that became part of the mix once we began the conversation) were applied during my twelve-year tenure. Some ideas worked; some didn't. But overall the strategy worked. The achievement gap was mostly closed to the standard in the early grades and narrowed in secondary school. The process we employed was based on a set of core beliefs and principles that has applicability in thousands of school districts across this country.

Initially, it was my job as district leader to build a community consensus about the need for fundamental change. Through GIS mapping, we were able to graphically illustrate regions of poverty, high mobility, and low academic performance in order to build understanding of the downward spiral of educational outcomes that was the long-term trend. In meetings with community leaders from every corner and interest sector, we culled the best ideas about how to "bend the trend"—including a funding formula for schools that was based on need rather than enrollment count. To their lasting credit, the citizens of Montgomery County understood that improving education for every student was in the long-term interests of the county.

Within the school system, we embarked on a process of continuous improvement. This process has been employed in industry, and the strategy is applicable to any institution, including school systems. In essence, the goal is to encourage a long-term, ultimately self-sustaining progression of change. I believe the culture of transparency initiated by the public disaggregation of student performance data was the first step on the road to developing public schools that provide high-quality educational opportunity to every student. Exposing performance data not only forced an acknowledgment that the excellent public schools in the county were not serving all the children equally well, but also brought the issue of race squarely to the table.

After we defined the problem, we began to come to consensus about the goals we sought to achieve. Broadly stated, school system leaders agreed to pursue the interrelated goals of excellence—developing a curriculum that would ensure career and college-ready graduates—and equity, providing equal access to that challenging curriculum by preparing all children for success equally well. Working collaboratively, we moved on to a phase that caused us to identify existing conditions and evaluate our efforts to determine if our resources were being used to best effect. Having had decades of experience as a school superintendent, I had learned the importance of structuring change so as not to overrun the capacity of the people and the system. Sequencing a coherent structure through a series of independent and interrelated actions made sense and allowed employees and the community time to assimilate and adapt to new ideas and processes. Building this acceptance about the need for change was foundational to a long-term commitment to improve academic opportunities and outcomes for all children.

Courageous Conversations

During the early months, we began to have frank conversations about race. Those conversations never stopped during my twelve years in the district.

Most of the students who were not succeeding in our schools were black or Hispanic. Most teachers and school leaders were white. We had to ask ourselves what was going on in our schools that kept children from achieving their full potential. We could address inequities associated with family circumstances and economic challenges to some degree through food programs, co-located health facilities, and other outreach; however, our focus had to be on what was happening in school. In the words of one successful principal, the first conversations on race among staff at her high school were "almost explosive." But over time, the conversations became easier. The understandable initial defensive response morphed into awareness that unwitting practices and attitudes were factors that caused some students to feel excluded from the mainstream school community:

- Gatekeeping practices that tended to exclude black and Hispanic students from higher-level courses because access was based on the completion of prerequisites without review of other data
- Uneven provision of academic supports and differentiated instruction
- Inadequate communication with parents of minority children; dismissing them as uncaring though they may work multiple jobs or be intimidated by the school bureaucracy
- Failure to reach out to establish positive mentoring relationships with children who don't come forward to initiate them
- Displaying language or attitudes that convey disrespect or disregard of life experiences different from our own.

We began to gain an understanding of the power of language to incite or transform. There came to be an understanding, according to one member of my leadership team, that "the whole concept of 'color-blindness'—the belief that you should treat everyone the same . . . if you are expecting kids to act like you, that's a disconnect that leads to office referrals and poor student achievement."

The realizations implicit in those remarks from school leaders were catalyzed in part through Study Circles, facilitated conversations among individuals of different ethnicities and races. Administrators, school leaders, faculty, support staff, parents, and students all participated (and continue to participate) in these important gatherings. Usually organized into six sessions and offered in both Spanish and English, Study Circles have been successful at unifying diverse groups, helping each appreciate the benefits of that diversity while developing action steps to address the related challenges. They have sought to create an environment in which racial issues can be discussed openly and productively. We also regularly invited experts in the dynamics of cultural change, matters of race and equity, and the pedagogy of addressing the needs of minority children to address the quarterly meetings of administrators and to speak before school-based groups. We placed an emphasis on helping each staff member understand his or her specific role in improving student outcomes.

Trend-Benders

Through our early meetings on how to "bend the trend," agreement had been reached that it would be most productive to "begin at the beginning" with a focus on improving early childhood education. Studies show that high-quality early childhood education goes a long way to level the playing field as children enter kindergarten. Since the number of seats available in the school system's early childhood programs for low-income families was inadequate, we made partners of private early childhood caregivers, offering them training and curriculum materials that would allow them to align their services with those of the school system. This was an effective short-term solution to a long-term problem. Meanwhile, we initiated a rollout of full-day kindergarten, first in high-poverty schools. In those highly impacted schools, too, we kept class size in the early grades very small (fifteen children per class) and offered free summer school, including two free meals and enticements for good attendance. The board of education eventually accelerated the implementation of full-day kindergarten systemwide, making it available two years early.

Professional development (paid for in the first year by funds repurposed when ineffective programs were eliminated) was mandatory for teachers of the early grades, but we listened when they told us they couldn't track student progress on new formative assessments in a timely manner with existing tools. Ready access to good data was important if we all were to be partners in improving children's learning. Through an innovative enterprise, we provided those teachers with handheld devices that gave immediate feedback on children's performance on brief assessments in reading and

FIGURE 7.1   Kindergarten: Reading simple text

KINDERGARTEN:
READING SIMPLE TEXT

PERCENTAGE OF
STUDENTS
**READING SIMPLE
TEXT BY END OF
KINDERARTEN** BY
ETHNICITY/RACE

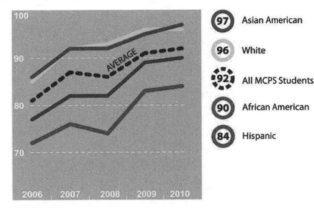

97 Asian American

96 White

92 All MCPS Students

90 African American

84 Hispanic

TEXT LEVEL 4

2006   2007   2008   2009   2010

Source: www.montgomeryschoolsmd.org/about/strategicplan/annualreport/2010/goal1/m2dp1.aspx.

math. Instruction could then be effectively targeted. The improvement in student achievement through the early grades was gratifying, and students of all races and income levels benefited from instructional improvements (see figure 7.1).

Bending the trend from the high school end of the continuum also was an objective. MCPS had long sent a majority of its graduates to higher education, but looking ahead to future workforce needs, we understood that career and college-ready graduates needed to meet equally demanding standards and that we were not preparing all our graduates equally well. Here again, data guided our decision making. Using available information, we back-mapped the course-taking history of our high school graduates who had been successful in college. It was clear that aligning our preK–12 curriculum from the highest national standard—Advanced Placement and International Baccalaureate courses—would provide challenging opportunities to all our children. Further analysis of those successful graduates' performance on standardized testing throughout their educational careers allowed us to benchmark performance levels on those assessments that were predictive of future success. These benchmarks became the Seven Keys to College Readiness, which was a flashy, easily understood communications tool for staff and, most importantly, parents (see figure 7.2). This graphic was widely disseminated in various media throughout the school district and to families of all students; it was also produced in multiple languages.

Accelerating Progress

Accelerating progress—engagement of staff, students, and families—did require effective communication and information sharing. Building a comprehensive, accessible database of student information became a progressive undertaking that ultimately gave every member of the instructional team access to student performance information, policies, practices, lesson-planning tools, curriculum materials, and more. But with the flood of data that became available, broader sharing was needed to get beyond anecdotal information and help data users understand that correlation is not necessarily causation, but a piece of a bigger picture. Modeling a program on one used by the New York City Police Department, we developed M-Stat. Through M-Stat, data were developed around particular challenges, such as improving student readiness for success in Algebra 1 by grade 8. Instructional leaders from schools where success had been achieved would lead meetings of peers from other schools to share the processes and pathways that were effective in that work. These meetings proved to be highly successful in addressing the attainment of the objectives set by the school system each year as part of the strategic plan.

Our progress toward closing the achievement gap was hopeful but uneven. Some schools struggled, and we assigned School Improvement Teams to them for a year. Typically, members of these teams did Walk-Throughs at the school, a formal protocol that was developed and shared systemwide. These planned school site visits were intended to provide "a catalyst for informative, non-evaluative collegial discussion; an examination of current school practices; and a vehicle to acknowledge school strengths, address challenges, and raise questions about teaching and learning."[11] Even seasoned professionals acknowledged having new insights into their teaching styles after these no-holds-barred discussions about the importance of personal relationship building; promoting a positive academic identity by

FIGURE 7.2   Seven keys to college readiness

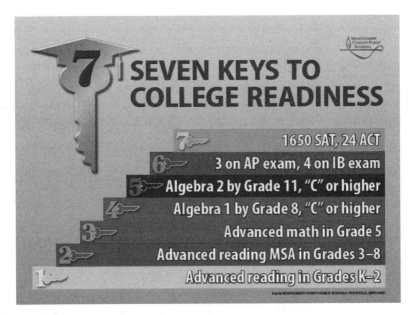

Source: © 2010 Montgomery County Public Schools, Rockville, MD

making struggling students feel competent; making connections between content and what is familiar; keeping language for ELLs clear with use of action verbs; providing more white space on papers for an ELL audience; allowing time for student discourse/discussion of assignments.

Partnerships were essential to progress. Key among these was the development of collaborative working relationships with all three of the employee associations (teachers, administrators, and classified employees), which had not been treated equally by the school system. We eliminated those inequalities as a first step. The union leaders also agreed to interest-based bargaining on contracts and to proceed with negotiations on salaries and benefits simultaneously, not one association at a time. We brought association leaders, as well as the leader of the County Council of Parent-Student-Teacher Associations, into the process of developing the annual operating budget from the outset. And over the course of several years, we developed groundbreaking Professional Growth Systems, each including a Career Lattice and a Peer Assistance and Review process for removing underperformers.

In recognition of the findings of significant studies from the Coleman Report on, we learned to look also to parents as partners in their children's learning. In the case of immigrant students in particular, that meant that parents sometimes needed assistance in order to gain the knowledge and confidence required of effective partners. Developing these partnerships—building a community of leaders, teachers, and parents—was important to students' success. As Coleman observed in 1988, children are "embedded in the enclaves of adults, first the family and second a surrounding community." The relationships nurtured within their community shape the adults that children will become. To bring reluctant parents into the process of educating their children, we delivered communications from the school system in several languages (English, French, Spanish, Chinese, Korean, Vietnamese, and Amharic); established an Office of Family and Community Partnerships through which, among other things, we offered Parent Academies in the evenings at several schools to share with parents ways in which they can help their children succeed in school, answer parents' questions, and provide information on timely topics; established an annual Back to School Fair with support of local retailers and community agencies, all of which provide information and supplies that are distributed to the thousands of families who attend each year. Among many active community collaborations, members of the school system's Retirees' Association banded together to provide books for young readers as well as backpacks and school supplies.

Student success in the early grades was gratifying. In secondary school, on national measures such as the SAT and Advanced Placement examinations, high school completion rates, and intermediate hurdles such as completion of Algebra 1 by grade 8, the gap among children of different races has greatly narrowed. For example, African American students in MCPS now participate and succeed in Advanced Placement at rates higher than for all students nationally; 2010 saw the highest male African-American high school graduation rate in the nation among districts with large African American populations; and African American students are increasingly enrolling in college (see figures 7.3–7.5). The district has a long way to go, but we are proud of what we have accomplished.

FIGURE 7.3   AP participation and performance: MCPS all African American graduates

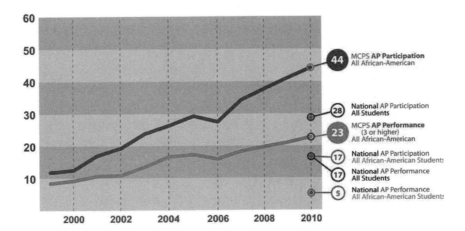

Source: Montgomery County Public Schools, Rockville, MD

FIGURE 7.4   2010 MCPS male African American graduation rate highest in nation

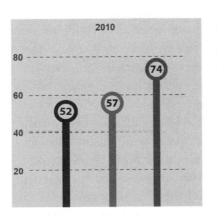

Source: Schott Foundation for Public Education 2013 Report, "The Urgency of Now"

FIGURE 7.5   MCPS African American graduates college enrollment

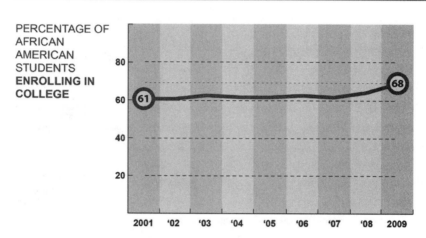

MCPS African American Graduates
COLLEGE ENROLLMENT

Note: 83 percent participation due to FERPA and college nonparticipation in data collection.
Source: MCPS Office of Shared Accountability, June 2012

Lessons Learned

What can be taken away from the Montgomery County story that can be applied in other districts to benefit children whose life circumstances put them at risk of lives of insufficiency and struggle? The goals and objectives we set included improved early childhood education, a curriculum back-mapped from a college-ready standard all the way to preschool, and professional development for teachers, leaders, and school teams to build skills and strategies to address the complex needs of the children entering their classrooms. The importance of curriculum aligned to a high standard cannot be overstated. As our children's performance is increasingly measured against a global norm, we do them and our future prosperity as a nation a great disservice if we don't challenge our students to excel. The Common Core State Standards are a good-faith attempt to raise the bar and establish a national standard that will prepare U.S. high school graduates to compete worldwide. The Common Core is similar to the aligned curriculum developed in Montgomery County and is an effort I support.

The process of continuous improvement, of establishing a self-sustaining culture that encourages initiative and innovation, does require effective leadership, but most of all, it demands collaboration if it is to succeed. There is neither a master blueprint of the individual actions that bring success nor a silver bullet that will make things right. The goals any district sets must be its own; the evaluation of what's working and what is not must be accomplished uniquely in each district. Only through a collaborative process can there be developed an awareness of the need for change and a climate in which change can be undertaken without fear of failure or retribution. It is the job of the district leader, the superintendent, to set that tone, communicate the vision, and provide political leadership that supports the people who are doing the work.

It is a mistake to believe that only the leader of an organization can make good decisions. If the leader is making all the decisions, those charged only to implement become disengaged. Disengaged staff don't feel they have any ownership of results. Nor does a leader necessarily have the expertise or perspective that will allow him or her to make the best decision. Empowering others to be decision makers—a responsibility that requires each person to gather information and advice from others before reaching a conclusion—pays dividends to the organization exponentially. As more people are encouraged to take ownership of the work through involvement in the decision-making process, more people become invested and far more likely to bring the best of themselves to their work each day. I am reminded of an administrative secretary in my office who was to provide technical support for me at a national conference where I was to present a paper. My flight was canceled, but his was not. He made the presentation for me, as effectively as I would have. Another employee, aware that minority students were being excluded from higher-level courses because of residual gatekeeping practices, took it on himself to develop a tool easily created at each school that monitored key test scores to identify capable students who were missing academic opportunities. They were engaged in their work!

We brought stakeholders to the table in Montgomery County, where leaders of the three employee unions participated fully in developing the district's goals and objectives, policies and processes, and even the operating budget. The trust that resulted from this cooperative venture allowed us to get through the economic recession without rancor. Everyone understood the sacrifices that we all would have to make—no raises for a start—in order to maintain high-quality instructional programs. That partnership, in which each constituency had an equal voice, was instrumental in developing a culture in which every employee felt a part of the whole.

The best organizations create value for those they serve by bringing out the best performance of all constituencies. With the right people, the right plan, the right process, and a healthy dose of persistence, we finally created in Montgomery County what I had strived for the whole of my career: to ensure that race and class were not predictors of academic success. That wasn't accomplished by attacking the competencies or the intentions of our workforce but instead by ensuring we created and supported a culture of the best people doing their best work—a fully engaged team.

While competent and committed employees follow directions, *engaged* employees form an attachment to the work that taps a reserve of discretionary effort, fuels perseverance, and stimulates creative problem solving. Nationwide, according to surveys of employee engagement conducted by Gallup in 2010, only 29 percent of employees are actively engaged in their jobs. People who are actively engaged help move an organization forward. Nearly all highly engaged employees, motivated by intrinsic factors such as personal growth and working toward a common and meaningful purpose, believe they positively impact their organization's performance; few who are disengaged feel this way.

A well-run education system coordinates the talents and efforts of all employees, allowing them to thrive in careers they love. As they thrive, the larger effect is the emergence of engaged and inspired students who also have a greater opportunity to succeed in school and in the wider world.

The process of developing an engaged and effective workforce is relevant to closing the achievement gap in school districts large and small across this country. Contemporary research finds that more than 40 percent of children attend high-poverty schools and that these students disproportionately are taught by "out-of-field" and early-career teachers. If, as research also indicates, the single most significant change agent in a child's education is the classroom teacher, it is imperative that we focus our efforts on improving the quality of that workforce over time. [12]

As a district confronts its own issues around student achievement, stakeholders must begin with a comprehensive assessment of current conditions by looking at student performance data at the individual and school levels. Districts must evaluate their interactions and then demonstrate the courage to redirect resources that are misaligned with the goals the district has defined and jettison ineffective programs. This evaluation process is not costly. By doing so in Montgomery County, we were able to offer professional development initiatives through cost savings.

Changes at the school level can be catalyzed not only by a visionary district leader but also by effective school and central office administrators who understand the mission. To the extent that individuals with these understandings are not available in the district, they must be developed or hired. Distributed leadership was key to cultivating the values and attitudes that led to the implementation of best practices and a "grow your own" process to developing future leaders. In Montgomery County, distributed leadership began at the highest levels of the school system through creation of an Executive Leadership Team that was vested with policy-making decisions and process development and that vetted all significant reports prior to publication or release. The team included the district's senior leaders from all offices, union presidents and executive directors, and staff whose responsibilities were relevant to the topic being discussed. As superintendent, I met with the group to provide goals and broad vision, but I did not directly participate in its day-to-day work. It was important for me to maintain an oversight role but not to micromanage. For any leader, finding the right loose/tight balance in supervision is critical.

Distributed leadership occurred at the school level in Leadership Teams, which made decisions about all aspects of the education process at the school, and in the grade-level teams or content-area teams that operated to coordinate delivery of instruction. The Professional Learning Communities Institute, created as part of our professional development structure, educated whole school staffs on ways to improve instruction, collaborate, differentiate delivery of the curriculum to a diverse community of learners, and create a welcoming climate in all interactions within the school and the wider community.

Technology offers solutions to accelerate the learning process that is part of a whole-system cultural shift, tools that were not available even ten years ago: video conferencing, webinars, and facilitated discussions all are relatively inexpensive tools. MCPS leadership teams read widely about creating professional learning communities and structuring schoolwide interventions. At "job alike" meetings, individuals with similar responsibilities—school principals, assistant principals, resource teachers, curriculum specialists, career coordinators, school business managers—shared and discussed good ideas. We tapped our local business leaders for their expertise in helping us organize more effectively and thereby improve how we did our work. These relationships helped all to develop a common language and a shared set of beliefs and expectations and build trust among colleagues to support a culture of continuous improvement.

We agreed that a "gotcha'" mentality would be counterproductive. The current movement to tie teacher evaluations closely to the performance of students on standardized tests has the potential to destroy the environment in which educators feel able to share, experiment, and take risks. Rather, in Montgomery County we developed for teachers, administrators, and classified staff professional growth systems that provide mentoring and consultation for every new teacher and for struggling professionals. This helped establish a culture of respect across the district.

Central to developing that culture of respect, paradoxically, was the process the professional growth systems provided—called Peer Assistance and Review—for exiting staff who demonstrated an inability or unwillingness to improve after being provided with a year or more of guidance and support from a consulting (mentor) teacher. Peer Assistance and Review replaced a more punitive dismissal process but has resulted in discharging about ten times as many underperforming teachers, both novice and tenured.

Looking Ahead

The process of improving public education can be accelerated by changes in how we prepare our teachers and district leaders—the pedagogy provided by our colleges of education and the training available to those who aspire to lead the nation's fifteen thousand school districts. Colleges of education have been criticized for failing to provide teacher education programs that prepare teachers to address the needs of all the children in their classrooms. Linda Darling-Hammond outlines three concepts on which our teacher training programs should focus:

- The kinds of knowledge teachers must have about their subject matter and about the learning processes and development of their students
- The skills teachers need to provide productive learning experiences for their students, to provide them with informed feedback, and to evaluate their own performance and improve on it
- The professional commitments teachers need to help each child succeed and to develop their own knowledge and skills as members of a professional teaching community.[13]

Improving teacher preparation will require our best thinking and an investment over time to reorganize, restructure, and redesign the pathways to teacher certification. We should pay heed to the routes to certification that produce confident teachers who stay in the profession for the long term. The National Board for Professional Teaching Standards' rigorous certification process is a model assessment program designed to develop, retain, and recognize accomplished teachers and to encourage ongoing improvement in schools nationwide. We should aim for all our teachers to attain this standard of excellence.

District leaders, too, require professional training, mentoring, and consultation that is currently absent. Too many superintendents move along a continuum from classroom to school leader to district leader without having an opportunity to develop the leadership qualities they already possess or the big-picture-thinking that is required to move a system of schools from adequate to excellent. Both professional associations (such as the American Association of School Administrators) and university programs (such as Harvard's Public Education Leadership Program) have roles to play in this endeavor.

I do not believe that there is a Big Idea lurking on the horizon that will transform public education to make it equitable and challenging for all children. Rather, there are a series of unglamorous but foundational changes that can be undertaken in any school district, whether it serves 1,000 students or 100,000. The evidence is there in Socorro Independent School District in Texas; in Union City, New Jersey; and in Montgomery County. Their success has been documented in recent research by Harold Kwalwasser and David Kirp.[14] These districts have implemented and evaluated strategies we now know work:

- Review performance data so you know where you are.
- Decide collaboratively what you want your students to achieve.
- Evaluate the effectiveness of programs, technologies, and resource allocations in place.
- Get rid of what doesn't work or is misaligned and reallocate resources to support your goals.
- Identify the real and artificial impediments to student success: processes, attitudes, values, and beliefs.
- Change the processes; begin courageous conversations about the attitudes, values, and beliefs to develop a culture of respect and a commitment to high expectations for all students.
- Invest in high-quality early education.
- Align the curriculum to a high standard, preK to grade 12.
- Review performance data so you know where you are.
- Repeat the process outlined above.

A well-run education system coordinates the talents and efforts of all employees, allowing them to thrive in careers they love. Educators undertake the responsibility of providing students with an excellent education that will equip them with the tools to succeed in this twenty-first century and become productive members of their communities. Most importantly, providing equal access to opportunity for all of the children of this large and diverse country is a moral imperative—indeed, it is the foundation of the American Dream.

CHAPTER 8

Rising Inequality and the School Performance of Low- and High-Income Children

GREG J. DUNCAN AND RICHARD J. MURNANE

America has always taken pride in being the land of opportunity, a country in which hard work and sacrifice result in a better life for one's children. Economic growth has made that dream a reality for generations of Americans, including many people who started out poor. The quarter-century following World War II was a golden era for the U.S. economy, as the benefits of substantial economic growth were shared by both high- and low-income families.[1] But storm clouds began to gather in the 1970s. Economic changes favoring highly educated workers plus demographic shifts, such as the rise of single-parent families, produced sharply growing income gaps between high- and low-income families.

In this chapter, we explore some of the consequences of growing income inequality for American children. We first document the degree to which income inequality between children growing up in low- and high-income families has increased over the past forty years and then show that growing income gaps have been more than matched by increases in the gaps between the amount of money low- and high-income parents spend on enrichment activities for their children.

Most distressingly, these growing income and expenditure gaps have been accompanied by a steady divergence in the achievement and schooling attainment of children living in low- and high-income families. Differences in the reading and math achievement levels of low- and high-income children are much larger than they were several decades ago, as are differences in college graduation rates.

What accounts for these widening gaps? Drawing from our book *Whither Opportunity? Rising Inequality, Schools and Children's Life Chances*, we examine the role families and schools play in the linkages between increasing family income inequality and the widening gaps in schooling.[2] In addition to growing differences in what poor and rich families spend on their children, stagnant incomes for low-income families have likely continued to affect maternal stress, mental health, and parenting. At the school level, rising residential segregation by income has led to increasing concentrations of low- and high-income children attending separate schools. Peer problems, geographic mobility, and difficulties in attracting and retaining good teachers have made it difficult to provide consistently high-quality learning experiences in schools serving high concentrations of low-income students. We close the chapter with some ideas about proven policy approaches that might be considered as we tackle the enormous task of restoring the kinds of educational opportunities that our children need to lead healthy and productive lives.

Widening Gaps

The left bar in each set of bars in figure 8.1 shows the average income in a particular year (in 2012 dollars) for children at the twentieth percentile of the nation's family income distribution.[3] This means that, in a given year, 20 percent of children lived in families with incomes below that level while 80 percent had incomes above it. In 1970, the dividing line was drawn at $37,664 (in 2012 dollars). The middle bar shows the average family incomes in a given year at the eightieth percentile of the distribution, which was about $100,000 (in 2012 dollars) in 1970. The right bar shows the average income for very high-income families—those with incomes higher than 95 percent of U.S. families, which was a little more than $150,000 in 1970 (in 2012 dollars).

In contrast to the two decades before 1970, when the rising tides of economic growth boosted the incomes of these three groups grew at virtually identical rates, economic growth over the next four decades failed to lift all boats. Compared with 1970, the 2010 family income at the twentieth percentile fell by more than 25 percent. In contrast, the incomes of families at the eightieth percentile grew by 24 percent to $125,000, while the incomes

FIGURE 8.1 Children's family income over time

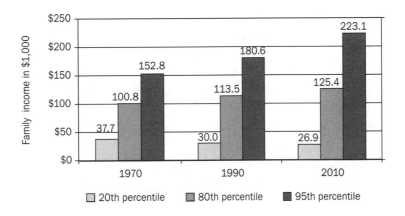

Note: Chart shows 20th, 80th, and 95th percentiles of the distribution of family incomes for all children ages 15–17. They are based on data from the U.S. Census Bureau and are adjusted for inflation. Amounts are in 2012 dollars.

Source: Reprinted with permission from Greg J. Duncan and Richard J. Murnane, eds., *Whither Opportunity? Rising Inequality, Schools, and Children's Life Chances* (New York: Russell Sage Foundation and Spencer Foundation, 2011), © Russell Sage Foundation.

of the richest 5 percent of families rose even more. The stagnation of the incomes of families at the lower end of the spectrum is also reflected in the nation's child poverty rate, which at 21.9 percent in 2011 was up sharply from 15.1 percent in 1970.

A consequence of increasing income inequality is substantial growth in the gap between the average reading and mathematics skills of students from low- and higher-income families. As illustrated in figure 8.2, among children who were adolescents in the late 1960s, test scores of low-income children lagged behind those of their better-off peers by four-fifths of a standard deviation about 80 points on an SAT-type test. Forty years later, this gap was 50 percent larger, amounting to nearly 125 points.[4] We were surprised to discover how much the income-based gap grew during this period in view of the fact that racial gaps in test scores have diminished considerably in the fifty years since *Brown v. Board of Education*.[5]

Given the importance of academic preparation in determining educational success, it should come as no surprise that growth in the income-based gap in children's reading and mathematics achievement has

FIGURE 8.2   Race and income-based gaps in reading achievement in SAT-type units

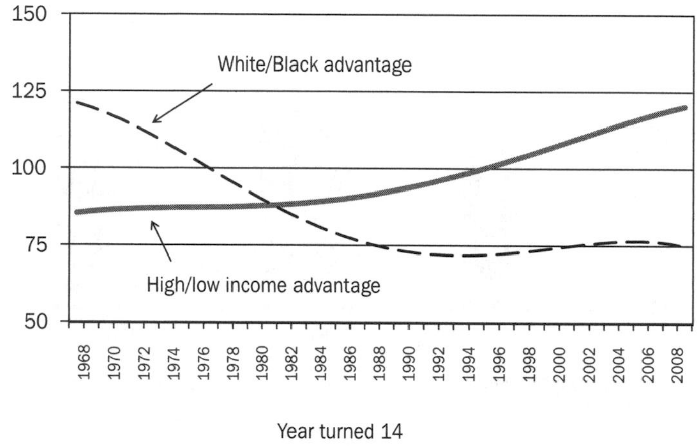

Year turned 14

Source: Reprinted with permission from Sean F. Reardon, "The Widening Academic Achievement Gap between the Rich and the Poor: New Evidence and Possible Explanations," in Duncan and Murnane, *Whither Opportunity?* © Russell Sage Foundation.

contributed to a growing gap in the rate of four-year college completion (see figure 8.3). The number of children raised in affluent families who completed college jumped by 18 percentage points—from slightly more than one-third to more than one-half—for students entering high school in the mid-1990s relative to their counterparts entering high school in the mid-1970s. Among children from low-income families, in contrast, the graduation rate was only four percentage points higher. Analysts differ in their assessments of the relative importance of college costs and academic preparation in explaining the increasing gulf between the college graduation rates of affluent and low-income children in our country.[6] However, all are rooted, at least in part, in the growth in family income inequality.

How Rising Inequality Influences Children's Skills and Attainment

American society relies on its schools to level the playing field for children born into different circumstances. More than any other institution, schools are charged with making equality of opportunity a reality. During a period

FIGURE 8.3   College graduation rates for high- and low-income children

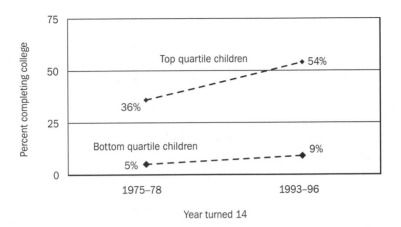

Source: Reprinted with permission from Martha J. Bailey and Susan M. Dynarski, "Inequality in Postsecondary Education," in Duncan and Murnane, Whither Opportunity? © Russell Sage Foundation.

of rising inequality, can schools play this critical role effectively? Or has growing income inequality affected families, neighborhoods, and local labor markets in a manner that undercuts the effectiveness of schools serving disadvantaged populations?

Our edited volume *Whither Opportunity?* attempts to answer these questions, while our companion book, *Restoring Opportunity: The Crisis of Inequality and the Challenge for American Education,* explores education- and family-based solutions to the growing gaps schooling outcomes between high- and low-income children.[7] In organizing the twenty-five chapters of *Whither Opportunity?* we adopted an ecological perspective to help understand the impact of growing inequality. Income inequality affects families and neighborhoods. Changes in these social contexts may in turn affect children's skill acquisition and educational attainments directly as well as indirectly by influencing how schools operate. For example, growing income inequality increases the gap between the resources rich and poor families can invest in their children.

Growing disparities in parental investments may also indirectly widen skill gaps by contributing to residential segregation, as the wealthy purchase housing in neighborhoods where less affluent families cannot afford to live. Indeed, residential segregation by income has increased in recent decades.[8] This can reduce interactions between rich and poor in settings ranging from schools and child care centers to libraries and grocery stores. Without the financial and human resources and political clout of the wealthy, institutions in poorer neighborhoods, perhaps most importantly schools, may decline in quality, which can have detrimental effects on the education and life chances of children born into poor families.

Low family income makes it more difficult for parents to gain access to high-quality child care that prepares children for kindergarten. It can also lead to classrooms filled with low-achieving, inattentive classmates. Crime in low-income neighborhoods may provide tempting alternatives to working hard at school and at the same time make it more difficult for neighborhood schools to recruit high-quality teachers.

Families

Very young children tend to be completely dependent on their families to provide what they need for healthy development.[9] Children growing up in families with greater financial resources score higher on many dimensions of school readiness on entering kindergarten. It is a challenge to identify the extent to which these differences are caused by income itself as opposed to differences in innate capabilities or other family characteristics (e.g., two-parent family structure, parental education levels).

An obvious advantage of a higher family income is that it provides more resources to buy books, computers, high-quality child care, summer camps, private schooling, and other enrichments. In 1972–1973, high-income families spent about $2,850 more per year on child enrichment than did low-income families.[10] By 2005–2006, this gap had nearly tripled to $8,000. Spending differences are largest for enrichment activities such as music lessons, travel, and summer camps.[11] Differential access to such activities may explain the gaps in background knowledge between children from high-income families and those from low-income families that are so predictive of reading skills in the middle and high school years.[12]

Parents also spend different amounts and quality of time interacting with their children and exposing them to novel environments, and these factors can make a difference in their development.[13] These experiences, financed in part by the higher incomes of more affluent families, contribute to the background knowledge that is so critical for comprehending science and social studies texts in the middle school grades.

It is difficult to untangle the precise effects of all these family-related factors—income and expenditures, family structure, time and language use—on the disparities in children's school readiness and success that have emerged over the past several decades. But the evidence linking income to children's school achievement suggests that the sharp increase in income gaps between high- and low-income families since the 1970s and the concomitant gap in children's school success by income is hardly coincidental.

In particular, two experimental studies involving three sites conducted in the 1970s examined the overall impacts on children of income supplements that boosted family income by as much as 50 percent.[14] In two of the three sites, the researchers found that children in families randomly assigned to receive an income supplement did significantly better with respect to early academic achievement and school attendance than children in families that received no supplement.

Still more evidence on policy-relevant impacts of income increases come from a study that takes advantage of the increasing generosity of the U.S. Earned Income Tax Credit between 1993 and 1997 to compare children's test scores before and after it was expanded.[15] Most of the children in this study were between the ages of 8 and 14, and the study's authors found improvements in low-income children's achievement in middle childhood that coincided with the EITC expansion. A second study, conducted in Canada, took advantage of variations in the generosity of the National Child Benefit program across Canadian provinces to estimate income impacts on child achievement.[16] Among children ages 6–10 residing in low-income families, policy-related income increases had a positive and significant association with math scores and a negative link with the likelihood of a child receiving a diagnosis of a learning disability. For 4- to 6-year-olds, the income increases were associated with higher scores on a test of receptive vocabulary for boys but not for girls.

All in all, the strongest research evidence appears to indicate that money matters, in a variety of ways, for children's long-term success in school. While some children have always enjoyed greater benefits and advantages, the income gap has widened dramatically over the past four decades, and the implication of these research studies is that, partly in consequence, the gap in children's school success has widened as well.

Schools

Researchers have long known that children attending schools with mostly low-income classmates have lower academic achievement and graduation rates than those attending schools with more affluent student populations. Less well understood are how environmental influences shape school functioning and the particular ways in which schools affect children's developmental trajectories and long-run outcomes.

In recent decades, increasing income-based segregation of schools has been a mechanism through which growing family income inequality has affected the educational attainments of the nation's teenagers. From 1972 to 1988, schools became more economically segregated, and teenagers from affluent families were less and less likely to have classmates from low-income families.[17] The result is that a child from a poor family is two to four times as likely as a child from an affluent family to have classmates in both elementary and high school with low skills and with behavior problems. This sorting matters, because the weak cognitive skills and greater behavioral problems among low-income children have a negative effect on the learning of their classmates. Once again, economic disadvantage is passed on from one generation to the next.

Despite this segregation, differences among schools account for a relatively modest, although growing, part of the variation in high school graduation rates, college enrollment rates, and labor market earnings. But modest does not imply unimportant. Moving a high school student in 1972 from a school in the tenth percentile of school quality to one in the 90th percentile would increase the student's probability of enrollment in a four-year college by about twenty percentage points, a very big change. The corresponding change for a high school student in 1992 or 2002 is even larger.[18]

Another threat to achievement is student mobility. Urban families living in poverty move frequently, and, as a result of school sorting by socioeconomic status, children from poor families are especially likely to attend schools with relatively high rates of new students arriving during the school year. Furthermore, children attending elementary schools with considerable student mobility make less progress in mathematics than do children attending schools with a low level of student mobility. Moreover, the negative effects apply to students who themselves are residentially stable as well as to those who are not, and the effects are likely to be associated with the disruption of instruction caused by the entry of new students into a class.[19]

Teacher quality is another factor contributing to the weak performance of students in high-poverty schools. A substantial body of research has shown that schools serving high concentrations of poor, nonwhite, and low-achieving students find it difficult to attract and retain skilled teachers. In addition to preferring schools with relatively low proportions of nonwhite and low-achieving students, teachers also favor schools in neighborhoods with higher-income residents and less violent crime.[20] Teacher commitment, parental involvement, and student achievement in these schools all tend to be low. Such schools are also likely to be in high-crime neighborhoods, although it is important to note that student arrest rates are not high in all schools located in high-crime neighborhoods.[21]

These patterns highlight the difficult challenges facing schools in high-crime neighborhoods. On the one hand, schools need to deal firmly with students who have been arrested, especially for violent crimes, because these students may disrupt the learning climate of their school. On the other hand, expelling students who have been arrested reduces the probability that these students will graduate from high school. This is one of many issues that occupy the time and resources of teachers and administrators in high-poverty schools and detract attention from teaching and learning.

Yet another challenge facing many of the nation's schools concerns the placement of new immigrants, many of whom speak little English. Today's immigrants are more likely than those in the early 1970s to come from high-poverty countries. Black and Hispanic immigrants to New York City are much more likely to be poor than are white immigrants from eastern Europe, and they are more likely to attend elementary and middle schools with native-born black and Hispanic students who are poor.[22] Thus, while immigrants are not segregated from the native-born in New York City schools, their residential patterns contribute to segregation by socioeconomic status and race.

Improving the Life Chances of Low-Income Children

These widening gaps in educational opportunities between children from low- and higher-income families are increasing income inequality and jeopardizing the upward socioeconomic mobility that has held our pluralistic democracy together. Closing these large income-related gaps in educational outcomes is critical to the nation's future. To do this, we need a combination of policies that support low-income families and that improve the quality of schools that low-income children attend.

Several recent studies suggest that childhood income does matter for some key child and adolescent outcomes. A better understanding of the role of the timing of income in how it affects children's development, across a wide range of outcomes, is important, because policies that target specific stages of childhood or adolescence will be more efficient than those that do not.

If the evidence ultimately shows that poverty early in childhood matters the most for development during childhood and adolescence, then it may make sense to consider income transfer policies that provide more income to families with young children. In the case of work support programs like the Earned Income Tax Credit, this might mean extending more generous credits (or reallocating existing credits) to families with young children. In the case of refundable child tax credits, this could mean providing larger credits to families with young children. Another step might be to ensure that sanctions and other regulations embedded within welfare policies do not deny benefits to families with very young children. Not only do young children appear to be most vulnerable to the consequences of poverty, but mothers with very young children are also the least able to support themselves through employment in the labor market.

Improving the quality of the schools low-income children attend poses even more important, and difficult, challenges. As a nation, we have failed to appreciate the extent to which technological changes over the past several decades have altered the skills needed to succeed in today's economy. Moreover, the rising economic and social inequality produced by technology and globalization has weakened neighborhoods and families in ways that make effective school reform that much more difficult. For a variety of historical reasons, our nation has not learned how to provide the consistent supports that schools and teachers—especially those serving large numbers of low-income children—must have to succeed.

Discussions of school reforms often center on simplistic "silver bullets"—more money, more accountability, more choice, new organizational structures. None of these reforms has turned the tide because each fails to effectively improve what matters most in education: the quality and consistency of the instruction and experiences offered to students.

What are the building blocks for an "American solution" to the serious problems facing our nation's schools? We argue for school supports designed to improve teachers' ability to provide effective instruction for their students, among them:

- High-quality, grade-by-grade academic standards, such as those in the Common Core, accompanied by curricula that are well aligned with the standards
- Assessments that measure students' mastery of the standards well
- School leaders who know what good instruction looks like and how to create an organization committed to continuous improvement
- Well-educated, well-trained teachers
- Teacher access to expertise on a host of topics, including improving instruction, identifying the strengths and weaknesses of individual students, creating and implementing norms for student behavior, and dealing with students' emotional problems.[23]

A second key building block is a well-designed accountability system that promotes a willingness to use resources in new ways and offers incentives for school faculties to work together to develop the skills of every student. We saw this in the three case studies we feature in our book *Restoring Opportunity*. In the case of one Boston preK program, accountability came in the form of the expectation that each school would obtain and retain accreditation from the National Association for the Education of Young Children (NAEYC). For the University of Chicago charter schools and some small schools of choice in New York City, accountability included the requirement that their students score well on state-mandated examinations.

But it was also the case that in these schools, teachers, and school leaders experienced a more immediate and more important type of accountability:

a responsibility to their colleagues for educating every student. For Boston preK teachers it included taking advantage of the instructional coaching provided by the system. For Chicago charter school teachers it included working together to make implementation of the sophisticated literacy curriculum more consistent. For the ninth grade teachers in New York City, it meant embracing their shared responsibility to develop the skills of all incoming students, including those reading far below grade level.

The country's future prosperity, and our ability to make the dream of upward mobility a reality, depend on reversing a trend toward increasingly divergent destinies in the education and lives of high- and low-income children. Successful educational interventions demonstrate that we, as a nation, have learned and continue to learn a great deal about how to educate low-income students well. We need to secure a nationwide commitment to put our knowledge into action so that every child has the opportunity to succeed, despite the barriers and challenges posed by increasing income inequality.

VULNERABLE CHILDREN

CHAPTER 9

Beyond Child Protection

Helping All Families Provide Adequate Parenting

MICHAEL S. WALD

Policy makers, advocates, and researchers all agree that four major factors influence children's development: genes, the nature and quality of the economic and other resources provided to the child by parents and the state, neighborhood, and the quality of parenting the child receives.[1] Each of these factors affects the others. Over the past forty years, societal efforts to promote children's well-being and development have expanded significantly. Most of the attention has been on expanding access to, and improving the quality of, the nonfamily institutions that serve children, especially the health, child care, and education systems. There also have been increases in economic resources available to low-income families.[2] As the other chapters in this volume show, many of these efforts are helping children.

There has been far less attention, however, to improving parenting.[3] Yet, especially with respect to protecting and promoting the *basic* physical, emotional, social, and cognitive development of children, parenting is of critical importance. I estimate that at least 20 percent of all children in the United States live in families where the parenting is highly problematic with respect to supporting their children's basic development. The only system with responsibility for addressing the needs of these children is child protective services (CPS), which is charged with responding to parenting that is legally defined as abusive or neglectful (maltreatment). Under most state laws, abuse and neglect are defined primarily in terms of physical harms to, or sexual conduct with, a child.[4] CPS systems focus primarily on children who have already suffered, or are in imminent danger of suffering, threats to their safety due to parental actions. The primary goal of intervention is to prevent the recurrence of these threats, not to promote children's long-term development. In most states, the majority of children reported to CPS are not brought under its jurisdiction or provided with any services.[5]

A variety of parenting programs and other support services are available to parents who seek them out, but no system has responsibility for trying to identify and help children whose emotional, social, or cognitive development is adversely affected by problematic parenting that does not fall within the definition of maltreatment. Voluntary services do not reach a significant proportion of the parents and children who need them the most, either due to lack of availability or the failure of the parent to seek or accept the services.

A new discussion is needed regarding government policies toward parenting. The current approach leaves far too many children at risk of injury during childhood and very poor outcomes in adulthood with respect to both economic well-being and mental health. In this chapter, I focus in particular on two outcomes for children that are central goals of public policy: safety during childhood, and the development of the skills needed to earn a *basic* living in adulthood. In order to substantially increase the likelihood that all children will attain these two minimum outcomes, it is necessary to reduce the scope of the child protection system and create a new system of services focused on improving parenting. Although these services would be voluntary, participation would entitle parents to economic and other benefits.

Outcomes

In order to develop and assess alternative policies toward children, it is necessary to identify the outcomes that government seeks to achieve through its policies and investments. The benefits and costs of alternative policies and investments in producing these outcomes can then be examined.

While government policies focus on helping children achieve many outcomes, four are especially important to policy makers and child advocates: safety during childhood, the ability to be self-sufficient in adulthood, economic "success" in adulthood, and equal opportunity for economic and social mobility.

Protection from physical and mental harm during childhood. One clear outcome relates to children's health. The promotion of children's basic health and safety (including nutritional needs) is the goal of significant public policies and spending. While the focus generally is on access to general health care, maltreatment laws are designed to protect children from parenting that substantially impairs (or threatens to impair) their physical or mental health. Recent evidence indicates that the health or safety of at least 15–20 percent of all children is put at risk by parental conduct considered maltreatment at some point before they turn eighteen.[6]

Self-sufficiency. Most government policies regarding children primarily aim to help children acquire the academic and social/emotional skills considered necessary for economic success in adulthood, rather than to provide them with a particular quality of life as children. The minimum goal is to provide children with the capabilities needed to be self-sufficient during adulthood, usually operationalized as trying to minimize the number of children who will live in poverty as adults. While nearly half of all adults experience a period of living in poverty, at least 10 percent of adults in the United States are poor over an extended period of time during adulthood.[7] Failure to graduate high school is the strongest factor leading to long-term poverty.

Economic well-being. A more expansive economic outcome is that each child attains the skills needed to earn a "middle-class" income. Defining middle-class income as three times the poverty level, Sawhill estimates that about 60 percent of children born in the United States now attain middle-class incomes by age forty.[8] Earning a middle-class income generally requires attaining a postsecondary credential; in recent years, the need for higher education has become even greater.

Economic and social mobility. Another outcome is the elimination of differences in educational achievement and economic success in adulthood that are highly correlated with the income, race, or ethnicity of a child's parents. This outcome often is framed in terms of closing the educational achievement gap, which is seen as necessary to increasing economic or social mobility. This goal does not require that children attain any particular level of well-being or economic accomplishment in adulthood; reducing the inequality of outcomes and, by implication, opportunity related to parental income or ethnicity is the target. Over the past thirty years, there has been no progress in closing the achievement gap or promoting relative economic mobility, although most children are better off economically than their parents.[9]

Parenting and Outcomes

In developing options aimed at promoting these four outcomes, policy makers must decide how much to invest in services focused primarily on the child (especially schools and preschool), in policies that increase family income, in efforts at improving neighborhoods, and in services directed at improving parenting. While these approaches are not mutually exclusive, and all are needed, choices must be made regarding how much to invest in different alternatives since resources are limited.

Which of the above outcomes require a major focus on parenting? The need to focus on parenting is definitional with respect to protecting children from maltreatment, since the parent is causing the harm. There also are strong reasons to focus heavily on parenting in order to enable all children to reach young adulthood capable of being self-sufficient and avoiding poverty. Most children will achieve basic self-sufficiency in adulthood if they graduate from high school, do not give birth to a child before age twenty, do not engage in serious or repeated delinquent behaviors, and are not drug or alcohol dependent or suffering from significant mental health problems. Twenty to 25 percent of children do not enter adulthood having met all these milestones.[10] The nature of the parenting a child receives appears to be strongly associated with whether the child engages in these behaviors or suffers from serious mental health problems.[11] To be sure, other factors, especially prolonged living in poverty and in neighborhoods with high violence and poor schools, may lead children to engage in these behaviors and/ or drop out of school even when the child receives adequate parenting.[12] And programs that are not focused on parenting do help many children avoid problem behaviors and graduate from high school.[13] But helping all children gain the skills and engage in the behaviors needed to achieve basic self-sufficiency in adulthood will require a focus on problematic parenting; without this focus, other approaches will be insufficient for many children.

The role of parenting is important, but less critical, with respect to helping children achieve the skills needed to attain a middle-class income. About 30 percent of all children graduate high school, do not give birth to a child as a teen, but still do not get a postsecondary degree and thus are unlikely to earn a middle-class income. Unlike the children just discussed, most of these children receive basically adequate parenting. While family environment likely influences the academic attainment of many of these children,[14] these families do not require the same types of intensive parenting services that are needed to alter the trajectories of children who do not graduate high school. Investing in high-quality preschool and K–12 education, plus offering these parents programs to help them provide cognitive stimulation to their children, is likely to be the most cost-effective way of helping more of these children attain a postsecondary degree, thereby increasing the likelihood that they will achieve a middle-class income. This is also the case with respect to promoting economic and social mobility.[15]

Thus, the parenting policies and programs I propose are designed to increase the likelihood that all children will have safe home environments throughout their childhood and acquire the skills needed to be self-sufficient in adulthood. A coordinated set of services is needed to support those families having, or likely to have, significant difficulty in providing the type of parenting needed if their children are to achieve these outcomes.

In developing any systemic approaches, it is important to have a reasonable idea of the extent of such parenting. I estimate that at least 20 percent of all children will experience seriously deficient parenting that will significantly affect their basic development at some point during their childhood; 10 percent of children will experience such parenting for an extended period. This includes both parenting that falls within the definition of maltreatment and other forms of parenting that are likely to substantially impair children's basic emotional, social, and cognitive development, as well as their health and safety.[16]

The starting point for any estimate is the number of children considered maltreated. In 2011, more than 6 million children (in 3.3 million families) were reported to CPS, which is more than 8 percent of all children in the United States. CPS agencies investigated reports involving over 3 million children. Almost 700,000 children (1 percent of all children) were found to have suffered from maltreatment as defined under various states' laws.[17]

These are annual numbers. Based on findings from several recent studies, 10–15 percent of all children born in the United States in 2000 will have substantiated instance of maltreatment at some point before they turn eighteen.[18] For children from poor families, that number goes up dramatically; for example, a recent study of all children born in California in 2000 found that approximately 35 percent of children born to native-born low-income mothers had been reported to CPS by age five.[19] Numerous studies have found that children reported to CPS agencies are considerably more likely to evidence serious behavioral problems over time than are children from similar socioeconomic households and neighborhoods who have not been reported to CPS.[20]

On the positive side, reports and substantiations of physical and sexual abuse have declined dramatically since 1994. However, neglect, which constitutes more than two-thirds of all reports, has not decreased. While neglect often includes some threat to physical safety, the core problem generally is highly chaotic, disorganized, nonresponsive, or emotionally hostile parenting. Such parenting can severely impair a child's ability to develop self-regulation, which is a "cornerstone of early childhood development that cuts across all domains of behavior."[21]

The number of maltreated children is a minimum estimate of the children experiencing highly inadequate parenting. A number of studies find widespread underreporting of parenting that constitutes maltreatment.[22] In addition, some types of parenting that put children at a high risk of poor long-term development do not fall under the legal definitions of maltreatment.[23] Based on reports to CPS and other indicators, such as the number of children living in deep poverty and/or with highly depressed or substance-abusing parents, I believe that 20 percent is a conservative estimate.[24]

State Involvement with Parenting

Prior to the 1960s, state agencies, other than schools, had very limited active involvement with families. During the 1960s, spurred by the "discovery" of the battered child syndrome, all states passed laws requiring physicians to report suspected cases of physical abuse to child welfare agencies. In 1974, Congress enacted the Child Abuse Prevention and Treatment Act (CAPTA), which offered states funds to deal with child abuse, provided that the state's reporting law included suspected instances of neglect and serious harm to a child's emotional well-being, in addition to physical abuse. This led to an enormous increase in reports. In 1967, approximately 10,000 cases of child abuse or neglect were reported. This rose to nearly 300,000 cases in 1975 and, as noted earlier, to more than 3 million in 2011.

Although CPS practice is regulated by a number of federal laws, provision of services is a state or local function. There is great variation in quality within and between states around the nature and quality of services.[25] It is widely accepted that few systems are able to promote the long-term development of the children under CPS supervision.[26] There have, however, been improvements. Jane Waldfogel describes these in her chapter and proposes some directions for further improvement.

Even if CPS agencies are improved so that they meet the needs of children who are brought under their supervision, this would not address the needs of the parents and children in the 70 percent of reports labeled "unsubstantiated" following investigation, as well the needs of the families experiencing major parenting problems that are not reported to CPS. In recent years, many states have begun referring reported cases that involve less risky situations to voluntary services; this is generally referred to as differential response (DR). While it is too early to assess these efforts fully, this approach will not meet the needs of children in many of these families. DR does not create a *system* for helping families with multiple problems.[27] An effective system for working with multiproblem families requires a dedicated funding stream, clear mandates regarding outcomes, clear criteria for who is served, performance standards, accountability measures, regular monitoring, consistent data collection and evaluation, and effective professional development. It is highly unlikely that such a system can be developed under the auspices of CPS. Moreover, a maltreatment framework is not a useful way of conceptualizing the problem. In addition, DR does not involve primary prevention.

Other than CPS, all programs addressing parenting are voluntary. These programs are delivered at the local level. There has been substantial growth in the availability of one type of voluntary services: home visiting following the birth of a child. The federal government is now funding a large research demonstration project seeking to determine how to make these services most effective. At least one home visiting model has documented significant success in producing positive long-term outcomes for children.[28] There also has been some growth in the availability of voluntary parenting programs and services for parents experiencing difficulties in interacting with their children.[29] Several research-based programs, such as Triple P and Incredible Years, appear to be reasonably effective for the parents who seek out these services.[30] Still, the availability and quality of services is highly variable, and attrition rates are very high in voluntary programs.

A new system is needed to support and *monitor* families suffering from multiple problems that seriously affect their capacity to provide adequate parenting. Developing such a system will not be easy, however. There is far too little recognition of the extent of highly problematic parenting. Many people remain suspicious of any government efforts to influence parenting other than addressing maltreatment. More public debate about alternative approaches is needed. Implementing services will be challenging. In particular, because most services for these families have been poorly funded, there is a shortage of qualified service providers; recruitment and training structures are needed. In addition, services to families are organized and funded in silos, usually related to a specific problem (mental health, substance use, etc.), even though families have multiple problems that often need to be addressed comprehensively. Many policy makers also believe that we do not know how to improve parenting and that current approaches are ineffective. Yet, there is now evidence that some programs do improve parenting.

Toward a New System of Support for (and Regulation of?) Parenting

Ensuring that all children live in safe homes and develop the capacities needed to become self-sufficient will require substantial changes in policies and resources devoted to helping multiproblem families improve parenting. At least three major alterations in policy are needed.

Restrict CPS to Only Providing Protection from Imminent Serious Harm

At noted above, most families reported to CPS are not brought under CPS jurisdiction. Given that many of the children in nonsubstantiated cases show long-term developmental problems, some commentators argue for more CPS involvement with these families.[31] This would not be wise. To the contrary, there is a strong case for reducing the role of CPS and changing mandatory reporting laws. Fewer than 25 percent of substantiated cases involve physical or sexual abuse; in only a small portion of the physical abuse cases has the child been treated in a manner that caused, or significantly threatened, bodily injury.[32] Most reports involve neglect. While neglect may lead to severe physical harm, and even death, the primary threat to most of these children relates to their academic and emotional development over a long period of time, not their immediate physical safety.

CPS systems are not dealing effectively with cases of neglect that are currently in the system. I doubt that CPS could get the additional resources needed to work effectively with the 75 percent of families in investigated cases that do not receive supervision or services.[33] CPS must compete with schools, child care, and health coverage for funds. Each of these systems has politically powerful advocates. Support for services to these children is much more likely through the health or education systems, which also are far more attractive approaches to parents. Focusing CPS on situations with the threat of serious injury also increases the possibilities for better protecting and helping these children.

Build a System to Improve Parenting

While expanding CPS is not the right approach to helping children achieve basic outcomes, neither is relying on the disjointed, limited, totally voluntary approach to helping parents that is the current alternative. Even the piecemeal expansion of "evidence-based" parenting programs will not be sufficient to produce adequate outcomes for many children. Parents experiencing the types of problems—mental health, substance use, domestic violence, deep poverty—that are generally associated with highly disorganized or unresponsive parenting need an adequately funded, coordinated set of services, one ideally managed by a single agency that is accountable for outcomes. While such a system should not have the coercive powers of CPS, it should include active outreach and some monitoring of parental conduct, not just provision of services to parents who seek help.

My purpose in outlining what a parenting-support system might look like for parents with infants and young children is to generate discussion; I cannot examine in detail the many issues that must be confronted in developing a viable, cost-effective approach.[34]

The system would build on a number of existing programs, including the Women, Infants, and Children Program (WIC), home visiting programs (HV), Early Head Start (EHS), Head Start (HS), and various evidence-based parenting programs (see figure 9.1).[35]

WIC and HV would be provided to pregnant women and new parents on a universal or targeted basis.[36] The issue of targeting is very difficult. Policy makers should approach investments in improving parenting with caution. Policies aimed at changing parenting are controversial and parenting programs are difficult to implement. Thus, major efforts to improve parenting should focus on those families for whom changing parental behaviors is critical to achieving the desired outcomes for the children. A targeted approach also is preferable from a cost and efficiency perspective, especially since the target population may vary for different services. However, targeting runs a very high risk of stigmatization, which would undermine any voluntary program. This is an area that needs careful discussion.

Home visiting would play a central role both in providing services directly and in monitoring the quality of parenting and helping parents access other services, beginning at the birth of a child. Many states are now expanding HV services, and there is a growing body of knowledge on how to make them more effective.[37] But states should not wait for the results of various experiments before establishing programs; rather, they should adopt a program and develop procedures for continuously improving the delivery system.

In addition to providing services directly, home visitors would recommend that the family follow one of three tracks for additional services.[38] In homes where the parenting is basically adequate, parents would be helped in finding high-quality child care and preschools designed to help prepare children for academic success in K–12 and higher education. A second track would be available to families that need more help with parenting and would include EHS and special HS programs that work closely with the parent, as well as the child. EHS would need to be redesigned and significantly expanded.[39] Finally, especially troubled families would be offered more intensive services, which might include full-day child care in special developmental centers (beginning at birth) and/or some form of parent-child therapy. Depending on local community resources, these services might be coordinated through a family resource or community health center.

There are other possible systemic approaches that might be less expensive and easier to implement. For example, Aber and his colleagues have suggested that pediatricians be at the center of the delivery system and that parents be encouraged to participate in two far less intensive parent-

FIGURE 9.1 Service system for parents

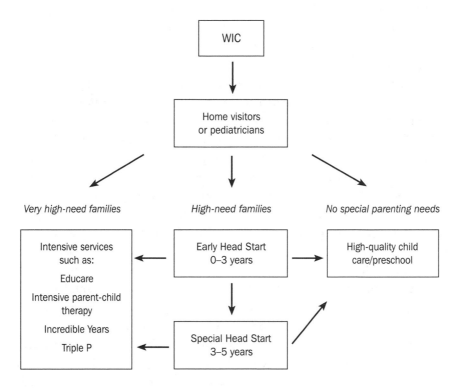

ing programs than home visiting.[40] But regardless of who does the screening, it must lead to services that are adequate to address the parents' and children's needs.

Create Incentives to Encourage Parental Involvement

There are a number of challenges, both political and practical, in designing and implementing a system of services that will adequately serve the target population. Two central issues are how to address the income needs of the vast majority of target families and how to get parents to engage in needed services. These need to be considered together.

Poverty, especially deep and persistent poverty, is a critical factor in the lives of many parents who struggle to provide adequate parenting. Reducing poverty is a necessary aim for any approach to helping children achieve the desired outcomes. Coping with poverty creates major obstacles "to attentive and nurturant child-rearing."[41] Moreover, with more income, parents can invest in more resources for their children.[42]

Current approaches to reducing poverty make addressing parenting more difficult. Poverty policy revolves largely around connecting all parents with jobs. This approach has had successes, but many parents are not able to connect to the labor force on a consistent basis and thus live in persistent, often deep, poverty. And the emphasis on work makes it more difficult for some parents to have the time or energy to engage in activities relating to improving parenting. There needs to be more flexibility in the Transitional Aid to Needy Families (TANF) program to allow parenting activities to count as "work" activity in families with children under three; other poverty-related programs also need to be modified to provide easier access and coverage.[43]

But more than just reform of existing programs is needed. One possibility is the adoption of a children's allowance for low-income families; most developed countries provide this to families as part of their social benefit system. The allowance would be made conditional on certain parental behaviors.[44] For example, the allowance might be obtained at pediatricians' offices or during home visits and conditioned on regular pediatric visits or involvement with the home visitor. Other possible program models include New York City's experiment in using Conditional Transfers to influence behavior.[45] A less extensive approach currently being tested is combining parenting education with "hard" services to parents. For example, there are job training and parenting education programs being offered in many localities throughout the country, generally in coordination with child care centers, including with both EHS and HS.[46]

There are many challenges in developing a fair and effective system of implementation of contingent benefits.[47] But the plight of the children living with highly disorganized or depressed parents who are often far too unresponsive to their children's needs demands new thinking. Income transfers alone are not likely to substantially alter the well-being of these children.[48] Given low engagement and high attrition rates in various programs, serious consideration must be given to adopting an incentive program focused on improving parenting.

Moving Forward

My aim here is to move the issue of parenting into a more central place in policy discussions regarding children. I have not analyzed the costs and benefits of investing in my proposed system versus other approaches (especially child-focused approaches) to reaching the same outcomes.

Clearly, my system would be expensive. Moreover, there is only limited evidence regarding the types of parenting programs that are likely to be effective, and for whom. It might be argued that these factors require a slow, cautious approach using experiments to test various alternatives. Several such experiments are now under way.[49] However, experimental research generally requires many years and often does not yield clear policy directions. There has been little progress over the past forty years in altering the situation of the worst-off 20 percent of children. Given the magnitude of the problem, I believe that policy makers should consider immediately adopting some version of the system I have outlined and then working to improve it over time. There is a moral imperative to help the most disadvantaged children and their parents *now,* both to reduce long-term social costs and to remedy long-term social injustices.[50] We cannot wait forty more years to address this.

CHAPTER 10

Child Protection and Child Welfare

Meeting the Needs of Vulnerable Children

JANE WALDFOGEL

The child protection and child welfare system (commonly known as CPS) has three main goals: to promote child safety, permanency, and well-being.[1] However, for most of CPS's history, attention to safety and permanency has been paramount. This is understandable. CPS is mandated by law to receive and respond to reports about children at risk of abuse or neglect, and thus its primary focus must be to ensure their safety. CPS also administers a system of ongoing services for children who, due to parental abuse or neglect or other needs, require state supervision and, sometimes, out-of-home placement. For this reason, permanency—ensuring that children are returned to their parents or placed in an alternative permanent living arrangement in a timely manner—must also be a focus for CPS. With resources stretched to the limit and with the public and policy makers holding CPS accountable for any failures related to safety or permanency, it is perhaps not surprising that child well-being—the third overarching goal—tends to receive less attention. Indeed, when the federal government proposed including child well-being as a dimension on which state systems would be monitored, some states objected. Fortunately, the issue was resolved in favor of including well-being, so, in principle, CPS agencies are responsible for meeting all three goals; however, it is still the case that well-being tends to receive less attention than the other two.

A similar tension arises with regard to the priority accorded to prevention. Public health scholars distinguish among three levels of prevention: tertiary (indicated), which entails services for children who have already been abused or neglected; secondary (selected), which involves programs for children who have been identified as being at elevated risk of abuse or neglect; and primary (universal), which involves efforts to prevent mal-treatment in the general population. Again due to limited resources and the high value placed on safety and permanency, most of the resources of the child protection and child welfare system are devoted to tertiary level prevention, to preventing repeat maltreatment and promoting permanency for those children who have already been identified as victims of abuse or neglect. In contrast, relatively few resources are devoted to the sizable share of families who come to the attention of CPS and are screened out at the time of the initial referral or to families whose cases closed after an inves-tigation. The cases that receive services from CPS on an ongoing basis thus constitute a minority of those referred—a minority made up of the highest-risk families.

This focusing of resources on the relatively small number of highest-risk families is illustrated in figure 10.1, which shows the flow of families (and children) into the CPS system using data from the most recent report on child maltreatment issued by the U.S. Department of Health and Human Services.[2] The first step in the process is an initial screening. Of the 3.4 million families reported to CPS agencies nationwide in 2011, 61 percent (2 million families, involving 3 million unique children) were screened in for investigation or fuller assessment. Of the 3 million children who were investigated or assessed, only 22 percent were ultimately substantiated for abuse or neglect, and only half of those children (53 percent) went on to receive postinvestigation services. The main focus of these services is to prevent any further maltreatment, whether by delivering services to the intact family or, if that is not possible, by removing the child to some form of out-of-home setting (e.g., placement with kin, foster care, group care), which occurred in just over a third (37 percent) of the cases substantiated and receiving postinvestigation services. (Some cases receive no postinves-tigation services at all, even after being substantiated, because the perpe-trator no longer has access to the child, the family has moved, or services are being provided by another agency.)

As figure 10.1 shows, 224,000 children were provided in-home services in 2011 as a result of having been reported, investigated, and substanti-ated by CPS that year. The figure shows that almost three times as many—645,000—were provided in-home services as a result of having been reported and investigated but *not* substantiated by CPS. The fact that there are more children referred for in-home services from the not-substantiated group than from the substantiated one in large part reflects the larger number of children in the first group. Thus, even though children whose reports are not substantiated have a much lower rate of being opened for services than substantiated children, that low rate still yields a large resulting number.

The services delivered to intact families typically include case management and supervision by a CPS worker (or perhaps a worker from an agency under contract with CPS), often supplemented by one or more other preventive services. Which services are delivered to any given family depends on the family's assessed need, their willingness to engage in and accept specific types of services, and the availability of services in the area.

Problems with both the quantity and quality of services delivered to families are long-standing concerns.[3] Analyses of data from the National Survey of Child and Adolescent Well-Being (NSCAW) and its companion survey, Caring for Children in Child Welfare (CCCW), suggest that many cases opened for services don't actually receive very many services beyond periodic visits by usually overburdened caseworkers.[4] Researchers have also found poor quality of services coupled with insufficient dosage. For example, although proven parent training programs exist, fewer than half of families opened for services receive any parent training, and those who do typically receive fifteen hours or less of programs that have not been proven to be effective in rigorous studies and have little or no monitoring to ensure that providers are implementing those programs as intended.[5] These service delivery issues limit the ability of the system to promote children's safety and permanency, as well as their well-being.

As shown in figure 10.1, there are substantial numbers of children in lower-risk cases not opened or kept open for services with CPS: approximately 3.1 million children annually reported to CPS but screened out; 1.7 million children whose cases are reported to CPS but not substantiated and not kept open for services with CPS; and just over 300,000 children whose cases are substantiated but not kept open for services with CPS. It is likely that some children from each of these groups go on to receive preventive services from a community-based agency, even though they are not open

FIGURE 10.1   Pathways for children

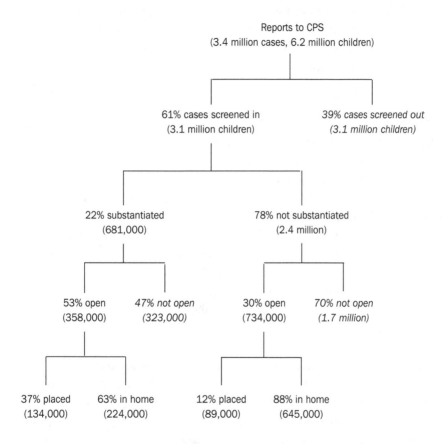

for ongoing services with CPS. Another group, not shown in the figure, consists of children not reported to CPS but referred directly for preventive services, whether as a result of applying voluntarily or being advised to do so by someone in the community.

Looking ahead, what types of steps should CPS be taking to better meet the needs of the vulnerable children being referred to it? I would emphasize three main points. First, it is essential to continue to strengthen efforts to provide a more differentiated response to children referred to the child protection and child welfare system. Second, CPS should continue to draw on the best available evidence to strengthen the services it provides to the highest-risk families. Third, CPS should do a better job of referring lower-risk children and families to key preventive services in their communities—in particular, child care—that could help meet safety and permanency goals while also promoting child well-being.

Expanding and Strengthening Differential Response

Historically, CPS systems have responded to screened-in reports of abuse and neglect by sending out an investigator to determine whether a child has been maltreated and, if so, who the likely perpetrator is and what actions are required to ensure the child's safety. Although this kind of investigative response is needed for high-risk cases, increasingly CPS agencies have come to believe that this kind of response may not be appropriate—and indeed may be counterproductive—for lower-risk cases. As a result, agencies nationwide have experimented with differential or alternative response systems that provide a family assessment, in place of an investigation, for low- and moderate-risk cases and focus on developing a service plan for the family, rather than identifying a perpetrator and producing a substantiation decision.[6]

The intent of differential response reforms is to provide services in a way that is more engaging for families and more attentive to the needs of lower-risk families so that CPS agencies can effect more lasting change in parents' behavior than with a more traditional adversarial investigative response. Differential response is, of course, not a panacea. But it can provide a more effective response to families who are referred to CPS by separating families at the highest risk who need a strong investigative response from families at lower risk who could benefit from a more assessment- and service-oriented response.

One question that has been raised about differential response is whether it might risk compromising children's safety by moving away from a narrowly focused investigative response. A related question is whether some high-risk cases might fall through the cracks if they are inappropriately categorized as low-risk at the initial screening. For this reason, a good deal of the research to date has focused on how well differential response systems have performed in terms of preventing maltreatment, as well as how far they have succeeded in engaging families and promoting child and family well-being.

Although the research base is somewhat limited, the evidence thus far suggests that CPS agencies that have adopted a differential response approach appear to be more effective at preventing future maltreatment, engaging families, and promoting well-being, compared with agencies that use a more traditional investigative approach.[7] The strongest evidence comes from an experimental study in Minnesota in which cases reported to CPS were randomly assigned to receive an alternative response or an investigative response.[8] The researchers found that cases assigned to the alternative track were less likely to be re-reported than cases assigned to the investigation track, a finding that was linked to the provision of increased services to families (funded in part by a grant from the McKnight Foundation and by additional government funding). Moreover, families were more engaged; workers delivering an alternative response reported that the caregiver was uncooperative at initial contact only 2 percent of the time, compared with 44 percent of the time in the control group (investigation track) cases. In addition, families received more services. Families receiving the alternative response were more likely to have their cases opened for services (36 percent versus 15 percent). They were also more likely to receive both the types of services traditionally prescribed and paid for by CPS (such as counseling) as well as less traditional services and services from other community resources not funded by CPS (such as assistance with employment, welfare programs, and child care). At the one year follow-up, families in the alternative response group reported lower levels of financial stress and stress associated with relationships with other adults as well as lower levels of drug abuse problems and domestic violence, although there were few impacts on other outcomes for the children and families.

Although the evidence from Minnesota is promising, a few limitations should be noted. We do not know whether the Minnesota results would have been as positive in the absence of the additional funding (which allowed families to receive services costing an average of $490 per year in the alternative response group as compared to only $150 per year in the control group); this is important given that most states implementing differential response have not had access to the kinds of resources that Minnesota had. And most reforms in other states, while yielding some promising evidence, have not been subject to a random assignment evaluation. More experimentation, and in particular more studies with augmented service provision, are needed to inform CPS strategy.

Strengthening the Services CPS Provides to the Highest-Risk Families

CPS agencies have worked hard in recent years to improve the services they deliver to the highest-risk families. These service improvement efforts have focused on enhancing both safety and permanency. However, services to promote child well-being and to engage families in meaningful ways to prevent future maltreatment remain limited.

Service plans for families involved with CPS prescribe a familiar roster of services, with programs such as parent training and parent education prominently featured. Unfortunately, the evidence base on these types of programs is fairly weak. Few such programs have been subjected to rigorous evaluation, and, when they have, results have often been disappointing.[9] As a field, child welfare has been slow to learn the lessons of evidence-based parenting programs such as Triple P, which is highly structured and uses trained staff and media materials to ensure program fidelity.[10]

CPS agencies must do a better job of identifying, developing, and implementing programs that have a sound evidence base; and, where such programs do not exist, policy makers and researchers must conduct randomized trials to build such an evidence base. To do so, they will need help from outside agencies—the federal government and/or foundations—to fund trials of programs that aspire to not only promote safety and permanency but also to improve children's well-being and prevent future maltreatment.

Having worked in CPS and having studied CPS systems for many years, I have no illusions about the magnitude of the challenge involved in improving services for the highest-risk families, but I am also optimistic that meaningful improvements can be implemented. New York City's child protection system, the Administration for Children's Services (ACS), provides a compelling example. Historically, it is hard to point to a more beleaguered child welfare system than New York City's. Yet, during the 1990s, under the leadership of a truly remarkable commissioner, Nicholas Scopetta, dramatic improvements in child safety were accomplished through reforms such as reductions in caseload size, enhanced training, and, most importantly, an unrelenting focus on child safety.[11] Following Scopetta's tenure, Commissioner John Mattingly brought about substantial improvements in permanency by instituting more neighborhood-based systems of foster care and also implementing performance-based contracts for foster care providers. And now, Commissioner Ronald Richter is pushing the system to implement evidence-based programs to improve child well-being and prevent maltreatment, starting with reforms to improve the capacity of the foster care system to meet the needs of children and move them more swiftly to permanent settings. New York City's system and other CPS systems still have a long way to go to address the problems that have historically plagued them.[12] But their recent reforms certainly provide reason to believe that they can be improved to provide services that are more effective and more oriented to child well-being as well as safety and permanency for the highest-risk families.

Providing Key Preventive Services, Such as Home Visiting and Child Care, to Lower-Risk Children and Families

As discussed earlier, many families referred to CPS do not receive services because they have not crossed the threshold into abuse or neglect and hence are screened out or not substantiated; others receive ongoing monitoring from CPS but little in the way of meaningful service provision. But such families may still be at risk of future maltreatment or have children in need of services. Some of these families are referred to community-based agencies or services, and such referrals have likely increased as a result of differential response reforms and also in response to the 2003 Child Abuse Prevention and Treatment Act (CAPTA) reauthorization, which requires states to have procedures to refer children not at imminent risk of harm to community organizations or voluntary child protective services. But there is more to be done.

In particular, CPS and community partner agencies should do more to provide preventive services for young children, who are at higher risk than their older peers for initial and repeat maltreatment. Because infants are at particularly high risk, there has been considerable interest in home visiting programs for pregnant women and women with infants. However, not all such programs have been demonstrated to be effective at preventing mal-treatment.[13] In general, the most successful programs have been those that adhered closely to program guidelines and used appropriately trained and professional staff.[14]

The home visiting program with the strongest track record in terms of preventing maltreatment is the Nurse Family Partnership (NFP), in which highly trained nurses provide home visits to at-risk first-time mothers, beginning prenatally and continuing into the first few years after the birth. Randomized evaluations of NFP in two sites (Elmira, NY, and Memphis, TN) have found decreased rates of substantiated child maltreatment and fewer emergency room visits for accidents and injuries among the families randomly assigned to receive home visits.[15] These benefits are in addition to a host of other positive outcomes for home-visited mothers and children, which together have resulted in impressive cost-benefit ratios.[16] The Early Start Program, which delivered home visits to high-risk pregnant women and new mothers in New Zealand, also stands out as a successful preventive program, having been found to reduce parent-reported abuse.[17]

In contrast to home visiting, child care has received less attention as a way to prevent maltreatment. This is unfortunate, because child care pro-grams could play an important role. The developmental benefits of child care are well-documented, and high-quality care is likely to be particularly beneficial for vulnerable infants and toddlers.[18] But child care could also play a role in preventing maltreatment by relieving parental stress, making parents aware of alternative forms of discipline, and/or making the child more visible to potential reporters (e.g., child care providers).[19]

The strongest evidence on the potentially protective role of child care comes from studies of Head Start, a compensatory early education program for low-income children. The recent randomized study of Head Start found that parents of three-year-olds who had been randomly assigned to Head Start were less likely to report spanking their child in the prior week and reported spanking less frequently, with especially pronounced effects for teen mothers (however, there were no significant effects for parents of four-year-olds).[20] Further evidence is provided by the randomized evaluation of Early Head Start, for children under age three, which found that the program improved parenting and reduced the use of spanking by both mothers and fathers.[21]

Reduced spanking was also found in a random assignment study of the Infant Health and Development Program (IHDP), an early child care program for low birth weight children, and in analyses of observational data from the Early Childhood Longitudinal Study-Birth Cohort and Kindergarten cohort.[22] Finally, a quasi-experimental evaluation found that the Chicago Child-Parent Centers, which provided preschool child care to children from disadvantaged neighborhoods, reduced court petitions related to maltreatment by approximately 50 percent.[23]

Thus, I think there is scope for child care programs to play a greater role as a preventive service for at-risk preschool-age children. Such programs could nicely complement, and follow on from, evidence-based home visiting programs for at-risk pregnant women and women with infants.

Concluding Thoughts

The child protection and child welfare system has a heavy set of responsibilities: to promote child safety, permanency, and well-being. It is also expected to prevent maltreatment not just among the relatively high-risk cases opened for services but also among the lower-risk families who come to its attention but do not meet the thresholds for case opening or ongoing service delivery. Failing to prevent maltreatment among open cases is a signal that CPS intervention has failed in its primary role of promoting child safety, permanency, and well-being among the most vulnerable group of children. But failing to refer lower-risk families for effective preventive services is also a failure, as it represents a missed opportunity to intervene before the risk of maltreatment escalates into full-blown abuse or neglect and before children's early developmental risks translate into a lifetime of lesser chances.

CPS services have improved in recent years, but it is still too often the case that CPS provides "a somewhat haphazard set of services that aim to help abusive families and their children . . . [with] a shortage of effective intervention programs to provide needed services [and] a dearth of prevention services."[24] Given that CPS is the main, and often only, service provider for our nation's most vulnerable families, we can and must do better. Providing a more differentiated response to families reported to CPS, delivering evidence-based services to families in the system, and providing more preventive services such as home visiting and child care to children both in and out of the system would all be important steps in the right direction.

JUVENILE JUSTICE

CHAPTER 11

The Wheel Turns

Recreating a System of Justice for Juveniles

ROBERT G. SCHWARTZ

> Dear Lord, be good to me. The sea is so wide, and my boat is so small.
> —*Children's Defense Fund*

> The voyage of the best ship is a zigzag line of a hundred tacks.
> —*Ralph Waldo Emerson,* "Self-Reliance"

Progress in juvenile justice rarely appears as a straight line. At its best, it is like the path of Emerson's ship. At its worst, it is a journey with many false starts coursed by navigators who steer us in the wrong direction.

Juvenile justice goes through cycles of reform.[1] The good news is that we are now at an upbeat moment. Today there is powerful public recognition of the science showing that teens are different: adolescent development is a unique time of experimentation and risk taking. Policy makers and advocates agree that youth need room to make mistakes; that the justice system should not be used for minor, normative misbehavior; and that public safety can be maintained while giving youth room to discover the people they will become.

At the same time, state juvenile justice systems are riddled with vestiges of a punitive past. Too many youth are still labeled "delinquent" for typical adolescent misbehavior. Too many youth are unnecessarily confined. Too many suffer life-long consequences from their involvement with the juvenile justice system. Too many are tried as adults.

The coming decades will require zealous advocacy to create more opportunities for youth who are in conflict with the law to make successful transitions to productive adulthood.

The First Century

In 1899, Lucy Flower and Julia Lathrop—working in a progressive environment nurtured by Jane Addams and her Hull House colleagues—established in Chicago the nation's first juvenile court.[2] The experiment in individualized attention to youths who misbehaved led other states to emulate Illinois. The new juvenile court system was accompanied by a service-delivery system that ranged from specialized juvenile probation to locked reform schools. As originally imagined, the juvenile court aimed to treat children differently from adults, a theme that has itself zigzagged back and forth over the last century on its way to being reconfirmed by research.[3]

The United States today has a patchwork approach to juvenile justice. There is no single American juvenile justice system; each state has fashioned its own. Nevertheless, there are consistencies. States dealt with two kinds of youthful misbehavior through the first seventy-five years of the formal juvenile court. They addressed conduct that would be criminal if committed by an adult. And they created a category of crimes called "status offenses," such as being "ungovernable," that could be committed only by children.

In 1974, led by Senator Birch Bayh (D-IN), Congress passed the Juvenile Justice and Delinquency Prevention Act (JJDPA). In addition to removing children from adult jails, the new law provided federal funds to states that eliminated status offenses from the jurisdiction of the juvenile court. JJDPA was largely successful, even though later Congresses amended JJDPA to give states wiggle room.[4] There has been a strong movement in the last decade to phase out the federal exception that allows courts to confine status offenders for violation of court orders. The odds are excellent that federal law in the near future will once again strip juvenile courts of their power to incarcerate status offenders.

While the juvenile justice system has wavered on whether it should have jurisdiction over status offenders, it has never lost its focus on youth who commit "crimes"—that is, who engage in misbehavior that would constitute a violation of the state's criminal code. The cycles of juvenile justice reform have reflected different views of how to respond to crimes committed by teens.

Until the early 1990s, America's juvenile court responses had evolved through two phases. The first involved the court as a kind of parent, exercising *parens patriae* powers to do whatever it thought was best for a child.

This led to many children being helped by probation officers, judges, or other caring adults who gave them second chances and connected them with opportunities. But it also led to many children being harmed by the juvenile court, which had become a random, arbitrary agent of power. The capriciousness of the juvenile court led the U.S. Supreme Court to inject due process into the juvenile justice system, ending the *parens patriae* era.

In re Gault (1967) illustrated how the juvenile court could harm children. Fifteen-year-old Gerald Gault was accused of making a lewd and adolescent phone call to a next door neighbor. He was tried without notice of the charges. He had no lawyer. The judge in Arizona sent him to a state training school for up to six years. The Supreme Court overturned Gault's adjudication of delinquency, holding that children were persons within the meaning of the Fourteenth Amendment; juveniles had a constitutional right to a lawyer, among other rights that were at the core of a fairly administered system of justice. *Gault* ushered in the due process era of the juvenile court.

The late 1980s saw an increase in juvenile crime and led to another shift in juvenile justice system responses. The increase in crime, which peaked around 1993, was due to a lethal combination of guns and crack cocaine. Almost every state in the early nineties entered a third, retributive phase of juvenile justice. This punitive period was characterized by increased prosecutorial power, including the power to send juveniles to the adult system. More youth were automatically excluded from juvenile court jurisdiction. Juvenile training schools became more punitive. States adopted bumper-sticker philosophies like "adult time for adult crime."

Knowledge Informs Policy

In response to the punitive cycle of the early 1990s, the MacArthur Foundation in 1996 launched a Research Network on Adolescent Development and Juvenile Justice. The Network's insights led the U.S. Supreme Court nine years later to end the juvenile death penalty and ushered in a paradigmatic shift in thinking about kids and crime. Led by Temple University professor Laurence Steinberg, the Network included some of the nation's leading psychologists, criminologists, and academics.

The Network's research was bolstered by new findings in neuroscience that described ways adolescent behavior, specifically emotional regulation, is a function of the developing teenage brain. Collectively, the new knowledge has led to legislative reform like that in Connecticut and Illinois— which recently raised the age of juvenile court jurisdiction, treating youth as adults when they turn eighteen—and to case law that has reshaped juvenile justice in America. It is fair to say that in 2014, social science, behavioral science, and neuroscience require that the law treat juveniles differently than adults. Courts—especially the Supreme Court—began recognizing those differences in the most serious cases, those in which youth tried as adults had been convicted of murder or other serious felonies.[5]

Developmental differences, however, were not only recognized by the Supreme Court in cases of youth being tried as adults; the Court affirmed the constitutional significance of adolescent development in juvenile court cases. Most notably, the Court interpreted *Miranda v. Arizona* (1966) to accommodate the youth of a suspect. In *J.D.B. v. North Carolina* (2011), Justice Sotomayor's majority opinion declared, in the case of a thirteen-year-old, that

> the age of a child subjected to police questioning is relevant to the custody analysis of *Miranda* . . . It is beyond dispute that children will often feel bound to submit to police questioning when an adult in the same circumstances would feel free to leave. Seeing no reason for police officers or courts to blind themselves to that commonsense reality, we hold that a child's age properly informs the *Miranda* custody analysis.

Justice Sotomayor added in a footnote: "Although citation to social science and cognitive science authorities is unnecessary to establish these commonsense propositions, the literature confirms what experience bears out. See, e.g., *Graham v. Florida* . . . ('[D]evelopments in psychology and brain science continue to show fundamental differences between juvenile and adult minds')."

Unfortunately, these cases, like states raising the age of juvenile court jurisdiction, have not undone prior cycles of American juvenile justice policy. Youth can still be sentenced as adults to life sentences. Many juvenile justice facilities remain unsafe places. After years of action and reaction, today's system is a blend of *parens patriae*, due process, and punishment, infused with a dose of social science and neuroscience.

The Need for Vigorous Advocacy

For the vast majority of youth who misbehave, the tug-of-war over juvenile justice policy is largely about three questions: What kind of youthful misbehavior should we criminalize? What should be the consequences of court involvement? Should youthful offending be addressed by juvenile courts or by adult criminal courts?

Advocates today celebrate states that are returning to an early, Hull House notion of juvenile justice, appropriately constrained by constitutional safeguards and fortified by new insights into adolescent development. Recent progressive reforms, during decades of declining juvenile crime, have been advanced by an increasingly robust advocacy movement. The Children's Defense Fund (CDF) opened its doors in 1973 and focused on issues of poverty, race, and justice. Led by Marian Wright Edelman, CDF sought to give every child a fair start in life as well as opportunities for education, health care, and economic security. CDF in the 1970s was followed by public interest law firms for children: Juvenile Law Center, Legal Services for Children, the Youth Law Center, and the National Center for Youth Law. These groups were augmented in the 1990s by Northwestern University's Children and Family Justice Center and the National Juvenile Defender Center. The next decade saw the W. Haywood Burns Institute, the Center for Children's Law and Policy, the Campaign for Youth Justice, and many others that added weight to the progressive side of the fulcrum. These public interest organizations, bolstered by an increasingly robust indigent juvenile defense bar and a growing group of progressive state juvenile justice administrators, are positioned to redefine justice for youth well into this century.

Vigorous advocacy remains essential. There will remain a vocal population of public policy Luddites that dismisses the differences between children and adults. This group includes too many legislators, judges, and prosecutors who choose to ignore the findings from social science and neuroscience. These folks focus on the harm that adolescents cause, excluding other components of justice policy. Yes, adolescents can commit horrific crimes. Every murder leaves a trail of grief. Retribution is a natural reaction. However, while public policy should acknowledge victims' grief—as it has with the victims' rights movement that emerged in the mid-1990s—

public policy cannot be bound by it. Society can recognize harms adolescents cause while building a justice system that mitigates punishments because of youths' lesser blameworthiness and capacities for change. Youth must be held accountable, but in developmentally appropriate ways.[6]

Opportunities

Juvenile justice advocates imagine a future that uses the juvenile justice system less. This means diverting youth from the system entirely. It means less frequent use of institutional care—through diversion and enhanced reentry policies that reduce length of stay and recidivism. And it involves having fewer life consequences for youth who are involved with the justice system.

Opportunities for juvenile justice reform can come from nontraditional sources. The Affordable Care Act and Medicaid, for example, will enable states to provide better health care for youth at risk of entering, in, or exiting the juvenile justice system. Since the late 1980s, states have used EPSDT to pay for services to youth involved with the juvenile justice system.[7] Many states have used Medicaid to pay for mental health screening, assessment, and treatment. Health care financing has multiple benefits. Medicaid can fund evidence-based practices that divert youth from institutional care. It can pay for new screening instruments, like the Girls Health Screen that Los Angeles introduced in 2012 in its juvenile justice system.[8] It can pay for reentry services that address youths' behavioral health and special education needs. (The only thing that Medicaid won't cover is care of youth who are in public, secure juvenile justice facilities.)

Diversion from the Juvenile Justice System

CDF has, since 2007, fought the cradle-to-prison pipeline. Juvenile justice advocates have focused in particular on that part of the pipeline that begins with schools. Organizations like the Advancement Project and the Legal Defense Fund have helped create a future in which the juvenile court is decreasingly used as a school's disciplinarian. Staff from those organizations and others have supported the Dignity in Schools campaign. This effort has offered solid, savvy alternatives to the pipeline, most notably a model code with a human rights framework. The model code addresses different aspects of a quality education, reflects core human rights principles, and recommends student-centered policies for states, districts, and schools.[9]

The effort to stem school referrals is part of a larger effort to promote diversion from juvenile court. The MacArthur Foundation's Models for Change initiative has supported a cultural shift in which diversion is again in fashion. Diversion, which is a concept as old as the juvenile court itself, recognizes that many youth in the juvenile justice system do not need to be in it. Public safety can be achieved through other means that are just as effective at preventing crime while reducing stigma to youth and giving them life chances. Diversion engages families. It saves dollars.[10]

Done well, diversion can often meet youths' needs better than the formal justice system. Many youth who enter the justice system have co-occurring behavioral disorders. The coming decades will see more refined screening and assessment tools that will do more than assess risks; they will also address youths' strengths and needs.[11]

Diversion from Placement

Diversion is about more than keeping youth out of the justice system. It also means reducing unnecessary use of institutional care. Since 1992, the Annie E. Casey Foundation has advanced this value through its Juvenile Detention Alternatives Initiative (JDAI). JDAI has shown how to advance public safety and save dollars while reducing the use of pretrial detention for youth charged with crimes.[12]

In the decades to come, juvenile justice advocates, supported by Casey, MacArthur, Pew, Open Society, Public Welfare, and other foundations, will promote a reduction in what James Bell of the Burns Institute describes as America's "addiction to incarceration." This trend began in states like California, New York, and Texas, which have reduced the use of training schools for delinquent youth. Other states, like Illinois, Ohio, and Pennsylvania, have shown how fiscal incentives can reduce unnecessary out-of-home placement.

The future will see systems in which fewer youth are incarcerated. Those who must be removed from their homes will be held in smaller, more youth-friendly facilities. Missouri has demonstrated that large congregate care programs for delinquents are not only counterproductive, they are unnecessary. Smaller programs, close to home and family, that treat youth with respect will increase the chances that youth leaving the system will become productive adults.[13]

Smoother Reentry

Thoughtful reentry—or aftercare—is also an essential part of the pathway to productive adulthood. The federal government invested in reentry through the Second Chances Act of 2007. The federal law gave most of its attention to adult offenders, but juvenile reentry has quietly advanced in many states. Reentry is the combination of services, planning, support, and supervision that begins at disposition, continues while a youth is in placement, anticipates the youth's release from placement, continues until the youth is discharged from juvenile court supervision, and extends thereafter through connections to other opportunities, supports, and services. Done well, reentry reduces lengths of stay.[14] It connects youth to caring adults, appropriate educational opportunities, and career and technical training. It ensures that youth have a safe place to live and continuity of health care.

Reducing Use of the Criminal Justice System

Related to progress in juvenile court is the movement to reform sentencing of youth as adults. This will address two issues. The first is reducing the number of youth who are *tried* as adults. Raising the age in the remaining states that start criminal court jurisdiction below age eighteen is one easy way to decrease the number of youth in criminal court. It is also important that discretion in this area be taken from prosecutors and returned to judges. Prior to the punitive legislation of the early-to-mid-1990s, most youth who were transferred to criminal court underwent a hearing overseen by a judge. At that hearing, prosecutors had to prove that a youth was not amenable to treatment in the juvenile justice system. That system changed in the nineties, when states increasingly gave prosecutors the decision to send adolescents to criminal court. States also increased the number of offenses for which youth under eighteen would automatically be tried as adults. Some commentators, like Marty Guggenheim of New York University Law School, have suggested that the rationale of *Graham v. Florida* makes automatic or mandatory transfer constitutionally suspect. Guggenheim argues that youth must have individualized transfer hearings before judges. We have seen a slow recent rollback in mandatory transfer laws, but there is much work to be done.[15]

The second issue is the need to change sentences for youth who are tried as adults. It is time for states to have different sentencing guidelines for youth and adults. The logic of the Supreme Court jurisprudence after *Roper v. Simmons* (2005) ended the juvenile death penalty is that less culpable youth should receive shorter adult sentences because they have the capacity for change. Unfortunately, in the year after *Miller v. Alabama* (2012) ended *mandatory* life sentences for juveniles, many states enacted new laws with mandatory minimum sentences of many decades. It will be a long time before we know whether life sentences for juveniles are uncommon.

Addressing New Barriers to Youths' Success

The juvenile justice system exists to give youth better life chances than the criminal justice system. While there has been choppy progress in many state juvenile justice systems, too many recent laws establish unnecessary barriers to success at the same time as they purport to provide room for reform. The general public believes that juvenile courts are closed to the public, that juvenile records are sealed or expunged, and that being in juvenile court gives a youth a free pass to adulthood. All of these beliefs are wrong.

Punitive "reforms" of the mid-1990s opened juvenile courts to the public in many circumstances. Juvenile records are rarely expunged. When expungement is available under state law, it is rarely automatic. Juvenile court involvement is hardly a free pass. Indeed, the American Bar Association (ABA) launched a Web site, www.beforeyouplea.com, that identifies states' collateral consequences of delinquency adjudications. Collateral consequences, the ABA notes, are hardships that "affect youth who have successfully completed a sentence imposed by the court. The hardships include barriers to education, employment, and public benefits."

Reentry should mean fresh starts, yet too many youth have records that haunt them for years. In some cases, these records will last for a lifetime.

There has long been a myth that juvenile court records disappear when youth turn eighteen. Advocates around the country are trying to make that myth more of a reality by creating greater opportunities for record expungement and by reducing collateral consequences.

This is particularly important to the effort to end racial and ethnic disparities in the juvenile justice system. Because youth of color are more likely than their white counterparts to be arrested and convicted for youthful crimes, they are also more likely to carry the stigma with them well into adulthood. Thus, it is even more important to these youth that their pathway to mainstream success not be inappropriately impeded by juvenile records.

Immigrant youth are also affected by juvenile records. Proposals for comprehensive immigration reform should ensure that true pathways to citizenship not have collateral consequences as bumps in the road. This will be challenging. There's a natural tendency, exemplified by western Europe's reaction to an influx of eastern Europeans after the breakup of the Soviet Union, to criminalize the misbehavior of "others." Sociologists have noted for a century that societies need to create Others who serve as the criminal class. Indeed, the American juvenile justice system was created, in part, to control an influx of immigrants at the dawn of the twentieth century. Progressive reforms will be harder to implement as the white culture recoils from a more diverse America.

Nowhere is the hardship greater than for youth adjudicated delinquent for so-called sex offenses. A minuscule number of youth commit crimes of the sort that raise public alarm. Youth are not serial pedophiles; recidivism rates among juvenile sexual offenders are exceedingly low.[16] And yet state and federal governments have enacted registration laws that shackle youth for life. In *Raised on the Registry*, published by Human Rights Watch, Nicole Pittman describes how almost forty states impose sex offender registration, notification, and residency restrictions on children adjudicated delinquent of certain sex offenses in juvenile court. After they have served their juvenile court dispositions, these children must comply with a complex array of legal requirements that permeate nearly every aspect of their lives for a lifetime. These restrict where and with whom youth sex offenders may live, work, attend school, or spend time. Youth on sex offender registries become targets of vigilante violence, suffer stigma and public humiliation, are barred from school, and perpetually have a hard time finding or keeping a job or home while struggling to pay high registration fees. They are often prohibited from living or even spending time in places where children typically gather, like schools, playgrounds, daycare centers, libraries, and bus stops.

The juvenile court has always tried to manage youth who are sexually active. That is one reason that the latest "status offense" is sexting. States have begun creating new crimes directed at minors who sext. Legislators have faith that the criminal law will deter teenagers from using technology to transmit sexually suggestive photographs. Their optimistic belief in the power of the crimes code does little to promote wise adolescent behavior; it does, however, create a new class of young offenders.

Advocates must challenge these regressive policies. The coming decades must see a reduction in collateral consequences, increased expungement of records, a retreat from sexting laws and other new status offenses, and a serious restructuring of sentences of youth convicted as adults.

Economic Benefits of Progressive Policies

It has long been clear that effective delinquency prevention is sound crime control policy.[17] Prevention programs teach youth to behave. They solve problems that undermine pro-social behavior. The good news is that research-based prevention programs are also cost-effective.[18]

An important recent trend has been the alliance of the Right on Crime group of conservatives with progressive activists in states like Texas to reduce the use of expensive out-of-home care. Some states, like Pennsylvania, have reinvested savings from institutional closures, spending on prevention programs, evidence-based programming, and system reform. Many jurisdictions have taken advantage of the Social Security Act's Title IV-E waiver program to use dollars that had been restricted to paying for out-of-home care to pay for community-based services.

The good news is that the cost of converting systems from institutions to community-based is relatively small. Juvenile Law Center and colleagues did a study twenty years ago that examined how debt financing might pay for deconstruction costs, much as it pays for the building of prisons and juvenile facilities. The surprising finding was that the cost of converting systems from institution- to community-based was relatively small. Conversion costs can easily be absorbed by state or local governments.[19]

In July 2013, Illinois governor Pat Quinn signed a bill that raised the state's age of juvenile court jurisdiction to seventeen. In Illinois, as in almost forty other states, youth who are under eighteen will now, for most offenses, be under the jurisdiction of the juvenile court. (Illinois, like every state, still sends some juvenile offenders to the adult system.) Illinois followed Connecticut, which raised its age of jurisdiction to sixteen in 2010 and to seventeen in 2012. Midway through 2013, New York and Massachusetts were close to raising the age of juvenile court jurisdiction to seventeen. The raise-the-age movement has been part of a larger, thoughtful effort to align juvenile justice policy with social science. This is progress in the early twenty-first century. Social science has given states permission to return to Illinois' 1899 belief that youth are less culpable and more capable of change than adults.

The Wheel Doesn't Turn on Its Own: Creating a Better Future for Teens

The juvenile justice system should be a last resort. When it must be used, it should avoid interventions that unnecessarily disrupt normal adolescent development. The system should give youth opportunities to reform and provide them with the skills necessary to be contributing members of society. This means reducing collateral consequences of arrest and adjudication for delinquent acts. It means more opportunities to expunge juvenile records. It means avoiding the impulse to create new crimes, like sexting, or cruel and knee-jerk policies like sex offender registries for children.

Initiatives like JDAI and Models for Change have helped communities save money, decrease recidivism rates, and develop alternatives to incarceration that hold kids accountable while giving them opportunities to become capable members of society. There are obvious benefits to creating a society in which youth become tax payers rather than tax takers. Aligning fiscal responsibility, public safety, and good kid outcomes is in our enlightened self-interest. It is also doable.

The pursuit of progress is a collective enterprise. It must involve lawyers who litigate and take appeals; defense lawyers who raise issues; advocates who work on budget policy; parents who call for diversion; judges who are attuned to adolescent development; and prosecutors who recognize the value embedded in every youth and who see diversion and community-based services as a core component of justice.

CHAPTER 12

Using Scientific Research to Transform Juvenile Justice Policy and Practice

A Modest Success Story and Some Suggestions for the Next Four Decades

LAURENCE STEINBERG

This article describes what I believe has been a genuine success story, one of those rare cases in which scientific research has been used to create a foundation on which a radical transformation in social policies affecting children and youth has been set in motion. When this work began, juvenile offenders were being demonized as "super-predators," and our nation's response to juvenile crime was growing increasingly harsh. That trend has clearly reversed, however, and several landmark cases decided by the U.S. Supreme Court in the past ten years have ensured that numerous aspects of this shift will be more than fleeting changes of opinion. The transformation is ongoing, to be sure, and much work remains to be done, though remarkable progress has been made in reforming juvenile justice policy and practice over the past fifteen years. Over the next few decades, it will be important to see that juvenile justice interventions focus more on rehabilitation than punishment, that more juvenile offenders are treated in the community rather than institutional placements, and that fewer juveniles are tried and sanctioned as adults.

Historical Background

Few issues challenge a society's ideas about both the nature of human development and the nature of justice as much as serious juvenile crime. Because we neither expect children to be criminals nor expect crimes to be committed by children, the unexpected intersection between childhood and criminality creates a dilemma that most people find difficult to resolve. Indeed, the only ways out of this problem are either to redefine the offense as something less serious than a crime or to redefine the offender as someone who is not really a child.[1]

For most of the twentieth century, American society most often chose the first approach—redefining the offense—treating most juvenile infractions as matters to be adjudicated as delinquent acts within a separate juvenile justice system designed to recognize the special needs and immature status of young people and to therefore emphasize rehabilitation over punishment. States believed that the juvenile justice system was a vehicle to protect the public by providing a system that responds to children who are maturing into adulthood. They recognized that conduct alone—that is, the alleged criminal act—should not be dispositive in deciding when to invoke the heavy hand of the adult criminal justice system. By providing for accountability, treatment, and supervision in the juvenile justice system—and in the community whenever possible—the juvenile justice system promoted short-term and long-term public safety.

In the latter decades of the twentieth century, as violent youth crime rates rose, attacks on the juvenile court intensified.[2] Critics railed at the depiction of young criminals as children, a characterization that was discordant with media images of teenage street gangs spreading fear in urban neighborhoods. By the 1990s, young offenders became "super-predators" in the popular imagination, teenage criminals without moral inhibitions who were eager to kill and maim those who came in their paths. Under the mantra of "adult time for adult crime," young offenders became subject to increasingly harsh punishments, many of them administered by adult criminal courts and sometimes carried out within correctional facilities that had been previously reserved for individuals eighteen and older.

Although the United States today continues to punish juveniles who commit serious crimes more harshly than does the rest of the industrialized world, research has played a role in pushing the pendulum back toward a more progressive position in which legislators, practitioners, and judges have become more likely to acknowledge that juveniles differ from adults in important ways that warrant their differential treatment under criminal law.[3] This trend has been manifested in numerous ways, including increased awareness that normally developing adolescents may lack the competence necessary to be tried in criminal court (and that some minimal level of competence is also necessary for a fair hearing in juvenile court), that minors need special protections during police interrogations, and that the transfer of juvenile offenders into the adult system is harmful both to the juveniles and their communities.

Nowhere has the impact of research on the shift toward more progressive policies been more visible than in a series of cases decided during the past decade by the U.S. Supreme Court, which has issued rulings that have banned the juvenile death penalty and limited the use of life without parole in cases involving juveniles. These cases were not the first ones in which the Court acknowledged that adolescents and adults are different in legally relevant ways, but they were the first to look to science for confirmation of what "any parent knows," as Justice Anthony Kennedy put it in his majority opinion in *Roper v. Simmons*, the 2005 case that abolished the juvenile death penalty.[4] An analysis of the Court's decisions in several cases that followed *Roper* suggests that they have been increasingly influenced by findings from studies of brain and behavioral development which show that adolescents are less mature than adults in ways that diminish their criminal responsibility.[5]

Roper is both a landmark case in juvenile justice jurisprudence and an impressive example of how developmental science can be marshaled to influence legal policy in ways that benefit young people. Writing for the Court's majority, Justice Kennedy, citing developmental research, explicated three characteristics of adolescents that distinguish them from adults in ways that mitigate their culpability. First, citing evidence of adolescents' overinvolvement in reckless behavior, Kennedy concluded that adolescents are characterized by immaturity and an underdeveloped sense of responsibility, which leads them to make impetuous and ill-considered decisions. Second, he noted that adolescents are more susceptible than adults to external influences, especially peer pressure, which makes it difficult for them to extricate themselves from "criminogenic" situations. Finally, referencing theories of identity development, Kennedy wrote that the personality traits of adolescents are less fixed than they are among adults, making it difficult to infer that even heinous criminal behavior during adolescence is evidence of "irretrievably depraved" character and stressing the fact that adolescents are better candidates than adults for rehabilitation. In response to arguments that the death penalty serves a general deterrent function, Kennedy noted that the same characteristics that diminish adolescents' blameworthiness make it less likely that people this age will be deterred by the possibility of capital punishment; individuals who commit crimes impulsively don't pause to consider the consequences they might face if they were to be arrested and convicted.

The basic logic of *Roper* was extended to *Graham v. Florida*, the 2010 case that banned life without parole in juvenile cases involving non-homicides, and *Miller v. Alabama*, the 2012 case that banned mandatory life without parole for juveniles.[6] The decisions in these cases, unlike *Roper*, explicitly referenced developmental neuroscience. In *Roper*, adolescent brain development was mentioned during oral arguments, but it was never referenced in the Court's opinions, which emphasized behavioral differences between adolescents and adults.[7] In *Graham*, adolescent brain development was mentioned in the opinion but mainly in passing, in a sentence about the maturation in late adolescence of brain regions important for "behavior control."[8] By the time the Court decided *Miller*, neuroscience warranted an entire paragraph in the majority opinion. The Justices noted that the behavioral science evidence had become even stronger since *Roper* and *Graham*, pointed out that the Court's conclusions in those earlier cases continued to be strengthened by brain science, and went into greater detail about the findings from neuroscience, mentioning adolescent immaturity in higher-order executive functions such as impulse control, planning ahead, and risk avoidance. The justices cited amicus curiae briefs filed in these cases by scientific organizations such as the American Psychological Association, the American Psychiatric Association, and the American Academy of Child and Adolescent Psychiatry, which summarized the literature on adolescent brain development and connected it to the legal issues facing the Court.[9]

It is difficult to know how much and in what ways the Court's conclusion was influenced by research, but the opinions issued in this series of cases increasingly referenced developmental research, and there was a concomitant decrease in the amount of time devoted during oral arguments to discussions of whether and in what ways adolescents and adults differed and at what age the law should draw an age boundary. In *Roper*, this question occupied a good deal of the exchanges between the attorneys and Justices. By way of contrast, in his dissenting opinion in *Miller*, Chief Justice John Roberts noted that "[*Roper* and *Graham*] undoubtedly stand for the proposition that teenagers are less mature, less responsible, and less fixed in their ways than adults—*not that a Supreme Court case was needed to establish that.*"[10]

From 1997 until 2007, I directed the John D. and Catherine T. MacArthur Foundation Research Network on Adolescent Development and Juvenile Justice. Our primary goal was to inform policy and practice in the justice system with findings from the scientific study of adolescence. Our three main programs of work—on the development of capacities relevant to juveniles' criminal culpability, on age differences in abilities relevant to competence to stand trial, and on the factors that contribute to juvenile offenders' desistance from crime—have had demonstrable impact on policy and practice. Findings from the culpability project were cited in the Supreme Court opinions in the juvenile death penalty and life without parole cases.[11] The dissemination of the results of the competence study has led to legislative changes in many states, and competence evaluations are now more common in cases in which juveniles have been prosecuted as adults.[12] And the results of our Pathways to Desistance study are being used by advocates to push for a return to more progressive sanctions that keep larger numbers of juvenile offenders from penetrating more deeply into the justice system than is beneficial for them or the community.[13] In ways that are easy to see but difficult to quantify, our research has changed the national conversation about juvenile offending—in courtrooms, in statehouses, and in the mass media.

There is plenty of room for continued reform, however. Although the juvenile death penalty and mandatory life without parole have been abolished, it is still possible for courts to sentence juveniles to very long terms in adult facilities—in some states, sentences so long that they might as well be life sentences. The justice system remains remarkably punitive in its response toward juvenile offenders. Although we now have evidence that certain rehabilitative approaches are more successful than others, evidence-based practices are not widely used, and, as a consequence, it often appears as if "nothing works."[14] Policy priorities continue to lean toward responding after the fact to juvenile crime rather than preventing it in the first place. And the connections among juvenile justice, mental health, and child welfare remain poorly understood—and poorly addressed by current practice and policy.

Obstacles to Reform

Although there remain numerous obstacles to further progress, the chief impediment to continued reform is attitudinal rather than financial. Juvenile justice systems generally have enough money but simply spend it on the wrong things—after-the-fact intervention rather than prevention, formal processing through the justice system rather than diversion, incarceration rather than community-based treatment. These ill-guided choices generally stem from a deeply held belief that punitive policies are effective at deterring juveniles from offending and reoffending, despite a general lack of evidence for this view and numerous studies indicating that harsh policies, whether within the juvenile or criminal justice system, tend to make things worse and increase, rather than decrease, recidivism. Persuading policy makers to set aside their intuitions and follow evidence-based practices is an enormous challenge.[15]

An important strategy, especially in the current economic climate, will be amassing and presenting evidence demonstrating that approaches that emphasize prevention, diversion, and community-based programs produce comparable (or even greater) reductions in crime at considerably lower cost. Prevention-oriented approaches, however, will require the cooperation of different types of youth-serving agencies, including those that are overseen by departments of education, parks and recreation, social services, and mental health. This, in turn, will require new approaches to funding programs for youth, because agencies are understandably concerned about cost savings that they themselves realize rather than those that benefit others. A mental health services agency has little to gain if a cost savings that is realized by a justice system organization is merely passed on to them.

Related to this attitudinal hurdle is the inclination of legislatures to make policy in response to the crime of the moment. In our book *Rethinking Juve-*

nile Justice, Elizabeth Scott and I detail how moral panics frequently drive juvenile justice policy making, often leading to legislative extremes that are unduly expensive and iatrogenic in their consequences.[16] It is indeed ironic that one of the very features of adolescence that is so commonly cited as a reason to treat juveniles differently under the law—their tendency to make impulsive, short-sighted decisions—is characteristic of many politicians who should have long outgrown this sort of impetuosity. This tendency makes it difficult to sustain progress, since a single, high-profile event can so easily derail sensible reform.

A third obstacle to reform is the lack of familiarity that justice system practitioners have with the basics of adolescent growth and development. Attorneys and judges whose cases involve juvenile defendants rarely have had training in how adolescents think, and, not surprisingly, hold many misconceptions about the period. Practitioners do not understand that someone who knows the difference between right and wrong in the abstract might be unable to resist peer pressure to behave in ways that contradict this knowledge, or that a young adolescent may think it is in his best interests to confess to a crime that he did not commit, or that an adolescent who fails to make eye contact during a judge's colloquy may be expressing respect or fear or even guilt rather than remorselessness.

Looking Forward

We have made great strides over the last two decades toward the ultimate goal of aligning our juvenile justice policies and practices with a scientifically based understanding of adolescent development. Over the next four decades, we can continue to make progress toward this aim by pursuing three specific research agenda, all of which have the potential to generate new knowledge that will resonate with policy makers and opinion leaders: (1) the study of developmental differences between adolescents and adults that have implications for their differential treatment under criminal law, with a particular focus on the neural underpinnings of these differences; (2) the study of the impact of variations in juvenile justice policy and practice on outcomes other than recidivism; and (3) the study of the financial costs and benefits of juvenile justice policy alternatives.

Research on Brain Development and Adolescents' Criminal Responsibility

For better or for worse, policy makers today are enamored with neuroscience. Psychological studies of differences between adolescents and adults are seen as confirming "what every parent knows," but in front of a legislative hearing, one brain scan is worth a thousand words. Several experiments, including a recent one in which judges were the subjects, showed that adding just one or two sentences referring to the brain to a description of behavioral findings makes the behavioral evidence that much more compelling.[17] A cynical reader may conclude that the introduction of adolescent neuroscience into the Supreme Court's deliberations about the juvenile death penalty or juvenile life without parole did little more than exploit the scientific ignorance of laypersons. I think it did more than this, however.

The contribution of neuroscience to discussions of adolescent blameworthiness lies not in what neuroscience tells us about differences in the ways in which adolescents and adults act but in what it implies about the source of these differences.[18] For example, findings of structural and functional differences between adolescent and adult brains that are plausibly linked to differences in individuals' ability to control their impulses and stand up to peer pressure suggest that these aspects of adolescent immaturity are not merely reflective of juveniles' poor choices or different values, but are at least partly due to factors that are not entirely under individuals' control, which makes immaturity a more convincing mitigator. Identifying the neural underpinnings of age differences in legally relevant capabilities and capacities does not indicate that these differences are immutable (indeed, adolescence is believed to be a time of heightened neuroplasticity). However, to the extent that patterns of brain maturation during adolescence follow a specific and predictable pattern that is consistent with predictable patterns of behavioral change, the neuroscientific evidence bolsters the basic argument that adolescents are *inherently* less mature than adults. Moreover, the knowledge that individuals will almost always become more deliberate and self-possessed as they gain experience and as their brains mature, without any special interventions designed to facilitate this process, adds strength to the argument that adolescent offending is unlikely to reflect irreparable depravity. This last point is important, since it provides justification for distinguishing between adolescents, whose immaturity is by definition transient, and fully developed but callow adults, whose immaturity undoubtedly also has neural correlates but is more likely to be an enduring part of their character.

Further neuroscientific research on three specific issues would be especially helpful to future discussions of adolescents' criminal responsibility. First, as critics of the use of neuroscience in these court cases have pointed out, few studies have linked changes in brain structure or function between adolescence and adulthood to changes in the legally relevant behaviors, especially as they play out in the real world.[19] It is certainly reasonable to speculate that adolescents who commit crimes make more impulsive decisions than their adult counterparts because their prefrontal lobes are less fully developed, or because their ventral striatum is more responsive to rewards or emotional stimuli. However, this remains largely a matter of what I would characterize as sensible conjecture. More research that directly links age differences in brain structure and function to age differences in legally relevant capacities and capabilities is needed. Second, although it is often assumed that adolescents are more amenable to rehabilitation than are adults (in part because adolescence is thought to be a time of heightened neuroplasticity), there is very little human neurobiological research that has examined this proposition directly. In recent years, however, several nonhuman studies have provided encouraging evidence that adolescence, like the early years, may be a time of heightened neuroplasticity.[20] Indeed, considerable evidence indicates that brain plasticity does not end at adolescence.[21] Finally, there is growing interest in whether neurobiological data, either alone or in combination with other types of data, can improve the prediction of future behavior at the individual level, either with respect to recidivism or responses to intervention. Although there are studies that have compared juvenile offenders' brain structures or functions with that of nonoffenders, using neuroscience to predict individuals' future behavior is a different (and more difficult) matter.[22]

Research on Juvenile Justice Policy Outcomes Other Than Recidivism

Studies of various justice system interventions find surprisingly few effects on rates of reoffending. The vast majority of juvenile offenders reoffend within a few years of their first offense, regardless of whether they have been treated in the community or in an institutional setting, and regardless of the specific intervention to which they have been exposed.[23] This absence of effects can be looked at through very different lenses. A pessimistic interpretation is that very little works. A somewhat more positive view is that if less expensive interventions are just as effective (or as ineffective) as more costly ones, resources can be saved by opting for the less expensive ones and reallocating the savings elsewhere, perhaps to prevention efforts. One of the best sources of information on this is the Washington State Institute for Public Policy (WSIIP), a nonpartisan organization funded by the state's legislature that conducts and publishes extensive reviews, meta-analyses, and cost-benefit analyses of alternative policy options across a wide array of topics, including juvenile justice interventions.[24] A third perspective, and one to which I subscribe, is that perhaps recidivism is not the only metric along which we should evaluate juvenile justice policies.

A major limitation of research on the consequences of justice system involvement is that it has focused almost exclusively on a single outcome—recidivism—ignoring other important developmental and behavioral outcomes.[25] Yet, adolescents' experiences with the justice system have the potential to substantially influence their life courses in both direct and indirect ways. For example, the few studies that have examined consequences of juvenile justice experiences other than recidivism have found that juvenile court involvement has a negative impact on educational outcomes, such as high school completion.[26] However, it stands to reason that involvement with the juvenile justice system could affect adolescents' lives in a range of domains. Adolescence is a critical period with regard to many aspects of development other than academic achievement—for example, social relationships, mental health, vocational preparation, and psychosocial maturity. Life events (such as incarceration) that disrupt functioning in one or more of these areas may have greater long-term consequences for adolescents than they do for adults. Apart from its impact on subsequent offending (whether positive or negative), justice system involvement may engender considerable human costs and/or benefits that have gone unrecognized and unaccounted for due to an exclusive focus on recidivism as the outcome of interest.

Research on the full array of outcomes of alternative responses to juvenile offending is sparse. Our tendency is to think of juvenile offenders as young criminals rather than as adolescents who have broken the law but who nevertheless have developmental capacities and needs that are characteristic of all people at this age, regardless of their history of antisocial behavior. As a consequence, research on the success or failure of alternative responses to offending (e.g., whether transferring juveniles to the adult system is good policy) is nearly exclusively focused on how the policy affects reoffending. But two policies may have equivalent effects on recidivism but may vary markedly in their impact on juveniles' psychological development, mental health, social relationships, progress in school, and plans for the future. A policy that facilitates healthy psychological development and increases the chances of an adolescent graduating from high school is obviously superior to one that has a comparable impact on recidivism but that stunts psychological development, contributes to mental health problems, or encourages dropping out. If these other, non-crime outcomes are not included in juvenile justice research, however, we have no way of knowing how the policies differ in these respects.

Benefit-Cost Analyses of Alternative Juvenile Justice Policies

Many of the relatively more progressive juvenile justice policies are also less costly than their harsher alternatives. For example, the price difference varies from state to state, but it costs three to four times more to treat an offender in the community than in an institutional placement.[27] Providing accurate benefit-cost analyses of various juvenile justice policy alternatives is an important component of any large-scale effort to improve policy and practice.

Benefit-cost analysis can help policy makers and voters assess policy alternatives by "monetizing" their costs and benefits, thus permitting the options to be compared along a common metric.[28] The monetization of juvenile justice policy alternatives requires more than an accounting of the dollars spent on the intervention and its measured impact on recidivism, however. On the expenditure side of the ledger, the intervention might be monetized with respect to the direct costs of providing the service (e.g., per diem cost of an institutional placement or the cost of providing treatment in the community) as well as the intervention's indirect costs (e.g., the cost of processing the case within the justice system). These expenditures then can be compared with the benefits gained as a result of the intervention—

most obviously, a reduction in crime. Reductions in crime have both easily monetized benefits (e.g., reduced emergency room costs for injured victims, reductions in expenditures for arresting and processing suspects), but they also have benefits that, while very real, are much more difficult to quantify (e.g., improvements in perceptions of public safety yield mental health benefits for residents).[29] In addition, a full assessment of the net cost of an intervention involves estimating the impact of the intervention on non-crime outcomes as well. These outcomes, many of which can be monetized directly, might include positive or negative impacts on truancy, grade retention, and graduation; mental health and substance abuse service utilization; nonmarital childbearing; and physical health and development.

There have been vast improvements in benefit-cost analysis methodologies in the past decade, but by and large these improvements have not been applied to the analysis of juvenile justice policy, because the details of any such analysis vary across jurisdictions, where expenditures and costs are usually region-specific (which makes it difficult to generalize the findings of one jurisdiction's benefit-cost analysis to another jurisdiction), and because the actual methods remain unfamiliar to justice system practitioners. The Washington State Institute for Public Policy uses benefit-cost analysis effectively to inform the state legislature about justice system policy alternatives, but this is a rare practice.[30]

Concluding Comment

It is astonishing to acknowledge that it took more than a decade of concerted effort to persuade policy makers, practitioners, and the public that "kids are different from adults." But juvenile justice policy and practice are much more aligned with developmental science today than they were fifteen years ago, in no small way because research on adolescent development was used as the foundation on which to mount this effort. This is no time to rest on our laurels, however, for it can take only one high-profile crime or a temporary uptick in the crime rate to derail the progress of the past ten years. Over the next four decades, we will need to shore up empirical support for the view that young people's developmental immaturity demands that they be treated differently under the law, drawing on both behavioral and brain science; show how the way we respond to juvenile offending affects not only the crime rate but also the mental health, schooling, and long-term prospects of our most vulnerable young people; and demonstrate to policy makers that the most sensible juvenile justice policy is often the most cost-effective one. This three-pronged strategy will help ensure that momentum generated by the reforms that have been put into place in the last decade will not abate.

CHILD POVERTY

CHAPTER 13

Policies to Reduce Poverty

Supporting Family Income as an Investment in Children's Futures

ARLOC SHERMAN, ROBERT GREENSTEIN, AND SHARON PARROTT

Without adequate family income, children generally do not have the same long-term opportunities as their better-off peers. Research has made increasingly clear that income-supporting policies can promote children's health and their achievement in school and beyond, making these policies an important complement to education, health care, and other services. In a world where education matters ever more, averting childhood poverty and its consequences is of growing importance.

Existing safety net programs fill part of this need. They keep millions of U.S. children out of poverty each year. Yet many of the nation's children remain below or only barely above the poverty line, in part because economic growth has not been equally shared and job opportunities remain limited. More can be done to enable families to earn more, meet their basic economic needs, and provide opportunities for their children.

Historical Overview

The United States has made more progress against child poverty over the past five decades than is widely understood. But child poverty remains widespread. Widening income inequality is restraining income growth on the lower rungs of the economic ladder. Furthermore, policy decisions have weakened parts of the safety net for jobless families, exposing some already-poor children to deeper poverty. Still, low-income children's household incomes (adjusted for inflation and changing household size) are higher than they were forty years ago.

During the 1960s, the official child poverty rate dropped roughly by half, falling from 27 percent in 1959 to 14 percent in 1969. The plunge, which resulted from evenly shared growth in wages and incomes together with stronger public antipoverty policies and reduced racial barriers, showed that large reductions in the nation's child poverty rate are possible.

Starting in the 1970s, progress slowed. After decades of shared prosperity, income growth slowed for middle- and lower-income households, although incomes at the top continued to grow strongly. By 2007, the concentration of income at the very top of the distribution had reached levels last seen more than eighty years ago. Policies designed to fight poverty had to fight a strong headwind of rising inequality and persistently low wages for many workers.

Yet, the reduction in poverty from the 1960s has been maintained and further progress has been made, despite what official poverty figures may suggest. By 2011, the *official* child poverty rate was about 22 percent, close to the levels in 1965 and after the recessions of the early 1980s and 1990s. But the official poverty measure is deceptive; it counts only families' pretax cash income and fails to count noncash benefits such as food assistance and tax credits, which make up most of the new government income assistance added since the early 1970s. In other words, it leaves out the good news for children's incomes.

A fuller accounting suggests that household incomes have probably improved somewhat for children at the bottom since the early 1970s. Census Bureau income figures from that era do not include noncash benefits, but such benefits were smaller then and can be approximated with budget data.[1] We analyzed incomes counting the value of food stamps (now called SNAP benefits), housing assistance, and the two largest tax credits for low-income families, the Earned Income Tax Credit (EITC), and the Child Tax Credit (CTC), both of which target working families. These are the largest noncash but cashlike benefits for which census data provide an estimated value.[2] We also adjusted for average household size, which shrank over this period. Our data are from the March Current Population Survey (see figure 13.1):

- Average incomes for the poorest fifth of households with children rose by 12 percent from 1973 to 2007, from about $20,300 to about $22,800 for a four-person household. These years represent comparable points in the business cycle, since both are economic peaks.

FIGURE 13.1 Average household income for the poorest fifth of households with children, selected years, in 2011 dollars

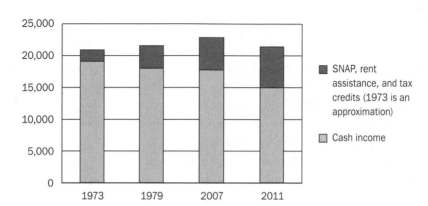

- By 2011, following the Great Recession, the figure had, not surprisingly, dipped to $21,400, about 5 percent above where it was in 1973.
- The $2,500 increase between 1973 and 2007 was driven by noncash benefits, which added an extra $3,300 to low-income children's household income. Earnings also rose slightly over this period, while welfare benefits and other cash income declined.

Thus, children's incomes improved at the bottom thanks largely to stronger government income-support policies.

For the poorest of these low-income households, incomes also rose over the last four decades. From 1973 to 2007, estimated household-size-adjusted real incomes rose 7 percent for the poorest tenth of households with children, from roughly $14,300 to $15,300.

Incomes for lower-income households with children would have grown much more if the benefits of economic growth had been shared more evenly across all income groups and if inequality had not increased sharply. For example, the nation's per capita personal income grew by 62 percent between 1973 and 2007 after inflation (not counting medical benefits and certain other compensation that is excluded from the survey data). If income had risen that rapidly for every quintile, per capita income for the bottom fifth of children would have grown by 62 percent since 1973—

several times faster than it actually grew—and by 2007 average income for these children's households would have been several thousand dollars higher than it actually was.

The full effect of benefit programs can be seen using the federal government's new Supplemental Poverty Measure, which, unlike the official poverty measure, counts noncash benefits and tax credits, but is only available for recent years. By this measure, safety net programs and the tax system kept 9 million children above the poverty line in 2011, cutting the number of poor children from 22 million when benefits and taxes are *not* counted to 13 million when they are counted.

Included in this 9 million are children kept out of poverty by the EITC and CTC (4.9 million), SNAP (2.1 million), unemployment insurance (1 million), housing assistance (1 million), and Temporary Assistance for Needy Families (TANF) and other cash welfare (400,000), among other programs. (The sum exceeds 9 million because children can be lifted out of poverty by more than one program.[3]) Social Security and Supplemental Security Income, though often thought of as programs for retirees, kept 2 million children out of poverty, sometimes by providing disability or survivor payments directly to a child and sometimes by providing retirement income or other benefits for an older family member who lives with a child and thereby lifting the family's income above the poverty line.

Deeper Poverty

The emergence of a strong EITC and CTC (and the extension of Medicaid and the State Children's Health Insurance Program to working poor families) have helped to strengthen the safety net in recent decades for working poor families. However, the safety net has weakened for families who experience significant periods with little or no earnings, leading to a disturbing trend: an increase in deep poverty among children.[4] Yonatan Ben-Shalom and colleagues find that the percentage of families living below *half* of the poverty line increased to 6.6 percent in 2004, up from 4.5 percent in 1993.[5] Among single-parent families, the deep poverty rate reached 11.8 percent.

This is the result of reducing assistance available to jobless families. In 1993, the average out-of-work family received cash and noncash benefits worth $718 per month (in inflation-adjusted 2007 dollars), usually enough to lift it out of deep poverty (though not out of poverty itself). By 2004, this monthly assistance had fallen to $544. One result was less effective protection from deep poverty. Among families with incomes (apart from public benefits) below half the poverty line, benefits kept 78 percent out of such deep poverty in 1993, but just 69 percent in 2004.

The prime cause of this rise in deep poverty was the 1996 law that fundamentally changed basic cash assistance programs for poor families with children. This law replaced the earlier Aid to Families with Dependent Children program with the more restrictive TANF and made cuts in certain other means-tested programs. While changes brought about by the law, in combination with expansions in the EITC and increased assistance with child care expenses and a booming economy in the late 1990s, pulled more single-mother families into the labor market and raised many of their incomes, the welfare changes deepened poverty for other single-mother families. As some families were lifted out of poverty by increased earnings supplemented by the EITC, others fell deeper into poverty as a result of having neither earnings nor cash assistance (or earnings that were more than offset by the loss of cash assistance).

The weakening of the safety net for the poorest families is evident in a recent study of extreme poverty by H. Luke Shaefer and Kathryn Edin, who find that the number of U.S. households with children that live on cash income of less than $2 per person per day—a standard that the World Bank uses to measure poverty in developing countries—has more than doubled since 1996, rising 159 percent to 1.6 million in 2011.[6] Counting the value of tax credits and noncash benefits (SNAP and housing assistance) lowers these numbers considerably. Even so, the increase in extremely poor households with children since 1996 is troubling: up 50 percent to 613,000 such families in 2011. To reveal the role of government benefits in this trend, Shaefer and Edin computed the trend in two ways, one including TANF income and one excluding it. In this comparison it is "obvious," they write, "that cash assistance was having a substantial impact in reducing extreme poverty in early 1996, and having a much smaller effect in reducing extreme poverty by mid-2011." Their findings show that TANF's protective effect against deep poverty dwindled in the 1990s and has remained at a reduced level ever since, changing little in response to the Great Recession.

Family Structure and Adult Choices

Poverty among families with children is complex and affected not only by job availability, wages, and safety net policies but also by such factors as lack of child care, inadequate parental education, disability, bad luck, discrimination, changing demographics, and family structure. Single-parenthood, in particular, increases childhood poverty.

Single-parent families have much higher poverty rates than do married families, and single parenting has become more common since the 1960s and 1970s. Most researchers believe that higher marriage rates would reduce child poverty and (apart from high-conflict marriages) would benefit children. But there is little agreement about what government can or should do that would result in more healthy marriages. Surprisingly, among interventions studied rigorously to date, some of the only successes in improving family stability and marriage rates have come from antipoverty experiments that set out to raise income and supplement low earnings, not to promote marriage.[7] These income interventions may succeed in part by reducing economic strains on couples living in poverty. One of these experiments, Milwaukee's New Hope Project, increased marriage rates of previously single mothers to 21 percent from 12 percent in the control group. In in-depth interviews, "financial stability was by far the most frequent prerequisite for marriage" cited by the women studied.[8] For already-married couples, receiving income in the form of earnings incentives in the second antipoverty experiment in Minnesota enabled second earners to partially reduce their work hours and sharply increased the chances of couples remaining married after three years, to 67 percent compared with 48 percent in the control group.[9]

The high poverty rates of single-parent families also partly reflect policy choices. British children were as likely as those in the United States to live in single-parent families in 2004, but children in single-parent families had lower poverty rates in the United Kingdom than they did in the United States because government benefits cut their poverty rate by more than half in the UK as compared to only one-fifth in the United States.[10]

While an increase in single parenting contributed to an increase in child poverty, other parental choices—such as having fewer children, completing more education, and, for mothers, greater employment—*reduced* children's poverty rates probably by about as much or more than marital changes increased them.[11]

Areas of Progress

Help for the Working Poor

One of the more positive trends in antipoverty policy has been the expansion of help for working poor families. Before 1975, little cash or noncash assistance was available for low-income working families, and families frequently faced subpoverty jobs or subpoverty welfare. That changed gradually with the creation of the EITC in 1975 and the CTC in 1998 and subsequent expansions of both credits, most recently in 2009. Federal and state child care assistance also expanded in the 1990s, and in the past decade SNAP has become more focused on working families.[12] As a result of these changes, Ben-Shalom and colleagues estimate that average monthly assistance for working families rose from $130 in 1984 to $210 in 2004 (in inflation-adjusted 2007 dollars).[13] Also, while medical benefits do not directly impact the poverty rate, expansions in health coverage for children in low-income working families through Medicaid and the Children's Health Insurance Program (CHIP) have improved the health and economic well-being of those families significantly.

Even so, cross-country comparisons calculated by Gornick and Jäntti show that the benefit and tax system did less to reduce the child poverty rate of working single-mother families in the United States than in any of the thirteen other comparably well-off countries studied, including Canada, Great Britain, Ireland, Australia, and countries in continental Europe and Scandinavia.[14] (The United States also had the weakest safety net for single mothers with little or no earnings.) And, as previously noted, the strengthening of government assistance for working families with children was accompanied by a weakening of the safety net for nonworking families.

Documenting Long-Term Effectiveness

Research supports the case for antipoverty policies. A growing body of evidence suggests that income-support policies can make a significant difference for children, both in the short term and in their long-term health and economic prospects. Studies of various antipoverty programs have found subsequent improvements for participating children in test scores, school completion, and long-term health status, labor-market outcomes, and self-sufficiency. Three examples are studies of the EITC, welfare-to-work and antipoverty experiments in the 1990s, and the introduction of the food stamp program starting in the 1960s.

Examining the EITC, Gordon B. Dahl and Lance Lochner find that children covered by a major EITC expansion of the 1990s had improved math and reading test scores.[15] Raj Chetty, John N. Friedman, and Jonah E. Rockoff likewise tie additional EITC and CTC income to significant increases in students' test scores and, drawing on evidence of the consequences of improved test scores, project improvements in students' earnings and employment rates when they become adults.[16]

Gordon Berlin, commenting on data from random-assignment evaluations of welfare-to-work and antipoverty programs, notes, "We have reliable evidence involving thousands of families in multiple studies demonstrating that 'making work pay' [through assistance that supplements low earnings] causes improvements in young children's school performance."[17]

A recent national study examined the rollout of the food stamp program by county in the 1960s and 1970s and found that food stamp access in early childhood and the prenatal year was associated with increased rates of high school completion and lower rates of metabolic syndrome (obesity, high blood pressure, heart disease, and diabetes) years later.[18]

Such long-term findings are a reminder that policies that ensure adequate childhood income not only enhance families' short-term consumption but also open doors of opportunity for children, and are an important complement to other efforts to improve opportunity such as early education, grants for college costs, and health coverage.

Barriers to Progress: Budget Realities and Misperceptions

Federal budget constraints—some real and some misperceived—may limit progress against child poverty. Budgets are likely to remain tight in coming decades due in part to fiscal challenges associated with an aging population and rising health care costs. At the same time, some of the current impetus for austerity draws from misperceptions about the federal budget and social spending.

One such misperception is that spending for antipoverty programs is growing explosively and fueling the deficit crisis. This belief has stoked calls for deep cuts in programs for low-income children and families; budget plans that the House of Representatives approved in 2012 and 2013 would take over 60 percent of their proposed multi-trillion-dollar budget cuts over ten years from programs targeted at low-income Americans.

In reality, most of the recent growth in spending for means-tested programs as a share of the economy is due to two factors: the recent recession and rising health care costs that are not particular to government health programs. As the recession's effects recede, the Congressional Budget Office projects that spending for low-income programs outside health care—for both entitlement and discretionary programs—will fall below its prior forty-year average, measured as a share of GDP. Since these programs are not rising as a percent of GDP, they do not contribute to our long-term fiscal problems (see figure 13.2).

Medicaid *is* projected to rise as a share of GDP, because of the growing cost of health care throughout the U.S. health care system, the aging of the population, and the expansion of Medicaid to cover more of the uninsured. But Medicaid is not the *cause* of systemwide health cost growth. It costs less per beneficiary and has been growing no more rapidly than the rest of the U.S. health care system.[19]

Deficit reduction is likely to continue to dominate discussions of federal budget priorities for a number of years. But the *quantity* of deficit reduction is not the only important issue; the *quality* of the deficit-reduction measures adopted matters as well. Deficit reduction can and should be secured through well-designed, balanced policies that do not impede the economic recovery, do not jeopardize future productivity growth (by providing inadequate resources for areas like education, infrastructure, and basic research), and do not increase poverty and inequality.

The most widely cited road map for deficit reduction, the bipartisan Bowles-Simpson plan of 2010, made it a core principle that deficit reduction should not increase poverty or harm the disadvantaged. Past deficit reduction efforts, including major deficit reduction legislation enacted

FIGURE 13.2   Federal spending on health and non-health low-income programs as a percent of GDP

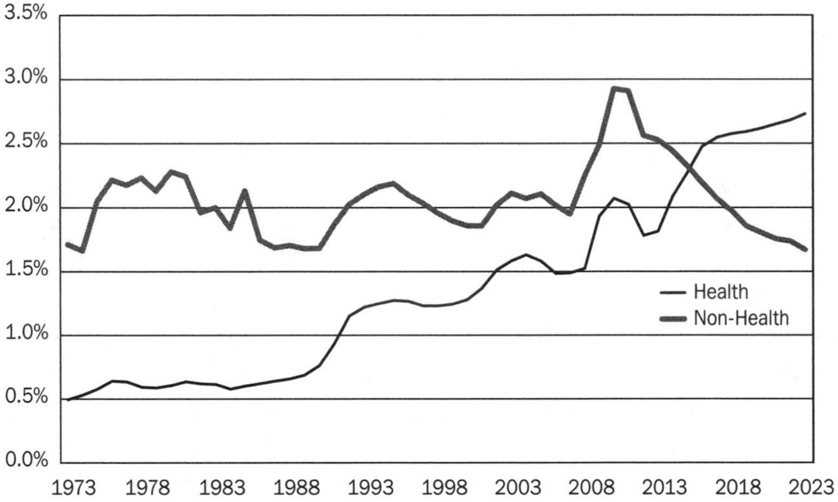

Note: Figures after 2012 are projections.
Source: Congressional Budget Office

in 1990 and 1993, indicate that adhering to this principle is politically possible.

Looking Forward

Progress against child poverty in the coming decades is more likely to come from a combination of solutions than from one or two big initiatives (although the Affordable Care Act will improve financial stability and well-being and parental access to health care for many families that could otherwise face high medical bills). This is both because families' needs vary and because the economy and safety net programs contain a number of distinct gaps and shortfalls. These include lack of secure jobs, especially for people with limited education and skills; continued widening inequality in wages and incomes; gaps in the safety net; and insufficient access to quality pre-school education and other services that can open doors of opportunity for the next generation.

A first duty of policy makers is to do no harm. Existing protections against poverty should be preserved. Some individual programs have weaknesses that merit improvement, and funding should be redirected from less-effective programs to more effective ones. But at a minimum, the overall level of resources for assisting society's most vulnerable members should not be cut.

Even in the current tight fiscal environment, progress is possible. Steps to improve employment and earnings include:

Subsidized jobs. The federal government should establish an ongoing Employment Fund to help states run subsidized jobs programs. Such programs were funded temporarily in the last recession through the TANF block grant and proved successful and popular with participating businesses, families, and state officials of both parties. During good economic times, the program should focus on people with major employment barriers; in bad economic times, it should ramp up to include those who have lost their jobs and have limited prospects of finding a new one in a reasonable period of time. The fund could help cover wages and other payroll costs as well as supportive services such as child care or transportation. Funding initially could come from redirecting the $612 million a year that is currently allocated to the TANF Contingency Fund, although in the long term more funds are likely to be needed. [20]

Training. Job training should be improved and expanded. One successful model involves sectoral training for well-paid jobs in high-demand employment sectors such as health care or computing, often accompanied by close ties to local employers. In a random-assignment evaluation, low-income participants in three such programs worked more and earned 18 percent more (about $4,500 more) than control group members during the two years of the study.[21] A low-cost approach would allow states to fund these and other activities that increase unemployed individuals' employability using a portion of the funds from the Employment Fund described above. With more adequate funding, economist Harry Holzer proposes a roughly $2-billion-a-year federal competitive grants program to fund and continuously evaluate state job training, education, and workforce development programs based on randomized controlled experiments.[22]

More child care assistance. One study estimated that additional child care assistance could lift as many as one-seventh of poor children above the poverty line, mostly by increasing their parents' employment.[23] Child care funding should support both improved quality of care and integration with other early education initiatives such as Head Start and other preschool programs, as high-quality early education not only serves as a work support but improves children's earning prospects.[24]

Steps to further improve wages and reduce inequality include:

Wage and labor market policies. Isabel Sawhill of the Brookings Institution estimates that raising the minimum wage to $9 an hour and indexing it for inflation, as President Obama has proposed, would raise the average earnings of the bottom third of households by 7 percent.[25] Other measures could include requiring employers to offer paid sick leave and stricter enforcement of existing labor laws, including laws on overtime pay and the misclassification of employees as contractors, who are not covered by employee benefits and protections.

College aid. Thirty years ago, the maximum Pell Grant covered nearly three-fourths of the cost of attending a four-year public college; today, it covers only about a third of those costs.[26] The federal government should expand Pell Grant funding and simplify the application process.

Using existing rental assistance to improve opportunity. Housing programs can do a better job of helping families move from high-crime neighborhoods to safer communities with better job opportunities and schools. For example, federal tenant voucher programs can streamline the process for moving with a voucher across jurisdictional lines and tailor subsidy levels to the rents in each zip code rather than the metropolitan-area average. Other housing programs—government-owned housing projects, privately owned sites that receive federal subsidies tied to the site, and housing tax credits—could be marshaled to help develop and maintain more affordable housing in high-opportunity neighborhoods.

Additional steps can help close gaps in the safety net, especially for those in deep poverty:

Assisting parents with moderate disabilities. Qualifying for existing disability programs (Social Security Disability Insurance and Supplemental Security Income) can take a long time and requires extensive medical documentation of a serious, long-lasting disability. Many parents with moderate mental or physical impairments or limited cognitive functioning do not qualify. These same parents may have difficulty finding and holding a full-time, adequately paid job or satisfying the work requirements that are a condition of receiving cash assistance from TANF. A new program, or new component of the TANF program, could focus on this group, providing them with alternative pathways to work (including part-time work if that is what they can do), along with income support and help in strengthening their parenting skills.

More housing assistance. Federal rental assistance programs (including housing vouchers, public housing, and other programs) help five million low-income households obtain affordable housing, and in so doing significantly reduce homelessness and destitution. Housing assistance is effective against deep poverty; no other set of programs lifts a higher proportion of its participants above half the poverty line. But because of funding limitations, only one in five poor households with children receives rental assistance. The federal government could make rental subsidy vouchers available to more poor households, as the Bipartisan Policy Center Housing Commission recommended.[27]

All of these steps would likely not only reduce the number of people in poverty but reduce the severity of poverty for those who remained poor, while lifting incomes for many who are only modestly above the poverty line. Three steps in particular—creating subsidized jobs, expanding housing assistance, and supporting those with moderate disabilities—are likely to be of particular importance for reducing deep poverty.

Our recommendations are directed chiefly at the federal government, which has more resources to act than states; however, states can and often do move ahead without federal action. For example, states can preserve and improve funding for child care and early education, raise state minimum wages, and use housing and transportation policy to help families live in safer neighborhoods with better schools and jobs. States can also create or expand state refundable tax credits based on the federal EITC. Of particular importance now, states can adopt the Medicaid expansion called for under the Affordable Care Act and thereby cover many uninsured poor parents, improving their access to health care, lowering their out-of-pocket medical expenses, and helping reduce the economic impact of illness on families..

States facing tight budget constraints may wish to explore options for freeing up resources. One such option is in the area of criminal justice reform, including but not limited to juvenile justice reform.[28] Alternatives to incarceration, such as effective addiction treatment, can generate savings in state budgets by reducing incarceration costs.[29] Such reforms may also help some nonviolent offenders remain productively employed, which itself may positively affect their families and communities and, in some cases, help to reduce poverty.

CHAPTER 14

The State of Research on Children and Families in Poverty

Past, Present, and Future Empirical Avenues of Promise

ERIC DEARING

Less than two decades ago, a perfect storm of favorable labor market conditions and federal policy changes led to historic declines in child poverty rates in the United States. With unemployment low and wages high, work requirements in the 1996 welfare reform and federal benefits to the working poor such as the Earned Income Tax Credit (EITC) combined to produce the lowest overall child poverty rate in twenty years in the late 1990s.[1] Yet, high unemployment and stagnant wages at the low end of the income distribution have led to rising numbers of children in poverty in the last decade and increasing disparity between those growing up rich and poor. Today, although poverty rates for black and Hispanic children remain below their peak levels during the 1980s and early 1990s, more than one in five children in the United States are poor, which is one of the highest rates among developed nations.[2] As Arloc Sherman, Robert Greenstein, and Sharon Parrott highlight in chapter 13, there is good news hidden within the bad news. Economic well-being has, on average, increased over the last few decades for families whose incomes fall below federal poverty thresholds, primarily because of increases in noncash benefits such as the Supplemental Nutrition Assistance Program (SNAP) and tax credits (e.g., EITC) to lower-income families. Nonetheless, the number of children in the United States living in deep poverty is on the rise, and disparities in healthy development between poor and non-poor children are widening: from child mortality rates to achievement on standardized tests, gaps between poor and non-poor children have persistently widened since the 1970s.[3]

Developmental differences between children in poverty and their non-poor peers have been documented repeatedly in fields as diverse as education, medicine, and many of the social sciences. Indeed, it is now an empirical truism that children growing up poor are at risk for dysfunction and delay in nearly every area of their growth, including cognitive and language development, physical health, and social-emotional well-being. Yet, just as poverty rates have shifted over the last few decades, so, too, has the field of research dedicated to understanding the consequences of poverty for children and families. Most notably, in contemporary work, there has been increased attention to isolating the causal effects of economic deprivation, per se. This contemporary focus has been driven by a zeitgeist that values the application of empirical findings to policy and practice.[4]

In this chapter, after briefly defining poverty and reviewing the cumulative knowledge on poverty and child development, I identify two priorities for future study that should further increase the relevancy of empirical work on children growing up poor: greater attention to immigrant children growing up poor and more evaluation work with comprehensive interventions that aim to protect children from toxic stress (or alleviate the effects of toxic stress) due to growing up with the chaos, deprivation, and dangers of poverty.

Defining Poverty

I prioritize empirical work that has defined poverty as economic deprivation—that is, poverty is defined as having too little money to purchase resources necessary to meet basic human needs. Although attempts to identify a precise, nonarbitrary threshold for "too little money" are not without controversy, the bulk of evidence on which I report is based on family income levels relative to the federal U.S. Census Bureau poverty thresholds.[5] Conventionally, researchers have identified families that are near or below those thresholds as being poor. Empirical work that has examined family income on a continuous scale, considering variations in developmental outcomes across the full distribution of family income levels, has also been critical to the field. And these approaches have been extended to measure economic resources within groups (e.g., neighborhoods and schools) using a composite of family poverty rates and/or family income levels within the group.

Negative developmental outcomes associated with poverty are most likely to occur, and appear most severe, when children live in very deprived conditions for extended periods of time, although even brief episodes of less-than-extreme poverty are associated with underachievement and social-emotional disturbances.[6] In turn, cognitive, physical health, and social-emotional problems linked with childhood poverty contribute, in the long term, to reduced earnings, involvement in crime, and health and mental health problems throughout life.[7] Due to these long-term consequences, in fact, the public costs of childhood poverty in the United States are estimated to be as high as $500 billion per year, or about 4 percent of the U.S. gross domestic product.[8]

Physical Health

A wide variety of health risks associated with poverty during early childhood have been documented, with new evidence indicating that chronic poverty in childhood may have life-long health consequences. Children living in poverty are exceptionally likely to: (1) be exposed, prenatally, to alcohol and drugs; (2) be exposed to environmental toxins such as lead; (3) be injured in household accidents; and (4) acquire diseases and illnesses such as AIDS, asthma, bacterial meningitis, and ear infections.[9] In turn, health problems associated with poverty during early childhood become risk factors for developmental problems in achievement and social-emotional domains (e.g., the direct effects of lead poisoning on intelligence and the indirect effect of illness on academic achievement via school absences).[10]

Mounting evidence also indicates that early and chronic exposure to poverty may have lasting harmful consequences into mid- and late-life, placing adults at an increased risk for health problems such as obesity and metabolic syndrome.[11] Mechanisms explaining associations between adversity in early life and later life health problems are not fully understood, but most evidence points to the harm of the chronic activation of the body's stress system leading to changes in central fat accumulation and lipid metabolism as well as more generalized progressive wear and tear on the nervous, endocrine, and immune systems. Although most empirical work in this area tends to collapse across related socioeconomic risk indicators (or addresses other forms of early adversity such as child abuse), there is good reason to speculate that poverty, per se, operates on health via pathways of toxic stress. Indeed, hallmark characteristics of toxic stress such as sustained deprivation and chaotic surroundings have been well documented as one explaination for underachievement and social-emotional problems evidenced by children growing up poor.[12]

Achievement and Cognitive Functioning

Within the first few years of life, infants and toddlers in poor households display an increased risk of language and cognitive delays.[13] In turn, across early childhood and the schooling years, children in poverty score, on average, about one-half of a standard deviation lower on tests of achievement and intelligence compared with children in middle-class families and more than one standard deviation lower than children in affluent families.[14] Furthermore, with rates of children living in deep poverty on the rise, depth of poverty matters: children living in extreme poverty (i.e., less than 50 percent of the U.S. Census Bureau's official poverty threshold) score, on average, as much as one-half of a standard deviation lower on tests of achievement and intelligence than children living just above the poverty line.[15] As sociologist Sean Reardon has noted, the magnitude of the achievement gap between poor and wealthy children is comparable to the average achievement gap between fourth and eighth grade students.[16] Equally startling is the gap in years of completed schooling; youth growing up in extreme poverty, for example, are about twelve times less likely to graduate from high school than youth in middle-class families.[17]

While the developmental timing of poverty experiences may, in part, determine the severity of achievement consequences, longer spells in poverty are riskier at any developmental stage than shorter spells. Some researchers have found that low performance on achievement tests and real-life academic failures are most likely to occur if youth experience poverty during early childhood, and others report greater harm associated with poverty during middle childhood.[18] Regardless, persistent deprivation throughout childhood appears more likely to limit children's cognitive potential compared with transient deprivation (i.e., three or fewer years) during any one developmental stage.[19]

Most evidence on why poor children underachieve points to a lack of learning stimulation and support at home, at child care/preschool, and at school. There is considerable evidence that poverty constrains families' investments in material (e.g., books) and psychosocial (e.g., parent time) resources that promote positive child learning. The homes of poor children are, on average, defined by inadequate access to materials such as books, age-appropriate toys, and computers; low levels and quality of parent-child talk and little parental engagement in learning or school-related activities with their children; and housing conditions that are not conducive to learning (e.g., poor lighting, limited space, and high noise levels).[20] Outside the home, children in poverty are less likely than other children to attend learning-enriched child care centers and preschools, and schools with high concentrations of children in poverty are exceptionally likely to have teacher shortages, high teacher turnover rates, teachers assigned to topics they are not qualified to teach, and instructional practices that are not empirically informed (e.g., cooperative learning and instructional conversation strategies).[21] In addition, compared with middle-class and wealthier children and adolescents, poor youth are less likely to engage in organized out-of-school activities such as clubs, music lessons, and sports.[22]

Social-emotional Functioning

Associations between poverty and social-emotional functioning are not as strong as those between poverty and learning and achievement. Yet, according to the observations of parents, teachers, and children themselves, growing up poor is a risk for social-emotional problems that are interpersonal (i.e., externalizing problems such as aggression, destructive behavior, and hyperactivity) and intrapersonal (i.e., internalizing problems such as anxiety, depression, and fearfulness).[23] Only a small percentage of children develop social-emotional disorders that meet clinical definitions, but poverty is a risk factor for the development of oppositional defiant and conduct disorders as well as anxiety and depressive disorders.[24]

Children growing up poor may be especially prone to externalizing problems. Behavior regulation problems such as aggression and hyperactivity are common responses to unpredictable disruptions and changes in children's lives, and poverty is a risk for limited verbal skills, which are themselves a risk for externalizing problems.[25] More specifically, children in families with limited income tend to experience more volatile and less predictable family environments in terms of living circumstances, family structure, and consistency of parenting practices.[26] Moreover, persistent poverty (as with other forms of chronic adversity) has harmful effects on children's neuro-biological stress systems (e.g., the hypothalamic-pituitary-adrenocortical system), which are intimately involved in the development of anxiety and depressive disorders.[27] Children living in poverty are, in fact, more likely to evidence neuroendocrine markers of chronic stress than youth who are not poor, and increasingly researchers have suggested that toxic stress is a critical mechanism relaying the harm of poverty to children.[28]

The lives of children growing up poor are characterized by an abundance of proximal and distal stressors, with exposure to these stressors often being chronic and beyond the control of children (or their parents). In the home, children in poverty are more likely than other children to experience frequent shifts in family economic well-being (gains and losses in family income), changes in parental employment status, and changes in family structure (e.g., changes in mothers' partner statuses and extended family and friend networks moving into and out of the household). In turn, poor children are at risk of experiencing higher levels of unresponsive, harsh, and/or inconsistent parenting compared with their wealthier peers, because economic volatility and pressures associated with poverty impair parent mental health and undermine cognitive, effort, and emotional resources that can be dedicated to positive parenting.[29]

In school, teacher-student relationships and classrooms for poor children are, on average, characterized by fewer positive interactions and lower levels of instructional support compared with the schooling experiences of middle-class and wealthier students.[30] In their communities, youth in poverty are often exposed to environmental toxins and stressors, such as high levels of air and water pollutants (e.g., sulfur oxides), overcrowding, poor municipal services, and few merchants or retail stores.[31] Further, youth in poverty are more likely than youth who are not poor to be exposed to antisocial behavior and violence in their neighborhoods.[32]

The "Consequences" of Poverty—Are They Really Causal?

Within the fields of economics, sociology, and developmental psychology, much of the contemporary work on poverty and child development has been focused on isolating the causal effects of income poverty, per se. In part, this advance has been fueled by researchers recognizing that the study of omnibus socioeconomic status variables—composites of social and economic family indicators such as low parent education, low occupational prestige, and low family income—are of limited relevancy to policy decision makers, because informing policy requires greater precision. As Greg Duncan and Katherine Magnuson sum up the issue, "Household income, parental education and occupational standing are distinct theoretical constructs, with distinct impacts on children's development and subject to manipulation through very different policy interventions."[33]

Although the majority of studies of poverty and child development have relied on nonexperimental methods, evidence on the harmful consequences of poverty has mounted from designs that closely approximate randomized experiments in terms of strict control for potential confounds. Specifically, support for causal links between poverty and children's achievement and mental health have been documented in longitudinal within-family studies of gains and losses in income, natural experiments whereby family income has been increased for some entire communities but not others, and studies taking advantage of exogenous forces that cause family income changes (e.g., random assignment to intervention in antipoverty experiments that, on average, changed family income to greater or lesser extents).[34] In short, the consequences of poverty appear across a wide variety of methods that estimate the developmental consequences of poor families gaining (and losing) money. Even so, recent demographic changes to the populous and political realities in the United States deserve attention when evaluating the relevancy and legitimacy of the cumulative knowledge on poverty and child development.

The Next Forty Years: Advancing the Relevancy of Research on Children Growing Up Poor

Immigrant Children and Poverty

As developmental psychologist and policy scholar Deborah Phillips has noted, the "legitimacy" of empirical work that intends to be policy relevant increasingly depends on its generalizability to the large and growing immigrant population.[35] By 2020, it is anticipated that more than one in four children in the United States will live in immigrant families, most coming from Latin America and Asia.[36] In turn, the life-chances of these children are critical for maintaining the U.S. workforce and its competition in the global marketplace.[37] Thus, it is disconcerting that while the number of immigrant children growing up poor is disproportionately large—about 30 percent of immigrant children live in poor households—the cumulative knowledge on the consequences of poverty for immigrant children is disproportionately small.[38]

Similar to other children, there are achievement disparities between poor and non-poor immigrants, but as many researchers have noted, there is also some evidence of a paradox involving generational status, family socioeconomics, and child achievement among immigrant children in the United States.[39] On average, first-generation immigrant children can display higher levels of achievement than second- and third-generation immigrants, despite first-generation families, on average, having the lowest levels of family income and parent education. Indeed, among immigrant children, there is consistent evidence of a suppression effect: statistically adjusting for family income leads to *stronger* associations between generational status and achievement that favor first-generation children, because first-generation children are achieving, on average, at relatively high levels despite relatively low family incomes.[40] And, a similar paradox is evident for school-level disadvantage: native-born youth of color appear more sensitive to the negative consequences of school poverty than do immigrant youth.[41]

In trying to account for why the immigrant paradox exists, most researchers and theorists point toward a complex interaction of psychosocial mechanisms: despite material and economic deprivation, recent immigrants appear to benefit from strongly valuing close connections between parents and children, optimism and high expectations of their children, and perceptions of self in relation to society that bolster achievement motivation.[42] In short, the way immigrants perceive their circumstances is a potential moderator of economic (and other) risk.

There is also indirect evidence that the effects of antipoverty policy approaches may differ for children of immigrants compared with children of U.S.-born whites. Although they did not investigate immigrant status, per se, Hirokazu Yoshikawa and colleagues found that antipoverty experiments varied in their effectiveness across ethnic groups.[43] In Riverside, California, for example, Latino children's school readiness was bolstered by education-first "treatment" (i.e., an experimental antipoverty treatment that tied parent education requirements to welfare receipt) more so than white children's readiness.[44] Recent evidence also suggests that the extent to which parent investments and family stress explain estimated income effects on youth outcomes may vary somewhat by ethnicity; investment in cognitively stimulating resources and family stress in the home environment may explain a greater proportion of estimated income effects for white youth than for black or Hispanic youth.[45]

Yoshikawa and colleagues suggest that differences may occur in racial/ethnic responses to antipoverty policy approaches that promote education in part because newcomer parents place a particularly high value on education as a tool for family success in the United States.[46] That is, the education-first policy lever is closely aligned with many immigrant family goals. It is worth underscoring how this possible explanation and speculation on the immigrant paradox emphasize ways that variations in sociocultural histories may affect perceptions of economic disadvantage among diverse groups of children and families.

It is also important to note poverty-related risks that are unique to immigrant populations. Due to obstacles such as language and documentation status, for example, low-income immigrant families are as much as two times less likely to participate in SNAP.[47] In turn, food insecurity among low-income families with young children is about two and a half times higher when parents are immigrants than when parents are U.S.-born.[48] Moreover, discrimination may compound the harm of poverty for immigrant children and families in so far as it increases poverty-related psychological stress and further limits access to adequate health care, housing, and employment opportunities.[49]

Psychologists have long known that stressful environments that feel out of one's control have more damaging psychological and physical effects than stressful environments that feel within one's control.[50] Compared with those who have endured economic disadvantage and obstacles to upward mobility across generations (e.g., institutionalized racism, stagnant wages at the low end of the income distribution), perceptions of control may be relatively high among recent immigrants who have voluntarily migrated to the United States despite high levels of economic stress; and given considerable variation across immigrant in their likelihood of upward mobility, perceptions of control may vary across immigrant groups.[51] Yet, to date, there is much too little empirical work to move beyond speculation on such matters. And regardless of whether more attention directed toward the effects of income and poverty among immigrant children does or does not reveal variations across groups (for the consequences of economic disadvantage or for the consequences of policy approaches to solving that disadvantage), until the empirical focus on poverty and policy effects for immigrant children and families is proportional to their demographic representation, we will not know whether our present estimates are policy relevant for how harmful poverty can be and how helpful moving out of poverty can be.

Comprehensive Intervention in the Context of Persistent Poverty and Persistent Stress

Over the next forty years, research on children growing up poor will retain high incidence validity because the number of children facing this developmental risk is likely to remain substantial into the near future. This research will best maximize its relevancy by addressing constructs that might, indeed, be policy relevant. When considering policy-relevant poverty research in the United States, the elephant in the room is the political unlikelihood of large-scale redistribution policies through progressive income taxation; there is little to suggest that substantial reductions in child poverty rates will, any time soon, be accomplished via redistribution policies similar to those that have been successfully used in other highly-developed, wealthy economies.[52] Consider, for example, the Scandinavian countries of Denmark, Finland, Norway, and Sweden: these nations have used progressive tax policies, as well as other forces such as strong labor unions, as a lever for keeping levels of income inequality low, intergenerational mobility high, and child poverty rates much lower than in the United States (i.e., presently, child poverty rates in these countries are well below 10 percent).[53]

Empirical work on the developmental consequences of new and likely forthcoming policies that will impact children in poverty (e.g., the Affordable Care Act and comprehensive immigrant reform) will be one priority for the scientific community. Yet, we must also expand our study of levers for promoting children's well-being despite growing up poor. For one, more evaluation work is needed on interventions that complement and extend the value of proven policy targets such as high-quality early childhood education and care.[54] In addition, given wider political support for in-kind versus cash transfers in the United States, the study of goods, services, and supports that might effectively help offset or prevent the harms of poverty offer unique promise.

Even powerful levers for redirecting developmental trajectories toward healthy development for poor children such as high-quality preschool classrooms are unlikely to function as inoculations against persistent exposure to chaos, deprivation, and danger. To the same extent that the risks of poverty are multipronged and consequential for children's lives at home, in child care and preschool and at school and in their neighborhoods, compensating for poverty will require multipronged intervention. And there is increasing evidence that attention to family and child stress should be a central component of such intervention.

Associations between early childhood poverty and physiological indicators of chronic stress response have been documented, with much of the work focused on elevated cortisol levels as a marker of chronic activation of the hypothalamic-pituitary-adrenal axis (HPA). In turn, elevated cortisol is associated with worse executive functioning and lower cognitive achievement in early childhood.[55] In a recent longitudinal study, Clancy Blair and colleagues repeatedly measured family poverty and household chaos for a large sample of children across infancy and into early childhood.[56] At forty-eight months, children with more cumulative time in poverty and those with more cumulative exposure to household chaos had higher cortisol levels than other children.

Importantly, these researchers have also demonstrated both physiological and contextual moderators (including parental sensitivity and time in child care) of links between poverty and elevated cortisol.[57] For example, in the same sample of children, links between cumulative risk and cortisol at forty-eight months were moderated by time in child care such that more time in care was associated with lower cortisol levels for children from high-risk home environments but higher cortisol levels for children from low-risk home environments. Sensitive parenting also appears to buffer children from the physiological chronic stress responses initiated by poverty, although parenting does not fully mediate links between poverty and cortisol. If parenting is only partially responsible for relaying toxic stress to children, then interventions that exclusively target parenting will, at best, only partially buffer children against contexts of stress in poor households.[58] Indeed, parenting, family income, and other aspects of household risk each have some unique contributions to elevated stress and, in turn, executive functioning and cognitive abilities in early childhood.[59]

This is not to say, however, that parenting is not a critical mechanism or, perhaps, even the primary mechanism accounting for the largest portion of variance when considering pathways of stress in the context of poverty. Indeed, poverty researchers should note the success of parenting interventions that were been designed to buffer children from early adversities other than poverty.[60] Mary Dozier and colleagues, for example, have demonstrated that a parenting intervention designed to improve caregiver sensitivity to the emotions and developing self-regulatory capabilities of young children in foster care resulted in normalized functioning of the HPA (measured via cortisol levels) and improved cognitive flexibility.[61] Nonetheless, buffering children in poverty from toxic stress is a tall order given the wide array of stress factors they encounter at home, at school, and in the neighborhood.

Comprehensive intervention services for children and families in poverty is not a new idea, but recent movements toward family-school-community connection models may offer benefits beyond models that relied on individual agencies (e.g., the Head Start center) to efficiently and effectively provide many services to children and families (e.g., early childhood education, family health, parent education, and social services). Consider, for example, City Connects, a school-based intervention in several high-poverty elementary schools in Boston and Springfield, Massachusetts.[62] The core practices of City Connects include placing school counseling or social work professionals in elementary schools to evaluate every child and family's unique strengths and needs, in collaboration with teachers and other school professionals; create a support plan that is tailored to align with these strengths and needs; and carry out the support plan through school-community agency partnerships that are initiated, evaluated, and nurtured by the support professional. In quasi-experimental studies that matched students on background characteristics and several domains of pretreatment achievement and social competence, my colleagues and I have found early positive consequences for children's cognitive and behavioral self-regulation (e.g., teacher ratings of effort, work habits, and classroom behavior).[63] In turn, compared with other children in the same district, those in intervention schools show lasting achievement gains in literacy and mathematics through middle school, across high-stakes state achievement tests and low-stakes nationally standardized assessments. Notably, these effects seem particularly strong for immigrant children.[64]

There appears to be much promise in family-school-community collaborations as intervention for the multipronged risks associated with growing up poor. Many questions remain in work like this, however. It is not yet clear, for example, which community resources and supports are working best for which children and families. Continued careful mapping of the mechanisms of risk in the context of poverty and aligning supports that buffer children from these risks remains a priority for the next forty years. In particular, work that targets stress-related risks will prove critical for the future of the field and for children growing up poor.

Looking Ahead: Concluding Thoughts

In the last forty years, family poverty has proved to be one of the most robust predictors of developmental delay and dysfunction for children. And during this time researchers have moved from a basic understanding of differences in developmental outcomes of poor and non-poor children to a close examination of poverty's causal consequences for growth and an increasingly nuanced detailing of the mechanisms of harm. Yet, with persistently higher child poverty rates in the United States than in other wealthy nations, with levels of economic inequality on the rise, and with evidence that developmental differences between poor and non-poor may be increasing, the next forty years deserve a refined attention to empirical questions that are policy relevant. For one, the legitimacy of future poverty research depends on an adequate representation of, and attention to, immigrant children and families; of special importance will be the study of contextual and psychosocial moderators of the effects of poverty and the effects of interventions—not only for immigrant versus native groups but also between diverse groups of immigrants.

In addition, recent advances on the harm of chronic stress in childhood suggest that furthering this line of work is one of the most exciting avenues for advancing science, policy, and practice on children growing up poor. In particular, the development and evaluation of comprehensive interventions that take a multipronged approach to interrupting or alleviating pathways of stress within children's homes, schools, and neighborhoods is a pressing priority. In his analysis of widening achievement gaps between poor and wealthy children, Reardon concludes that it is not so much the widening gap in family income between the rich and poor that explains the trend but rather the widening gap in investments that wealthy families have made in promoting their children's growth at home (e.g., home learning materials), at preschool and school (e.g., purchasing high-quality education and care in the early years and beyond), and in the community (e.g., extracurricular supports and activities).[65] At the other end of the income distribution remains a question of great relevance to policy: could increased supports and services across home, school, and community contexts prove equally or more vital in narrowing disparities?

Afterword

The test of the morality of a society is what it does for its children.
—Dietrich Bonhoeffer

The test of our progress is not whether we add more to the abundance of those who have much. It's whether we provide enough for those who have too little.
—Franklin Delano Roosevelt

This second decade of the twenty-first century is a crucial one for the children's movement and the nation's future, as poverty and child poverty have resurged in a prolonged recession and jobless "recovery" and with wealth and income inequality at near record levels. As this indispensable and wide-ranging book reminds us, there are urgent needs that must be addressed if all of America's children are to have the supports and opportunities necessary for success in a rapidly changing world. The Children's Defense Fund (CDF)'s most important work lies ahead, building on the foundation laid and the seeds sowed and nurtured over four decades to mount a transforming movement to invest in giving all children the healthy, head, fair, and safe starts they need. We must and will lead boldly and strategically, collaborating with others to prevent and end child poverty by protecting critical safety net programs, moving to scale successful policies and practices, and engaging new voices for new choices and values calling for a new measure of success in America to achieve a nation fit for our children and grandchildren.

Through continuing research, policy development and implementation, youth leadership development, grassroots organizing, multimedia communications, nonviolent direct action movement building strategies, and youth, parent, and community empowerment and civic engagement, we will push the nation to adopt and achieve goals of decreasing child poverty by half by 2020, eliminating child poverty by 2025, and ending the violence of guns, illiteracy, and innumeracy in our globalized competitive economy. Children who cannot read and write and compute and think are being sentenced to social and economic death.

To those who say the nation with the largest economy in the world cannot afford to invest in ensuring all children's basic survival needs, health, early childhood development, and education, I say, "Nonsense." We cannot afford *not* to do it if we want to be educationally, economically, and militarily competitive in the future.

Our children are in trouble and our nation is in trouble, and we must reset our moral and economic compasses. We must stanch a backward drift into a second post-Reconstruction era driven too much by ideology; the fear of some of "losing our country" because of changing demographics and a black president; a continuing structural racism and poverty that are hard to discuss honestly; and the redistribution of wealth and income from bottom and middle incomes to the very wealthiest at the top. Dr. Martin Luther King Jr. warned about what the nation is facing today, saying we were integrating into a burning house infected by excessive materialism, militarism, and racism. When asked what we must do, he said that we all had to become firemen. CDF has been sounding the siren with urgency and persistence over four decades and will not stop until it is heard and sufficient actions are taken to combat this triple threat. This immensely helpful book, with its clear delineation of critical problems facing the nation and its children, points us in the direction of measures we all must undertake.

In our fifth decade, CDF is committed to melding together the critical mass of leaders—especially young black, Latino, Native American, faith, and women leaders—required to build and sustain the moral and political will to do for all children what we know works for some children. We must band together, all of us, across all racial and income groups—especially as mothers, grandmothers, sisters, and aunts, as leaders in the black, Hispanic, Asian American, Native American, and white communities—and be clear that we cannot wait any longer to ensure our children's healthy development. Children have only one childhood, and it is now. We know what to do. We know what works. We must make it happen now by working together, and we must reject all excuses for inaction from our political leaders.

Incorporating decades of research, knowledge of best practices, and national, state, and local policy experiences, CDF has created a six-pillar child investment agenda to end the violence of guns, poverty, and school failure and ensure success for every child and economic success for our nation. We believe the best defense is a strong offense. We must fight to make sure we secure what our children need.

Increased investments in children, especially poor children, throughout their childhood and into young adulthood are critical to ensuring their future and our nation's future. There is no greater threat to our military and economic security than the fact that 66 percent of all eighth grade public school students and 79 percent or more of black and Latino eighth graders cannot read or do math at grade level and will be unable to succeed in our increasingly competitive global economy. And the fact that 75 percent of all 17- to 24-year-olds cannot qualify for the military because of poor literacy, obesity, or prior incarceration should be a loud wakeup call for all of us.

CDF's six pillars of support for children represent the essential investments needed for all our children to grow into successful productive adults and will produce both intermediate and longer term savings and gains. Children don't come in pieces; what happens to them early in life affects them throughout childhood and often into adulthood. Investments in the early years will create public- and private-sector jobs now while preparing them for the jobs of the future. We must ensure all children:

- Affordable, seamless, comprehensive, and accessible health coverage in every state
- Access to a continuum of quality early childhood development and learning
- High-quality education in all schools and during out-of-school time to close achievement gaps
- Service learning and employment opportunities while in school to make them job and citizenship ready
- Protection from poverty through public- and private-sector jobs that pay livable wages and increased investments in refundable Earned Income and Child Tax Credits and other measures to make work pay
- Safety through commonsense gun safety laws, improved mental health resources for children and their families, and a commitment to counter the culture of violence in America.

We must move forward together and courageously embrace our growing national diversity as an asset in a multiracial twenty-first-century world desperate for moral example and leadership. We can and must close the indefensible, huge, and costly gaps in education, race, income, and wealth that channel millions of poor children of color into the Cradle to Prison Pipeline. We cannot and must not allow 1 in 3 black and 1 in 6 Latino boys born in 2001 to spend part of their lives in prison. We can and must stop mass incarceration from becoming the new American apartheid that will undermine the last fifty years of social and racial progress. And we can and must ensure that our children and grandchildren inherit a better, safer, and more just nation and world.

As we look toward the future, the Children's Defense Fund remains steadily focused on helping catalyze and mount the transforming nonviolent social justice movement for children our nation desperately needs and on pursuing justice for children and the poor with urgency and persistence.

—Marian Wright Edelman

Notes

Introduction

1. Children's Defense Fund, Mission Statement, www.childrensdefense.org.
2. Washington Research Project, *Children Out of School in America: A Report* (Washington, DC: Children's Defense Fund, 1974).

Chapter 1

1. U.S. Department of Health and Human Services, Health United States, 2012, Table 25, http://www.cdc.gov/nchs/data/hus/hus12.pdf.
2. Death rates for children ages 1–4 declined from 84.5 to 26.4 over the same time period. Among children ages 5–14 the death rate declined from 41.3 to 12.9. U.S. Department of Health and Human Services, Health United States, 2012, Table 25
3. Sara Rosenbaum and Kay Johnson, "Children," in *Social Injustice and Public Health,* ed. Barry Levy and Victor Sidel (New York: Oxford University Press, 2013), citing the Luxembourg Income Study, Inequality and Poverty Key Figures (selected country from Waves I-VII).
4. "American's Children: Key National Indicators of Well-Being," Federal Interagency Forum on Child and Family Statistics (Childstats.gov), 2013, http://www.childstats.gov/americaschildren/tables/econ1a.asp.
5. U.S. Department of Health and Human Services, Health United States, 2012, Table 6, http://www.cdc.gov/nchs/data/hus/hus12.pdf.
6. Emmanuel A. Anum et al., "Medicaid and Preterm Birth and Low Birth Weight: The Last Two Decades," *Journal of Women's Health* 19, no. 3 (2010): 443–451.
7. "Inadequate Prenatal Care by Race/Ethnicity, United States 2000–2002 Average," March of Dimes, http://www.marchofdimes.com/peristats/ViewSubtopic.aspx?reg=99&top=5&stop=37&lev=1&slev=1&obj=1&dv=ms.
8. The low birth weight rate in 2010 among black infants stood at 13.53 percent, nearly double the white rate of 7.14 percent. Rates for Hispanic infants that year varied from a low of 6.49 percent to a high of 9.55 percent for Puerto Rican infants. U.S. Department of Health and Human Services, Health United States, Table 6.
9. UNICEF, "The State of the World's Children, 2012," Table 1, http://www.unicef.org/sowc2013/files/SOWC_2012-Main_Report_EN.pdf.
10. Barbara Starfield, "U.S. Child Health: What's Amiss and What Should Be Done about It?" *Health Affairs* 23, no. 5 (2004): 165–170.

11. Robert F. Anda et al., "Building a Framework for Global Surveillance of the Public Health Implications of Adverse Childhood Experiences," *American Journal of Preventive Medicine* 39, no. 1 (2010): 93–98.

12. Health conditions among children under age eighteen years, by selected characteristics: (affecting 7.5 percent of all poor children, compared with 4.7 percent of children with incomes 400 percent of poverty or greater over the 2009–2011 time period) and compare 9.0 percent for poor children to 3.9 percent for children with family incomes 400 percent of poverty or greater (U.S. Department of Health and Human Services, Health United States, Table 41). Compare 7.1 percent among poor children to 4.8 percent among children with family incomes 400 percent of poverty or greater (U.S. Department of Health and Human Services, Health United States, Table 6). Compare 26.1 percent for children with below poverty incomes to 14.7 percent for children with incomes 200 percent of poverty or greater (Centers for Disease Control and Prevention, "Untreated Dental Caries in Children Ages 2–19," http://www.cdc.gov/Features/dsUntreatedCavitiesKids/). Over the 2007–2010 period, obesity rates among poor children stood at 22.2 percent compared to slightly greater than 12 percent among children with family incomes of 400 percent of poverty or greater (U.S. Department of Health and Human Services, Health United States, 2012, Table 69).

13. "Facts on Children's Mental Illness in America," National Alliance on Mental Illness, http://www.nami.org/Template.cfm?Section=federal_and_state_policy_legislation &template=/ContentManagement/ContentDisplay.cfm&ContentID=43804.

14. "Mental Health Fact Sheet," Children's Defense Fund, March 2010, http://www.childrensdefense.org/child-research-data-publications/data/mental-health-factsheet.pdf.

15. U.S. Department of Health and Human Services, Health United States 2012, Table 122, http://www.cdc.gov/nchs/data/hus/hus12.pdf.

16. U.S. Department of Health and Human Services, Health United States 2012, Table 124, http://www.cdc.gov/nchs/data/hus/hus12.pdf.

17. Kaiser Family Foundation, *The Uninsured: A Primer—Key Facts About Health Insurance on the Eve of Expansion*, 2013, Table 2, http://kff.org/report-section/the-uninsured-a-primer-2013-tables-and-data-notes/.

18. Interagency Forum on Child and Family Statistics, Childstats.gov, http://www.childstats.gov/americaschildren/care3.asp.

19. The Carter administration proposed a coverage level of approximately half the federal poverty level; the House of Representatives would have set income eligibility at two-thirds the federal poverty level.

20. Family incomes up to 133 percent of the federal poverty level. Coverage was made mandatory for infants and children up to age 6 with family incomes up to 133 percent of the federal poverty level. Coverage for children ages 6–18 was mandated up to 100 percent of the federal poverty level. States were given the option of eliminating an asset test, and many did so.

21. Wendy Lazarus, *EPSDT: Does It Spell Health Care for Children?* (Washington, DC: Washington Research Project, 1977), 5–302.

22. Sara Rosenbaum and Paul H. Wise, "Crossing the Medicaid/Private Health Insurance Divide: The Case of EPSDT," *Health Affairs* 26, no. 2 (2007): 382–393.

23. Ian Hill, Bridgett Courtot, and Jennifer Sullivan, "Coping with SCHIP Enrollment Caps: Lessons from Seven States' Experiences," *Health Affairs* 26, no. 1 (2007): 258–268.

24. "FY 2012: Number of Children Ever Enrolled in Medicaid and CHIP," http://medi caid.gov/Federal-Policy-Guidance/Downloads/FY-2012-Childrens-Enrollment-04_09_13.pdf.

25. "A Nation of Immigrants," PewHispanic.org, January 29, 2013, http://www.pew hispanic.org/2013/01/29/a-nation-of-immigrants/.

26. Scott Harris and Joan Szabo, "Pediatrics Field in Subspecialist Shortage," Association of American Medical Colleges, June 2010, https://www.aamc.org/newsroom/reporter/june10/136278/pediatrics_field_in_subspecialist_shortage.html.

27. Robert Pear, "Lower Health Insurance Premiums to Come at Cost of Fewer Choices," *New York Times*, September 22, 2013, http://www.nytimes.com/2013/09/23/health/lower-health-insurance-premiums-to-come-at-cost-of-fewer-choices.html?pagewanted=all&_r=0.

Chapter 2

1. Center on the Developing Child at Harvard University, *A Science-Based Framework for Early Childhood Policy: Using Evidence to Improve Outcomes in Learning, Behavior, and Health for Vulnerable Children* (Cambridge, MA: Center on the Developing Child at Harvard University, 2007); Lynn A. Karoly, M. Rebecca Kilburn, and Jill Cannon, *Early Childhood Interventions: Proven Results, Future Promise* (Santa Monica, CA: RAND, 2005); Jack P. Shonkoff and Deborah A. Phillips, eds., *From Neurons to Neighborhoods: The Science of Early Childhood Development* (Washington, DC: National Academy Press, 2000).

2. Frances A. Campbell, Ronald Helms, Joseph J. Sparling, and Craig T. Ramey, "Early-Childhood Program and Success in School: The Abecedarian Study," in *Early Care and Education for Children in Poverty: Promises, Programs, and Long-Term Results*, ed. W. Steven Barnett and Sarane Spence Booncock (Albany: State University of New York Press, 1998), 145–166.

3. Frances A. Campbell et al., "Adult Outcomes as a Function of an Early Childhood Educational Program: An Abecedarian Project Follow-Up," *Developmental Psychology* 48, no. 4 (2012): 1033–1043; Craig T. Ramey and Frances A. Campbell, "Preventive Education for High-Risk Children: Cognitive Consequences of the Carolina Abecedarian Project," *American Journal of Mental Deficiency* 88, no. 5 (1984): 515–523.

4. W. Steven Barnett and Leonard N. Masse, "Comparative Benefit-Cost Analysis of the Abecedarian Program and its Policy Implications," *Economics of Education Review* 26, no. 1 (2007): 113–125.

5. Jeanne Brooks-Gunn et al., "Early Intervention in Low-Birth-Weight Premature Infants: Results Through Age 5 Years from the Infant Health and Development Program," *Journal of the American Medical Association* 272, no. 16 (1994): 1257–1262; Marie C. McCormick et al., "Early Intervention in Low Birth Weight Premature Infants: Results at 18 Years of Age for the Infant Health and Development Program," *Pediatrics* 117, no. 3 (2006): 771–780.
6. Marian F. MacDorman, Donna L. Hoyert, and T. J. Mathews, *Recent Declines in Infant Mortality in the United States, 2005–2011*, NCHS Data Brief No. 120 (Hyattsville, MD: National Center for Health Statistics, 2013).
7. Robert Wood Johnson Foundation Commission to Build a Healthier America, *Beyond Health Care: New Directions to a Healthier America* (Princeton, NJ: Robert Wood Johnson Foundation Commission to Build a Healthier America, 2009).
8. National Scientific Council on the Developing Child, *The Science of Early Childhood Development: Closing the Gap Between What We Know and What We Do* (Cambridge, MA: National Scientific Council on the Developing Child, 2007); Jack P. Shonkoff and Susan Nall Bales, "Science Does Not Speak for Itself: Translating Child Development Research for the Public and Its Policymakers," *Child Development* 82, no. 1 (2011): 17–32.
9. Harry T. Reis, W. Andrew Collins, and Ellen Berscheid, "The Relationship Context of Human Behavior and Development," *Psychological Bulletin* 126, no. 6 (2000): 844–872; Shonkoff and Phillips, *From Neurons to Neighborhoods*; Sharon E. Fox, Pat Levitt, and Charles A. Nelson III, "How the Timing and Quality of Early Experiences Influence the Development of Brain Architecture," *Child Development* 81, no. 1 (2010): 28–40; Michael J. Meaney, "Epigenetics and the Biological Definition of Gene × Environment Interactions," ibid., 41–79; National Scientific Council on the Developing Child, "Early Experiences Can Alter Gene Expression and Affect Long-Term Development" (Working Paper No. 10, National Scientific Council on the Developing Child, Cambridge, MA, 2010).
10. Bruce S. McEwen, "Protective and Damaging Effects of Stress Mediators," *New England Journal of Medicine* 338, no. 3 (1998): 171–179.
11. Jack P. Shonkoff, W. Thomas Boyce, and Bruce S. McEwen, "Neuroscience, Molecular Biology, and the Childhood Roots of Health Disparities: Building a New Framework for Health Promotion and Disease Prevention," *JAMA* 301, no. 21 (2009): 2252–2259; Jack P. Shonkoff, Andrew S. Garner, Committee on Psychosocial Aspects of Child and Family Health, Committee on Early Childhood, Adoption, and Dependent Care, and Section on Developmental and Behavioral Pediatrics, "The Lifelong Effects of Early Childhood Adversity and Toxic Stress," *Pediatrics* 129, no. 1 (2012): 232–246.
12. Jack P. Shonkoff, "Protecting Brains, Not Simply Stimulating Minds," *Science* 333, no. 6045 (2011): 982–983; Jack P. Shonkoff, "Leveraging the Biology of Adversity to Address the Roots of Disparities in Health and Development," *Proceedings of*

the *National Academy of Sciences of the United States of America* 109, supplement 2 (2012): 17302–17307.

13. Shonkoff, "Protecting Brains"; Jack P. Shonkoff and Philip A. Fisher, "Rethinking Evidence-Based Practice and Two-Generation Programs to Create the Future of Early Childhood Policy," *Development and Psychopathology* 25, no. 4, part 2 (2013): 1635–1653.

14. Center on the Developing Child at Harvard University, "Maternal Depression Can Undermine the Development of Young Children" (Working Paper No. 8 Center on the Developing Child at Harvard University, Cambridge, MA, 2009).

15. Mary A. Steinhardt, Shanna E. Smith Jaggars, Kathryn E. Faulk, and Christian T. Gloria, "Chronic Work Stress and Depressive Symptoms: Assessing the Mediating Role of Teacher Burnout," *Stress and Health* 27, no. 5 (2011): 420–429.

16. Greg J. Duncan, Pamela Morris, and Christopher Rodrigues, "Does Money Really Matter? Estimating Impacts of Family Income on Young Children's Achievement with Data from Random-Assignment Experiments," *Developmental Psychology* 47, no. 5 (2011): 1263–1279.

17. Shonkoff, "Protecting Brains"; Shonkoff and Fisher, "Rethinking Evidence-Based Practice."

18. Kirby Deater-Deckard, Nan Chen, Zhe Wang, and Martha Ann Bell, "Socioeconomic Risk Moderates the Link Between Household Chaos and Maternal Executive Function," *Journal of Family Psychology* 26, no. 3 (2012): 391–399.

19. Todd Grindal et al., "The Added Impact of Parent Education in Early Childhood Education Programs: A Meta-Analysis" (manuscript under review); Dietsje D. Jolles, Mark A. van Buchem, Serge A. R. B. Rombouts, and Eveline A. Crone, "Practice Effects in the Developing Brain: A Pilot Study," *Developmental Cognitive Neuroscience* 2, supplement 1 (2012): S180–191.

20. Adele Diamond, W. Steven Barnett, Jessica Thomas, and Sarah Munro, "Preschool Program Improves Cognitive Control," *Science* 318, no. 5855 (2007): 1387–1388; Jolles, van Buchem, Rombouts, and Crone, "Practice Effects in the Developing Brain"; M. Rosario Rueda et al., "Training, Maturation, and Genetic Influences on the Development of Executive Attention," *Proceedings of the National Academy of Sciences of the United States of America* 102, no. 41 (2005): 14931–14936.

21. Sonia J. Lupien, Bruce S. McEwen, Megan R. Gunnar, and Christine Heim, "Effects of Stress Throughout the Lifespan on the Brain, Behavior, and Cognition," *Nature Reviews Neuroscience* 10 (2009): 434–445.

22. Jeanne Brooks-Gunn, Greg J. Duncan, and J. Lawrence Aber, *Neighborhood Poverty: Policy Implications in Studying Neighborhoods* (New York: Russell Sage Foundation Press, 1997); Robert J. Sampson, Stephen W. Raudenbush, and Felton Earls, "Neighborhoods and Violent Crime: A Multilevel Study of Collective Efficacy," *Science* 277, no. 5328 (1997): 918–924; William Julius Wilson, *The Truly Disadvantaged: The Inner City, the Underclass, and Public Policy* (Chicago: University of Chicago Press, 1990).

23. James M. Radner and Jack P. Shonkoff, "Mobilizing Science to Reduce Intergenerational Poverty," in *Investing in What Works for America's Communities: Essays on People, Place and Purpose*, ed. Nancy O. Andrews, David Erickson, Ian Galloway, and Ellen Seidman (San Francisco: Federal Reserve Bank of San Francisco and the Low Income Investment Fund, 2012), 338–350.

Chapter 3

1. The 2011 preliminary estimate was 3,953,593 births. B. E. Hamilton, J. A. Martin, and S. J. Ventura, National Center for Health and Health Statistics, "Births: Preliminary Data for 2011," *National Vital Statistics Reports* 61, no. 5 (2012): 1–17, http://www.cdc.gov/nchs/data/nvsr/nvsr61/nvsr61_05.pdf.
2. An estimated 19,941,883 children were under five years of age in 2011 based on U.S. Census Bureau 2011 American Community Survey one-year estimates and calculated by multiplying the proportion of children under five (6.4%) by the total U.S. population estimate (311,591,919 people). U.S. Census Bureau, "Selected Population Profile in the United States [Table S00201]," http://factfinder2.census.gov/bkmk/table/1.0/en/ACS/11_1YR/S0201//popgroup~001.
3. National Center for Children in Poverty, "United States Early Childhood Profile," www.nccp.org.
4. Child Trends, "Family Trends," http://www.childtrends.org/?indicators=family-structure.
5. UNICEF Office of Research, "Child Well-Being in Rich Countries: A Comparative Overview," http://www.unicef-irc.org/publications/pdf/rc11_eng.pdf.
6. Council of Chief State School Officers and Child Trends, "Disparities in Early Learning and Development: Lessons from the Early Childhood Longitudinal Study—Birth Cohort (ECLS-B)," http://childtrends.org/wp-content/uploads/2013/05/2009-52 DisparitiesELExecSumm.pdf.
7. Child Trends, "Early School Readiness: Indicators on Children and Youth, Child Trends Data Bank," http://www.childtrends.org/?indicators=early-school-readiness #sthash.dKGnCaxC.dpuf.
8. S. F. Reardon, "No Rich Child Left Behind," *New York Times*, April 27, 2013, http://opinionator.blogs.nytimes.com/2013/04/27/no-rich-child-left-behind/._
9. Organisation of Economic Co-operation and Development (OECD) statistics, *Education at a Glance: 2013 OECD Indicators*, www.oecd.org/edu/eag2013%20(eng) .
10. Joan Lombardi, *Time to Care: Redesigning Childcare to Promote Education, Support Families, and Build Communities* (Philadelphia: Temple University Press, 2003).
11. Consortium for Longitudinal Studies, *Lasting Effects after Preschool: Final Report to the Administration on Children, Youth, and Families* (Washington, DC: Government Printing Office, 1979).
12. Lombardi, *Time to Care.*
13. National Education Goals Panel, "Goals," http://govinfo.library.unt.edu/negp/page3.htm.

14. National Association for the Education of Young Children, "Final Conference Agreement, American Economic Recovery and Reinvestment Act of 2009," February 19, 2009, http://www.naeyc.org/policy/ARRA."

15. The senior adviser on Early Learning position later became deputy assistant secretary for Policy and Early Learning.

16. Office of the Press Secretary: The White House, "Fact Sheet: President Obama's Plan for Early Education for All Americans," http://www.whitehouse.gov/the-press-office/2013/02/13/fact-sheet-president-obama-s-plan-early-education-all-americans. Note: As of the end of 2013, twenty states had received Early Learning Challenge funding.

17. Ibid. Note: In January 2014, federal funding for early childhood increased, including restoration of Head Start and childcare cuts made in sequestration, $500 million for expansion of Early Head Start, and $250 million for preschool development grants, among other investments.

18. OECD Family Database: Social Policy Division, Directorate of Employment, Labour, and Social Affairs, "PF2.5 Trends in Parental Leave Policies since 1970," fig. PF2.5.2, http://www.oecd.org/els/family/PF2.5%20Trends%20in%20leave%20 entitlements%20around%20childbirth%20since%201970%20-%2010%20oct%20 2012%20-%20FINAL.pdf.

19. U.S. Department of Labor, Wage and Hour Division, Table 3.1 Coverage of Establishments and Employees under the Family and Medical Leave Act: 1995 and 2000 Surveys, http://www.dol.gov/whd/fmla/chapter3_txt.htm.

20. Pew Center on the States, "States and the New Federal Home Visiting Initiative: An Assessment from the Starting Line," www.pewtrusts.org/uploadedFiles/ wwwpewtrustsorg/Reports/Home_Visiting/Home_Visiting_August_2011_Report. pdf.

21. U.S. Census Bureau, "Who's Minding the Kids? Child Care Arrangements: Spring 2011," http://www.census.gov/prod/2013pubs/p70-135.pdf.

22. U.S. Department of Health and Human Services, Office of the Assistant Secretary for Planning and Evaluation, "ASPE Issue Brief: Estimates of Child Care Eligibility and Receipt for fiscal year 2009," http://aspe.hhs.gov/hsp/12/childcareeligibility/ ib.cfm.

23. Office of Child Care, "Characteristics of Families Served by the Child Care and Development Fund (CCDF) Based on Preliminary Fiscal Year 2011 Data," http:// www.acf.hhs.gov/programs/occ/resource/characteristics-of-families-served-by-child-care-and-development-fund-ccdf.

24. National Institute for Early Education Research, "The State of Preschool 2012: State Preschool Yearbook," http://nieer.org/publications/state-preschool-2012.

25. See Christina Welland and Hirokazu Yoshikawa, "Impacts of a Prekindergarten Program on Children's Mathematics, Language, Literacy, Executive Function, and Emotional Skills," *Child Development* 84, no. 6 (2013); National Institute for Early Education Research: Education Forum, "Preschool Programs Can Boost School Read-

iness," http://nieer.org/resources/research/Gormley062708.pdf; National Institute for Early Education Research, "Abbott Preschool Program Longitudinal Effects Study: Fifth Grade Follow-Up," http://nieer.org/publications/latest-research/abbott-preschool-program-longitudinal-effects-study-fifth-grade-follow.

26. *Right from the Start: The Report of the NASBE Task Force on Early Childhood Education* (Alexandria, VA: National Association of State Boards of Education, 1988).

27. Collaborative for Social and Emotional Learning, "SEL in your State," Illinois, http://casel.org/policy-advocacy/sel-in-your-state/.

28. Ascend at the Aspen Institute, "Two Generations, One Future, Moving Parents and Children Beyond Poverty Together," http://www.aspeninstitute.org/sites/default/files/content/docs/pubs/Ascend-Report-022012.pdf.

Chapter 4

1. Harvard Center on the Developing Child, "*A Science-Based Framework for Early Childhood Policy* (Cambridge, MA: Harvard Center on the Developing Child, 2007); Patrice L. Engle et al., "Strategies for Reducing Inequalities and Improving Developmental Outcomes for Young Children in Low-Income and Middle-Income Countries," *The Lancet* 378, no. 9799 (2011): 1339–1353; Hirokazu Yoshikawa et al., "Investing in Our Future: The Evidence Base on Preschool Education" (policy brief, Society for Research in Child Development and the Foundation for Child Development, Ann Arbor, MI, and New York, 2013).

2. The Millennium Development Goals, the set of goals that informed UN member countries' development agendas from 2000 to 2015, did not include explicit consideration of early childhood development beyond goals and targets related to infant and maternal mortality. A target for comprehensive, quality early childhood development programs and policies, building on this new evidence, has been proposed for the post-2015 global development goals. Madhav Chavan, Hirokazu Yoshikawa, and Chandrika Bahadur, "The Future of Our Children: Lifelong, Multi-Generational Learning for Sustainable Development" (policy paper, UN Sustainable Development Network, New York, 2013); Consultative Group on Early Childhood Care and Development, *A Transformative Solution: Reducing Poverty and Inequality Through a Global Early Childhood Development Goal* (Toronto: Consultative Group on Early Childhood Care and Development, 2013).

3. UN General Assembly, "The Future We Want" (Resolution 66/288, United Nations, New York, 2012.

4. Ban Ki-Moon, "A Life of Dignity for All: Accelerating Progress Toward the Millennium Development Goals and Advancing the United Nations Development Agenda Beyond 2015" (report of the secretary-general, UN General Assembly, New York, 2013).

5. David Deming, "Early Childhood Intervention and Life-Cycle Skill Development: Evidence from Head Start," *American Economic Journal: Applied Economics* 1, no. 3 (2009): 111–134.

6. Yoshikawa et al., "Investing in Our Future."

7. Eric Dearing, Kathleen McCartney, and Beck A. Taylor, "Change in Family Income-to-Needs Matters More for Children with Less," *Child Development* 72, no. 6 (2001): 1779–1793; Greg J. Duncan, Kathleen M. Ziol-Guest, and Ariel Kalil, "Early-Childhood Poverty and Adult Attainment, Behavior, and Health," *Child Development* 81, no. 1 (2010): 306–325.

8. J. Lawrence Aber, Linda Biersteker, Andrew Dawes, and Laura Rawlings, "Social Protection and Welfare Systems: Implications for Early Childhood Development," in *Handbook of Early Childhood Development Research and Its Impact on Global Policy*, ed. Pia R. Britto, Patrice L. Engle, and Charles M. Super (New York: Oxford University Press, 2013), 260–274.

9. W. Steven Barnett and Milagros Nores, "Estimated Participation and Hours in Early Care and Education by Type of Arrangement and Income at Ages 2 to 4 in 2010" (working paper, National Institute on Early Education Research, New Brunswick, NJ, 2012).

10. Eric Dearing, Kathleen McCartney, and Beck A. Taylor, "Does Higher Quality Early Child Care Promote Low-Income Children's Math and Reading Achievement in Middle Childhood?" *Child Development* 80, no. 5 (2009): 1329–1349.

11. Jody Heymann, Alison Earle, and Jeffrey Hayes, "The Work, Family and Equity Index: How Does the United States Measure Up?" (report, Institute for Health and Social Policy, Boston and Montreal, 2007).

12. Katherine Magnuson, "The Effect of Increases in Welfare Mothers' Education on Their Young Children's Academic and Behavioral Outcomes: Evidence from the National Evaluation of Welfare-to-Work Strategies Child Outcomes Study" (Institute for Research on Poverty Working Paper, University of Wisconsin–Madison, 2003).

13. Ascend at the Aspen Institute, "Two Generations, One Future: Moving Parents Beyond Poverty Together" (policy report, Aspen Institute, Washington, DC, 2012).

14. Donald J. Hernandez and Jeffrey Napierala, "Diverse Children: Race, Ethnicity and Immigration in America's New Non-Majority Generation" (policy report, Foundation for Child Development, New York, 2013).

15. Hirokazu Yoshikawa, *Immigrants Raising Citizens: Undocumented Parents and Their Young Children* (New York: Russell Sage Foundation, 2011).

16. Nirmala Rao et al., "Is Something Better Than Nothing? An Evaluation of Early Childhood Programs in Cambodia," *Child Development* 83, no. 3 (2012): 864–876.

17. S. Anandalakshmy, "Cultural Sustainability and the Importance of the Collective: SEWA's Childcare Programme in Gujarat, India," *Early Childhood Matters* 71 no.1 (2011): 67–71.

18. Mario L. Small, *Unanticipated Gains: Origins of Network Inequality in Everyday Life* (New York: Oxford University Press, 2010).

19. Rahman, Atif, Abid Malik, Siham Sikander, Christopher Roberts, and Francis Creed, "Cognitive Behaviour Therapy–Based Intervention by Community Health Workers

for Mothers with Depression and Their Infants in Rural Pakistan: A Cluster-Randomised Controlled Trial," *The Lancet* 372, no. 9642 (2008): 902–909.

20. Daniel S. Shaw, Thomas J. Dishion, Lauren Supplee, Frances Gardner, and Karin Arnds, "Randomized Trial of a Family-Centered Approach to the Prevention of Early Conduct Problems: Two-year Effects of the Family Check-Up in Early Childhood," *Journal of Consulting and Clinical Psychology* 74, no. 1 (2006): 1–9.

21. Frances Duran et al., "What Works? A Study of Effective Early Childhood Mental Health Consultation Programs" (policy report, Georgetown Center for Child and Human Development, Washington, DC, 2009).

22. Christina Weiland and Hirokazu Yoshikawa, "The Impacts of an Urban Public Prekindergarten Program on Children's Mathematics, Language, Literacy, Executive Function, and Emotional Skills," *Child Development* 84, no. 6 (2013): 2112–2130.

23. UN Sustainable Development Solutions Network, "An Action Agenda for Sustainable Development: Report for the U.S. Secretary-General," 2013, http://unsdsn.org/files/2013/06/130613-SDSN-An-Action-Agenda-for-Sustainable-Development-FINAL.pdf.

24. UNESCO, *"Education for Sustainable Development: Good Practices in Early Childhood* (Paris: UNESCO, 2012).

25. Ibid., 11.

26. OECD, "Education at a Glance 2012" (policy report, OECD, Paris, 2012).

27. Hirokazu Yoshikawa et al., "Preschool Education in Mexico: Expansion, Quality Improvement, and Curricular Reform" (working paper, UNICEF Innocenti Research Centre, Florence, Italy, 2007).

28. Andrew J. Mashburn et al., "Measures of Classroom Quality in Prekindergarten and Children's Development of Academic, Language, and Social Skills," *Child Development* 79, no. 3 (2008): 732–749.

29. Aditya Natraj, "Kaivalya Education Foundation Principal Leadership Development Program: Overview," Harvard Graduate School of Education, January 2013, www.kefindia.org.

30. One recent initiative is the Pritzker Foundation/Goldman Sachs Early Childhood Innovation Accelerator, which seeks to fund innovations in the field as well as expansion of quality early childhood education with social impact bonds.

Chapter 5

1. The Civil Rights Act of 1964 and the Voting Rights Act of 1965, www.ourdocuments.gov/doc.php?doc=97.

2. James S. Coleman, "Equality of Educational Opportunity Study (EEOS)" [Coleman Report], 1966, Education Commission of the States, Document No. 4519, www.ecs.org.

3. Ronald R. Edmonds, "Programs of School Improvement: An Overview," *Education Leadership* (February 1982): 4–11; Pedro Noguera and Lauren Wells, "The Politics of

School Reform: A Broader and Bolder Approach to Newark," *Berkeley Review of Education* 2, no. 1 (2011), http://escholarship.org/uc/item/9mj097nv.

4. National Council for Excellence in Education, *A Nation at Risk* (Washington, DC: Department of Education, 1983), http://www2.ed.gov/pubs/NatAtRisk/risk.html.

5. Stan Karp, "Challenging Corporate School Reform and 10 Hopeful Signs of Resistance," Rethinking Schools, Northwest Teachers for Social Justice, 2011, http://www.rethinkingschools.org/cmshandler.asp?news/ NWTSJKarpOct11.shtml.

6. Coalition for Essential Schools, "Ted Sizer," http://www.essentialschools.org/items/27; Core Knowledge Foundation, "E. D. Hirsch," http://www.coreknowledge.org/ed-hirsch-jr; Lamar Alexander, "Time for Results: An Overview; The Governors 1991 Report on Education," *Phi Delta Kappan* 68, no. 3 (1986), http://www.jstor.org/stable/20403306.

7. Center for School Reform and Improvement, "A Nation Prepared: Teachers for the 21st Century: The Report of the Task Force on Teaching as a Profession," Carnegie Corporation, 1986, http://www.centerforcsri.org/ research/improvement.cgi?st=s&sr=SR001145.

8. U.S. Department of Education, "Great Nature Has Another Thing to Do to You and Me," http://eric.ed.gov/?id=EJ379937.

9. The corporate school reform model included a focus on school choice, vouchers, charter schools, state standards and assessments, Common Core State Standards, and teacher evaluations linked to student achievement. In 1992 the National Council on Education Standards and Testing issued a report recommending that voluntary national standards be created. In 1994 President Clinton signed into law the Goals 2000: Educate America Act. Examples include funding from the Bill & Melinda Gates Foundation that ushered in significant changes in the preK–16 landscape with initiatives such as the Gates Millennium Scholars Program (1999), the State Challenge Grant for Leadership Development (2000), and grants to create small high schools in select American cities (beginning in 2002). Through their foundation's funding, Bill and Melinda Gates also have had significant influence on the proliferation of charter school networks, such as their investment in the New Schools Venture Fund to increase the number of high-quality charter schools around the country by creating systems of charter schools through nonprofit charter management organizations, and in transforming how teachers are recruited, developed, retained, and rewarded, believing that teachers are the most important factor in students' success. See www.gatesfoundation.org.

10. Tenets of NCLB include higher standards and assessments to be developed by each state, the establishment of measurable and escalating yearly achievement goals, and the government's primary aid program for disadvantaged students, which is linked to students', schools', and districts' achievement outcomes around the provision of federal funding under Title I. See http://www2.ed.gov/nclb/overview/intro/execsumm.html.

11. Accountability is central to the success of NCLB; states need to set high standards for improving academic achievement in order to improve the quality of education for all students. Under the NCLB, each state establishes what constitutes AYP to determine the achievement of each school district and school. The new definition of AYP is diagnostic in nature and intended to highlight where schools need improvement and should focus their resources. See http://www2.ed.gov/policy/elsec/guid/secletter/020724.html.

12. U.S. Department of Education, "Statement on National Governors Association and State Education Chiefs Common Core Standards," http://www.ed.gov/news/press-releases/statement-national-governors-association-and-state-education-chiefs-common-core-.

13. Lewis C. Solomon et al., *The Challenge of School Reform: Implementation, Impact and Sustainability* (Charlotte, NC: Information Age, 2008).

14. Equality school reforms that focused on the integration of public schools were fueled by the civil rights movement, the judicial mandates to desegregate the nation's public schools, and the Johnson administration's War on Poverty. However, such coherence can be neutralized by political events and judicial decisions, such as the Vietnam War and resulting protests, and judicial decisions, such as *Milliken v. Bradley* (1977), which ended interdistrict busing for desegregation.

15. Jeff Howard, "You Can't Get There from Here: The Need for a New Logic in Education Reform," *Daedalus* 124, no. 4 (1995), http://www.efficacy.org/Portals/7/Article_Downloads/Writings_by_dr_jeff_howard/JeffHoward.DaedalusArticle-1.pdf.

16. During the time of greatest upheaval during my tenure as superintendent of Richmond Public Schools, recruiters from other districts secured some of the district's best and brightest teachers with promises of a better, more nurturing, and more professional learning environment. Unless we want the result of school reform to be a continuous cycle of recruiting, training, and losing high-quality teachers and administrators, our reliance on the heroic educator must end.

17. The collapse of the global economy in 2008 precipitated an economic crisis resulting in draconian austerity measures that affected education budgets at a time when schools and districts were most in need of funding to enhance the capacity and professional development of frontline teachers and principals.

18. Karp, "Challenging Corporate School Reform."

19. There are challenges and realities in the United States that make a complete side-by-side comparison to other countries, like Finland, unfair.

20. John Dewey, *The School and Society* (Chicago: University of Chicago Press, 1915), 7.

21. Diane Ravitch, *Left Back: A Century of Battles over School Reform* (New York: Touchstone, 2000), and "Why I Changed My Mind About School Reform," *Wall Street Journal*, March 9, 2010, http://online.wsj.com/article/SB10001424052748704869304575109443305343962.html.

22. Paul Reville, "Seize the Moment to Design Schools That Close Gaps," *Education Week*, June 5, 2013.

23. Chen, *Education Nation,* 25–27.
24. Robert Kegan and Lisa Laskow Lahey, *Immunity to Change* (Cambridge, MA: Harvard Education Press, 2009).
25. Anthony Jewett, "Creating and Expanding Capital Markets to Support Innovation and Entrepreneurship in U.S. Public Education" (doctoral capstone, Harvard University, 2013), 12.
26. Anthony Jewett is a member of the first cohort of the Doctor of Education Leadership Program at the Harvard Graduate School of Education; he completed his residency at the Tides Foundation in San Francisco. Crowd funding became an option as a result of the Jumpstart Our Business Startup (JOBS) signed into law by President Obama in April 2012. Jewett, *Creating and Expanding Capital Markets,* 10.

Chapter 6

1. See http://nces.ed.gov/nationsreportcard/pdf/main2008/2009479.pdf.
2. "High School Survey of Student Engagement, 2009," http://ceep.indiana.edu/hssse/images/HSSSE_2010_Report.pdf.
3. James Heckman, "The Case for Investing in Disadvantaged Young Children," http://heckmanequation.org/content/resource/case-investing-disadvantaged-young-children.
4. Andrea Berger et al., *Early College, Early Success: Early College Initiative Impact Study* (Washington, DC: American Institutes of Research, 2013).
5. William Symonds, Robert B. Schwartz, and Ronald Ferguson, *Pathways to Prosperity: Meeting the Challenge of Preparing Young Americans for the 21st Century* (Cambridge, MA: Harvard Graduate School of Education, 2011).
6. James J. Kemple, *Career Academies: Long-Term Impact on Work, Education, and Transitions to Adulthood* (New York: MDRC, 2008).
7. For more details, see Jal Mehta, *The Allure of Order: High Hopes, Dashed Expectations and the Troubled Quest to Remake American Schooling* (New York: Oxford University Press, 2013).
8. There are some examples of these kinds of collaboration in practice now. See Cynthia Coburn and Mary Kay Stein, *Research and Practice in Education: Building Alliances, Bridging the Divide* (Lanham, MD: Rowman & Littlefield, 2010).
9. Jal Mehta, Louis Gomez, and Anthony S. Bryk, "Building on Practical Knowledge: The Key to a Stronger Profession Is Learning from the Field," in *The Futures of School Reform,* ed. Jal Mehta, Robert B. Schwartz, and Frederick Hess (Cambridge, MA: Harvard Education Press, 2012), 35–64.
10. Paul Reville, Jeff Henig, and Helen Malone, "Addressing the Disadvantages of Poverty: Why Ignore the Most Important Challenge of the Post-Standards Era?" in ibid., 119–150.

Chapter 7

1. *Brown v. Board of Education,* 347 U.S. 483 (1954).

2. James S. Coleman, *Equality of Educational Opportunity* (Washington, DC: Department of Health, Education and Welfare, 1966).

3. National Center on Education Statistics [NCES], "Fast Facts Assessments 2010 NAEP: The Nation's Report Card," http://nationsreportcard.gov/ltt_2012/summary.aspx.

4. College Board, *Ninth Annual AP Report to the Nation* (New York, 2013), http://apreport.collegeboard.org/; Education Week, *Diplomas Count 2013,* June 2013, http://www.edweek.org/ew/toc/2013/06/06/.

5. Victor Hugo, BrainyQuote.com, Xplore Inc., 2013, http://www.brainyquote.com/quotes/quotes/v/victorhugo 104893.html.

6. Elise Gould and Hilary Wething, "US Poverty Rates Higher, Safety Net Weaker than in Peer Countries" (issue brief, Economic Policy Institute, Washington, DC, July 24, 2012).

7. Donald Hernandez, "Diverse Children: Race, Ethnicity, and Immigration in America's New Non-Majority Generation" (New York: Foundation for Child Development Disparities Among America's Children, 2013).

8. NCES, *The Nation's Report Card: 2011 National Assessment of Educational Progress (NAEP)* (Washington, DC: U.S. Department of Education, 2011).

9. Educational Testing Service, *"Parsing the Achievement Gap: Baselines for Tracking Progress* (Princeton, NJ: Educational Testing Service, 2003), http://www.ets.org/Media/Education_Topics/pdf/parsing.pdf.

10. McKinsey and Company, *The Economic Impact of the Achievement Gap in America's Schools: Summary of Findings*, April 2009, http://mckinseyonsociety.com/the-economic-impact-of-the-achievement-gap-in-americas-schools/.

11. Montgomery County Public Schools, "Local School Walk Throughs" (paper delivered at the National Staff Development Corporation Conference, Washington, DC, July 2006).

12. "Teacher Quality," *Education Week,* August 2004 and July 2011; Daniel Fallon (Carnegie Corporation), "Testimony before House Subcommittee on Higher Education, Lifelong Learning, and Competitiveness, May 2007," *Philanthropy News Digest,* May 21, 2007.

13. Linda Darling-Hammond and John Bransford, eds., *Preparing Teachers for a Changing World: What Teachers Should Learn and Be Able to Do* (San Francisco: Jossey-Bass, 2005).

14. Harold Kwalwasser, *Renewal: Remaking America's Schools for the Twenty-first Century* (Lanham, MD: Rowan & Littlefield Education, 2012); David Kirp, *Improbable Scholars: The Rebirth of a Great American School System and a Strategy for America's Schools* (New York: Oxford University Press, 2013).

Chapter 8

This chapter draws extensively from the introductory chapter in Greg J. Duncan and Richard J. Murnane, eds., *Whither Opportunity? Rising Inequality, Schools, and*

Children's Life Chances (New York: Russell Sage Foundation and Spencer Foundation, 2011). We thank the Russell Sage Foundation and the Spencer Foundation for supporting the book project and allowing us to summarize the lessons from the book here.

1. Claudia D. Goldin and Lawrence F. Katz, *The Race between Education and Technology* (Cambridge, MA: Belknap Press of Harvard University Press, 2008), 488.

2. Duncan and Murnane, *Whither Opportunity?*

3. These income figures are in 2012 dollars, drawn from the Current Population Survey and described in Greg J. Duncan and Richard J. Murnane, *Restoring Opportunity: The Crisis of Inequality and the Challenge for American Education* (Cambridge, MA: Harvard Education Press and the Russell Sage Foundation, 2014). We are grateful to Sean Reardon and Demetra Kalogrides for supplying these data.

4. Sean F. Reardon, "The Widening Academic Achievement Gap between the Rich and the Poor: New Evidence and Possible Explanations," in Duncan and Murnane, *Whither Opportunity?* 91–116.

5. Katherine A. Magnuson and Jane Waldfogel, *Steady Gains and Stalled Progress: Inequality and the Black-White Test Score Gap* (New York: Russell Sage Foundation, 2008), 355.

6. James J. Heckman and Alan B. Krueger, *Inequality in America: What Role for Human Capital Policies?* (Cambridge MA: Massachusetts Institute of Technology Press, 2005).

7. Duncan and Murnane, *Whither Opportunity?* and *Restoring Opportunity*.

8. For evidence on trends in residential segregation by income, see Paul A. Jargowsky, *Poverty and Place: Ghettos, Barrios, and the American City* (New York: Russell Sage Foundation, 1997), 288. Sean F. Reardon and Kendra Bischoff, "Income Inequality and Income Segregation," *American Journal of Sociology* 116, no. 4 (2011): 1092–1153; Tara Watson, "Inequality and the Measurement of Residential Segregation by Income in American Neighborhoods," *Review of Income and Wealth* 55, no. 3 (2009): 820–844.

9. Greg J. Duncan and Katherine Magnuson, "The Nature and Impact of Early Achievement Skills, Attention Skills, and Behavior Problems," in Duncan and Murnane, *Whither Opportunity?* 47–70.

10. All dollar amounts are inflated to 2012 price levels. We are very grateful to Sabino Kornich of the Center for the Advanced Studies in the Social Sciences at the Juan March Institute in Madrid for providing these data.

11. Neeraj Kaushal, Katherine Magnuson, and Jane Waldfogel, "How Is Family Income Related to Investments in Children's Learning?" in Duncan and Murnane, *Whither Opportunity?* 187–206.

12. Catherine Snow, *Reading for Understanding: Toward a Research and Development Program in Reading Comprehension* (Santa Monica, CA: Rand Corporation, 2002), http://www.rand.org/content/dam/rand/pubs/monograph_reports/2005/MR1465.pdf.

13. Betty Hart and Todd R. Risley, *Meaningful Differences in the Everyday Experience of Young American Children* (Baltimore: P. H. Brookes, 1995).

14. Rebecca A. Maynard, "The Effects of the Rural Income Maintenance Experiment on the School Performance of Children," *American Economic Review* 67, no. 1 (1977): 370–375; Rebecca A. Maynard and Richard J. Murnane, "The Effects of a Negative Income Tax on School Performance: Result of an Experiment," *Journal of Human Resources* 14, no. 4 (1979): 463–476.; Ibid.

15. Gordon B. Dahl and Lance Lochner, "The Impact of Family Income on Child Achievement: Evidence from the Earned Income Tax Credit," *American Economic Review* 102, no. 5 (2012): 1927–1956.

16. Kevin Milligan and Mark Stabile, "Do Child Tax Benefits Affect the Well-Being of Children? Evidence from Canadian Child Benefit Expansions," *American Economic Journal: Economic Policy* 3, no. 3 (2011): 175–205.

17. Joseph G. Altonji and Richard Mansfield, "The Role of Family, School and Community Characteristics in Inequality in Education and Labor Market Outcomes," in Duncan and Murnane, *Whither Opportunity?* 339–358.

18. Ibid.

19. Stephen W. Raudenbush, Marshall Jean, and Emily Art, "Year-by-Year and Cumulative Impacts of Attending a High-Mobility Elementary School on Children's Mathematics Achievement in Chicago, 1995–2005," in ibid., 359–376.

20. Donald Boyd et al., "The Effect of School Neighborhoods on Teachers' Career Decisions," in ibid., 377–396.

21. David S. Kirk and Robert J. Sampson, "Crime and the Production of Safe Schools," in ibid., 397–418.

22. Amy Ellen Schwartz and Leanna Stiefel, "Immigrants and Inequality in Public Schools," in ibid., 419–442.

23. Duncan and Murnane, *Restoring Opportunity.*

Chapter 9

The author wishes to thank Larry Aber, Jay Belsky, Ken Dodge, Jill Duerr-Berrick, Greg Duncan, Peter Edelman, Tara Ford, David Grusky, Frank Levy, Emily Putnam-Hornstein, Ross Thompson, Jane Waldfogel, Hiro Yoshikawa, and Charles Zeanah for their comments on earlier versions and Nisha Kashyap for invaluable research assistance.

1. Jack Shonkoff and Deborah Phillips, eds., *From Neurons to Neighborhoods: The Science of Early Childhood Development* (Washington, DC: National Academy Press, 2000).

2. There also have been various efforts at improving highly disadvantaged neighborhoods, although improving outcomes for children has not been the direct focus of most of these efforts. The federal government is now supporting a set of new place-based initiatives focused on improving outcomes for children modeled on the heralded Harlem Children's Zone. See U.S. Department of Education, "Promise Neighborhoods," www.ed.gov/programs/promiseneighborhoods.

3. One purpose of these other approaches, especially efforts to increase family income, is to facilitate better parenting; but there has been little investment in directly improving parenting.

4. Some state laws include emotional abuse and educational neglect, but only a small number of CPS cases involve these issues.

5. See Jane Waldfogel, "Child Protection and Child Welfare: Meeting the Needs of Vulnerable Children," chap. 10 this volume.

6. This includes only substantiated reports. See Christopher Wildeman et al., "The Prevalence of Confirmed Maltreatment among American Children, 2004–2011," *JAMA Pediatrics* (forthcoming); Emily Putnam-Hornstein, Barabara Needell, Bryn King, and Michelle Johnson-Motoyama, "Racial and Ethnic Disparities: A Population-Based Examination of Risk Factors for Involvement with Child Protective Services," *Child Abuse and Neglect* 37, no. 1 (2013): 33–46.

7. Carolyn Ratcliffe and Signe-Mary McKernan, "Child Poverty and Its Lasting Consequence" (Low-Income Working Families Paper 21, Urban Institute, Washington DC, 2012), 17–18.

8. Isabell Sawhill, Scott Winship, and Kerry Grannis, "Pathways to the Middle Class: Balancing Personal and Public Responsibilities" (working paper, Brookings Institution, Washington, DC, 2012).

9. Sean Reardon, "The Widening Socioeconomic Status Achievement Gap: New Evidence and Possible Explanations," in *Whither Opportunity? Rising Inequality, Schools, and Children's Life Chances*, ed. Greg Duncan and Richard Murname (New York: Russell Sage Foundation, 2011), 91–116; Pew Charitable Trusts, "Pursuing the American Dream: Economic Mobility Across Generations" (working paper, Pew Economic Mobility Project, Philadelphia, 2012).

10. Michael S. Wald and Tia Martinez, "Connected by 25: Improving the Life Chances of the Country's Most Vulnerable 14–25 Year Olds" (working paper, William and Flora Hewlett Foundation, Menlo Park, CA, 2003).

11. Emily Putnam-Hornstein et al., "A Population-Level and Prospective Study of Intergenerational Maltreatment," *Pediatrics* (forthcoming); National Research Council and Institute of Medicine, *Depression in Parents, Parenting, and Children: Opportunities to Improve Identification, Treatment, and Prevention* (Washington, DC: National Academies Press, 2009); Barbara Fiese and Marcia Winter, "The Dynamics of Family Chaos and Its Relation to Children's Socio-Emotional Well-Being," in *Chaos and Its Influence on Children's Development*, ed. Gary W. Evans and Theodore D. Wachs (Washington, DC: American Psychological Association, 2010), 49–66.

12. See Eric Dearing, "The State of Research on Children and Families in Poverty: Past, Present, and Future Empirical Avenues of Promise," chap. 14 this volume; Susan Mayer, "Revisiting an Old Question: How Much Does Parental Income Affect Child Outcomes?" *Focus* 27, no. 2 (2010): 21–26; Patrick Sharkey, *Stuck in Place* (Chicago: University of Chicago Press, 2013).

13. For example, over the past twenty years, teen births and juvenile crime have declined dramatically, and high school graduation rates have been rising since 2000, indicating that other investments are having payoffs.

14. Jane Waldfogel and Elizabeth Washbrook, "Early Years Policy," *Child Development Research* (2011): 9–12; James Heckman, "Role of Income and Family Influences on Child Outcomes," *Annals of the New York Academy of Sciences* 1136 (2008): 307–323.

15. Greg J. Duncan and Kathryn Magnuson, "Individual and Parent-Based Strategies for Promoting Human Capital and Positive Behavior," in *Human Development Across Lives and Generations: The Potential for Change,* ed. P. Lindsay Chase-Lansdale, Kathleen Kiernan, and Ruth Friedman (Cambridge, UK: Cambridge University, 2004), 93–138.

16. It is not possible to determine very precisely the percentage of children that will experience highly inadequate parenting over an extended period during their childhoods; no longitudinal studies track this. For a fuller discussion of how I define highly inadequate parenting and reach this estimated percentage, see Michael S. Wald, "Beyond Maltreatment: Developing Support for Children in Multi-Problem Families," in *Handbook on Child Maltreatment,* ed. Jill Korbin and Richard Krugman (Dordrecht, Germany: Springer, 2014), 251–280.

17. U.S. Department of Health and Human Services, Administration on Children, Youth, and Families, *Child Maltreatment 2011,* 2013, http://www.acf.hhs.gov/programs/cb/stats_research/index.htm#can.

18. Wildeman et al., "The Prevalence of Confirmed Maltreatment among American Children," n6.

19. Putnam-Hornstein et al. find much lower rates, 11 percent, for children born to low-income immigrant Hispanics Putnam-Hornstein , "Racial and Ethnic Disparities," 38n5. See also William Sabol, Claudia Colton, and Engel Polousky, "Measuring Child Maltreatment Risk in Communities: A Life Table Approach," *Child Abuse and Neglect* 28, no. 9 (2004): 967–983.

20. National Research Council and Institute of Medicine, *New Directions in Child Abuse and Neglect Research* (Washington, DC: National Academies Press, 2013); James Mersky and James Topitzes, "Comparing Early Adult Outcomes of Maltreated and Non-Maltreated Children: A Prospective Longitudinal Investigation," *Children and Youth Services Review* 32, no. 8 (2010): 1086–1096; Paul Kohl, Melissa Jonson-Reid, and Brett Drake, "Time to Leave Substantiation Behind," *Child Maltreatment* 14, no.1 (2009): 17–26.

21. Shonkoff and Phillips, *From Neurons to Neighborhoods,* 26.

22. Andrea Sedlak et al., "Fourth National Incidence Study of Child Abuse and Neglect (NIS-4)" (report to Congress, Department of Health and Human Services, Administration for Children and Families, Washington, DC, 2010).

23. See behaviors described in Fiese and Winter, "Dynamics of Family Chaos," 55–56; Alan Sroufe et al., *The Development of the Person* (New York: Guilford Press, 2005);

Alicia Lieberman and Patricia Van Horn, *Psychotherapy with Infants and Young Children* (New York: Guilford Press, 2008).

24. See Wald, "Beyond Maltreatment," 263–266.

25. Institute of Medicine and National Research Council, *Child Maltreatment Research, Policy, and Practice for the Next Decade* (Washington, DC: National Academies Press, 2012).

26. Ibid., 69.

27. Robert Hughes et al., "Issues in Differential Response," *Research on Social Welfare Practice* (2012): 1–28

28. David Olds et al., "Effects of Nurse Home Visiting on Maternal and Child Functioning: Age-9 Follow-Up of a Randomized Trial," *Pediatrics* 120, no. 4 (2007): 832–845; Diane Paulsell et al., "Home Visiting Evidence of Effectiveness Review" (executive summary, U.S. Department of Health and Human Services, Administration for Children and Families, Office of Planning, Research and Evaluation, Washington, DC, 2010).

29. There also are a number of programs designed primarily to help parents promote children's cognitive development.

30. Ron Prinz et al., "Population-Based Prevention of Child Maltreatment: The U.S. Triple P System Population Trial," *Prevention Science,* January 22, 2009, doi: 10.1007/s11121-009-0123-3; Carolyn Webster-Stratton, *The Incredible Years: A Training Series for the Prevention and Treatment of Conduct Problems in Young Children* (Seattle: The Incredible Years, 2005).

31. Elizabeth Bartholet, "Creating a Child-Friendly Child Welfare System: Effective Early Intervention to Prevent Maltreatment and Protect Victimized Children," *Buffalo Law Review* 60 (2012): 1315–1365; James Dwyer, "The Child Protection Pretense: States' Continued Consignment of Newborn Babies to Unfit Parents," *Minnesota Law Review* 93 (2008): 407–492.

32. U.S. Department of Health and Human Services, "Child Maltreatment 2011," 21.

33. Michael S. Wald, "Preventing Maltreatment or Promoting Positive Development— Where Should a Community Focus Its Resources?" in *Preventing Child Maltreatment: Community Approaches*, ed. Ken A. Dodge and Denise L. Coleman (New York: Guilford Press, 2009): 182–195.

34. Many of the issues regarding children over five are similar, but the types of systems needed to serve children ages 5–12 and teens have received little attention (except for teens in foster care) and are not covered here. There are some current efforts to put together comprehensive approaches. See, for example, Ken Dodge et al., "The Durham Family Initiative: A Preventive System of Care," *Child Welfare* 83, no. 2 (2004): 109–128.

35. These are described in Wald, "Beyond Maltreatment," 271–273.

36. WIC is already means-tested.

37. The Pew Charitable Trusts are working with a number of states on system improvement; see http://www.pewtrusts.org/our_work_detail.aspx?id=922.

38. This could be done using both risk assessment instruments and observations. While the initial assessment of parenting would be made by home visitors, other professionals working with children, including pediatricians and child care providers, also would be responsible for identifying parents needing greater support in parenting than they might be seeking or receiving.

39. The current focus often is solely on the child with the goal of promoting cognitive development. The focus should be on helping parents bond with their children and respond to them in ways that promote self-regulation.

40. Larry Aber et al., "From Birth to 3: A New Prevention Strategy to Improve School Readiness" (working paper, School Reform and Beyond, Center for Advancing Research and Solutions for Society, University of Michigan, Ann Arbor, March 2013); Thomas Dishion et al., "The Family Check-Up with High-Risk Indigent Families: Preventing Problem Behavior by Increasing Parents' Positive Behavior Support in Early Childhood," *Child Development* 79, no. 5 (2008): 1395–1414.

41. Robert Halpern, "Poverty and Early Childhood Parenting: Toward a Framework for Intervention," *American Journal of Orthopsychiatry* 60, no. 1 (1990): 6–18.

42. Dearing, "The State of Research on Children and Families in Poverty."

43. Olivia Golden et al., "Disconnected Mothers and the Well-Being of Children: A Research Report" (working paper, Urban Institute, Washington, DC, 2013).

44. Many states already impose conditions for receiving TANF, such as having children immunized or obtaining regular checkups for children. TANF provides basic support and should not be conditional.

45. James Riccio et al., *Conditional Cash Transfer in New York City* (New York: MDRC, 2013).

46. Olivia Golden and Karina Fortuny, "Improving the Lives of Young Children: Two-Generational Services and Interventions" (working paper, Urban Institute, Washington, DC, 2011); Aspen Institute, "Two Generations, One Future: Moving Parents and Children Beyond Poverty Together," 2012, http://ascend.aspeninstitute.org/resources/two-generations-one-future; C. T. King et al., "The Career/Advance/Pilot Project: Recommended Jobs Strategy for Families Served by the Community Action Project of Tulsa County" (report, Ray Marshall Center for the Study of Human Resources, Lyndon B. Johnson School of Public Affairs, University of Texas at Austin, 2009).

47. Larry Aber and Laura Rawlings, "North-South Knowledge Sharing on Incentive Based Conditional Cash Transfer Programs" (Discussion Paper No. 1101, World Bank, Washington, DC, 2011).

48. Lawrence M. Berger, Christina Paxson, and Jane Waldfogel, "Income and Child Development," *Children and Youth Services Review* 31, no. 9 (2009): 978–989; Jeanne Brooks-Gunn and Lisa Markham, "The Contribution of Parenting to Racial and Ethnic Gaps in School Readiness," *Future of Children* 15, no. 1 (2005): 139–168; Duncan and Magnuson, "Individual and Parent-Based Strategies for Promoting Human Capital and Positive Behavior," 114–120.

49. There currently are experiments testing the effects of home visiting, expanded EHS approaches, preschool for all, and new approaches to delivering neighborhood services. These are summarized at http://www.whitehouse.gov/issues/education/early-childhood; "Promise Neighborhoods," U.S. Department of Education www.ed.gov/programs/promiseneighborhoods.

50. Many of these parents were highly disadvantaged as children; in fact, many were in the child welfare system, which failed to help them. The challenges facing many of these parents also are due, at least in part, to historic and current patterns of discrimination and misguided social policies. See, Sharkey, *Stuck in Place*, 5–7; Wald and Martinez, "Connected by 25," 3. It is likely that somewhat more advantaged children will be the primary beneficiaries of child-focused versus parent-focused policies.

Chapter 10

1. Jane Waldfogel *The Future of Child Protection: Breaking the Cycle of Abuse and Neglect* (Cambridge, MA: Harvard University Press, 1998).

2. U.S. Department of Health and Human Services, Administration on Children, Youth, and Families, *Child Maltreatment 2011* (Washington, DC: Government Printing Office, 2013).

3. Waldfogel, *Future of Child Protection*.

4. Ron Haskins, Fred Wulczyn, and Mary Bruce Webb, "Using High-Quality Research to Improve Child Protection Practice: An Overview," in *Child Protection: Using Research to Improve Policy and Practice,* ed. Ron Haskins, Fred Wulczyn, and Mary Bruce Webb (Washington, DC: Brookings Institution Press, 2007), 1–33.

5. Michael Hurlburt, Richard Barth, Laurel Leslie, John Landsverk, and Julie McRae, "Building on Strengths: Current Status and Opportunities for Improvement of Parent Training for Families in Child Welfare," in Haskins et al., *Child Protection*, 81–106.

6. U.S. Department of Health and Human Services, Administration for Children and Families, "Differential Response to Reports of Child Abuse and Neglect" (issue brief, Child Welfare Information Gateway, 2008), www.childwelfare.gov; Waldfogel, *Future of Child Protection*; Jane Waldfogel, "The Future of Child Protection Revisited," in *Child Welfare Research: Advances for Practice and Policy*, ed. Duncan Lindsey and Aron Shlonsky (New York: Oxford University Press, 2008); Jane Waldfogel, "Differential Response," in *Preventing Child Maltreatment*, ed. Kenneth Dodge and Doriane Lambelet Coleman (New York: Guilford Press, 2009), 139–155.

7. Waldfogel, "Differential Response."

8. Anthony L. Loman and Gary L. Siegel, "Minnesota Alternative Response Evaluation" (final report, Institute of Applied Research, St. Louis, MO, 2004); Anthony L. Loman and Gary L. Siegel, "Alternative Response in Minnesota: Findings of the Program Evaluation," *Protecting Children* 20, nos. 2–3 (2005): 79–92; Anthony L. Loman and Gary L. Siegel, "Extended Follow-Up Study of Minnesota's Family

Assessment Response" (final report, Institute of Applied Research, St. Louis, MO, 2006). See also review in Waldfogel, "Differential Response."

9. Richard Barth, "Preventing Child Abuse and Neglect with Parent Training: Evidence and Opportunities," *Future of Children* 19, no. 2 (2009): 95–118; Jane Waldfogel, "Prevention and the Child Protection System," ibid., 195–210.

10. Barth, "Preventing Child Abuse and Neglect with Parent Training."

11. Waldfogel, *Future of Child Protection.*

12. Ibid.

13. Kimberly Howard and Jeanne Brooks-Gunn, "The Role of Home Visiting Programs in Preventing Child Abuse and Neglect," *Future of Children* 19, no. 2 (2009): 119–146.

14. Ibid.

15. David Thomas et al., *Emerging Practices in the Prevention of Child Abuse and Neglect* (Washington, DC: Department of Health and Human Services, 2004), https://www.childwelfare.gov/preventing/programs/whatworks/report/report.pdf.

16. Lynn A. Karoly et al., *Investing in Our Children: What We Know and Don't Know about the Costs and Benefits of Early Childhood Interventions* (Santa Monica, CA: RAND, 1998).

17. David Thomas et al., *Emerging Practices.*

18. See, for example, Margaret O'Brien Caughy, Janet A. DiPietro, and Donna M. Strobino, "Day-Care Participation as a Protective Factor in the Cognitive Development of Low-Income Children," *Child Development* 65, no. 2 (1994): 457–471; Sylvana Cote et al., "The Role of Maternal Education and Nonmaternal Care Services in the Prevention of Children's Physical Aggression Problems," *Archives of General Psychiatry* 64, no. 11 (2007): 1305–1312; Mary Dozier, Charles Zeanah, and Kristin Bernard, "Infants and Toddlers in Foster Care," *Child Development Perspectives* 7, no. 3 (2013): 166–171. See also reviews by Jane Waldfogel, *What Children Need* (Cambridge, MA: Harvard University Press, 2006); and Christopher Ruhm and Jane Waldfogel, "Long-Term Effects of Early Childhood Care and Education," *Nordic Economic Policy Review* 1 (2012): 23–51.

19. Katherine Magnuson and Jane Waldfogel, "Pre-School Enrollment and Parents' Use of Physical Discipline," *Infant and Child Development* 14, no. 2 (2005): 177–198.

20. U.S. Department of Health and Human Services, Administration for Children and Families, *Head Start Impact Study: First Year Findings* (Washington, DC: U.S. Department of Health and Human Services, 2005), http://www.acf.hhs.gov/programs/opre/hs/impact_study/.

21. John M. Love et al., *Making a Difference in the Lives of Infants and Toddlers and Their Families: The Impacts of Early Head Start. Final Technical Report* (Princeton, NJ: Mathematica Policy Research, 2002).

22. Judith R. Smith and Jeanne Brooks-Gunn, "Correlates and Consequences of Mothers' Harsh Discipline with Young Children," *Archives of Pediatric and Adolescent Medicine* 151 (1997): 777–786; RaeHyuck Lee et al., "Head Start Participation and

Mothers' Use of Spanking: Associations by Child Gender" (working paper, Columbia University, New York, 2013); Magnuson and Waldfogel, "Pre-School Enrollment."

23. Arthur J. Reynolds and D. Robertson, "School-Based Early Intervention and Later Child Maltreatment in the Chicago Longitudinal Study," *Child Development* 74, no. 1 (2003): 3–26.

24. Ron Haskins, Fred Wulczyn, and Mary Bruce Webb, "Using High-Quality Research to Improve Child Protection Practice: An Overview," in Haskins et al., *Child Protection*, 2.

Chapter 11

1. Thomas J. Bernard and Megan C. Kurlychek, *The Cycle of Juvenile Justice* (New York: Oxford University Press, 2010).

2. David S. Tanenhaus, "The Evolution of Juvenile Courts in the Early Twentieth Century: Beyond the Myth of Immaculate Construction," in *A Century of Juvenile Justice*, ed. Margaret K. Rosenheim, Franklin E. Zimring, David S. Tanenhaus, and Bernardine Dohrn (Chicago: University of Chicago Press, 2002), 42–73.

3. See Laurence Steinberg, "Using Scientific Research to Transform Juvenile Justice Policy and Practice: A Modest Success Story and Some Suggestions for the Next Four Decades," chap. 12, this volume.

4. In 1980, in response to judges' frustration, Congress amended JJDPA to allow, under certain circumstances, status offenders to be held in secure confinement for violations of a valid court order. 42 U.S.C. Sec. 223(11).

5. See Steinberg, "Using Scientific Research."

6. This principle is the subtext of Article 40 of the Convention on the Rights of the Child, which was adopted by the United Nations in 1989 and has been ratified by every country in the world except the United States, South Sudan, and Somalia.

7. The Early Periodic Screening, Diagnosis, and Treatment (EPSDT) Program is the child health component of Medicaid. It's required in every state and is designed to improve the health of low-income children by financing appropriate and necessary pediatric services. For information about how EPSDT works with public health, families, managed care organizations, pediatricians, and other health providers, go to http://www.medicaid.gov/Medicaid-CHIP-Program-Information/By-Topics/Benefits/Early-Periodic-Screening-Diagnosis-and-Treatment.html.

8. The Girls Health Screen was created by Leslie Acoca and the National Girls Health and Justice Institute.

9. Dignity in Schools Campaign, "A Model Code on Education and Dignity: Presenting a Human Rights Framework for Schools," http://www.dignityinschools.org/files/DSC_Model_Code.pdf.

10. The history of diversion is discussed thoroughly in the Models for Change Juvenile Diversion Workgroup, "Juvenile Diversion Guidebook," http://www.ncmhjj.com/pdfs/publications/juvdiversionguide0628.pdf.

11. Ibid.; National Center for Mental Health and Juvenile Justice, "Blueprint for Change: A Comprehensive Model for the Identification and Treatment of Youth with Mental Health Needs in Contact with the Juvenile Justice System," http://www.ncmhjj.com/Blueprint/pdfs/Blueprint.pdf.

12. Richard A. Mendel, "Two Decades of JDAI: From Demonstration Project to National Standard," http://www.aecf.org/~/media/Pubs/Initiatives/Juvenile%20Detention%20Alternatives%20Initiative/TwoDecadesofJDAIFromDemonstrationProjectto Nat/JDAI_National_final_10_07_09.pdf.

13. Richard A. Mendel, "The Missouri Model: Reinventing the Practice of Rehabilitating Youthful Offenders," http://www.aecf.org/~/media/Pubs/Initiatives/Juvenile%20 Detention%20Alternatives%20Initiative/MOModel/MO_Fullreport_webfinal.pdf.

14. Texas Public Policy Foundation, "Out for Life: Pathways to More Effective Reentry for Texas Juvenile Offenders," http://www.texaspolicy.com/sites/default/files/documents/2012-01-PP05-OutForLifePathwaysMoreEffectiveReentryforTexas JuvenileOffenders-CEJ-JeanetteMoll.pdf.

15. Martin Guggenheim, "*Graham v. Florida* and a Juvenile's Right to Age Appropriate Sentencing," *Harvard Civil Rights-Civil Liberties Law Review* 47, no 2 (2012): 457–500.

16. Franklin E. Zimring, *An American Travesty: Legal Responses to Adolescent Sex Offending* (Chicago: University of Chicago Press, 2004).

17. Peter W. Greenwood, *Changing Lives: Delinquency Prevention as Crime-Control Policy* (Chicago: University of Chicago Press, 2006).

18. Ibid.

19. The Conservation Company and Juvenile Law Center, *Building Bridges: Strategic Planning and Alternative Financing for System Reform* (Philadelphia: The Conservation Company and Juvenile Law Center, 1994).

Chapter 12

My work in on the topic of adolescent development and juvenile justice was made possible by an extraordinary commitment of generous and long-term support from the John D. and Catherine T. MacArthur Foundation. I am especially indebted to Laurie Garduque, director of Justice Reform at the Foundation, whose commitment to this program of research for the past two decades has been unflinching. Address correspondence to me at the Department of Psychology, Temple University, Philadelphia PA 19122, or by e-mail at laurence.steinberg@temple.edu.

1. Laurence Steinberg, "Adolescent Development and Juvenile Justice," *Annual Review of Clinical Psychology* 5 (2009): 47–73.

2. Elizabeth S. Scott and Laurence Steinberg, *Rethinking Juvenile Justice* (Cambridge, MA: Harvard University Press, 2008).

3. Laurence Steinberg, "The Influence of Neuroscience on U.S. Supreme Court Decisions Involving Adolescents' Criminal Culpability," *Nature Reviews Neuroscience* 14 (2013): 513–518.

4. *Roper v. Simmons*, 543 U.S. (2005), p. 15.
5. Steinberg, "The Influence of Neuroscience."
6. *Graham v. Florida*, 560 U.S. (2010); *Miller v. Alabama,* 567 U.S. (2012).
7. U.S. Supreme Court, "Transcript of Oral Argument in *Roper v. Simmons*," No. 03-633, October 13, 2004, http://www.supremecourtus.gov/oral_arguments/argument_transcripts/03-633.pdf.
8. *Graham v. Florida*, 17.
9. American Psychological Association, "Amicus curiae Brief in *Miller v. Alabama* and *Jackson v. Hobbs,*" http://www.apa.org/about/offices/ogc/amicus/miller-hobbs.aspx.
10. *Miller v. Alabama,* p. 9 (emphasis added).
11. Laurence Steinberg and Elizabeth S. Scott, "Less Guilty by Reason of Adolescence: Developmental Immaturity, Diminished Responsibility, and the Juvenile Death Penalty," *American Psychologist* 58, no. 12 (2003): 1009–1018.
12. Kimberly Larson and Thomas Grisso, *Developing Statutes for Competence to Stand Trial in Juvenile Delinquency Proceedings: A Guide for Lawmakers* (Chicago: MacArthur Foundation, 2011), http://modelsforchange.net/publications/330.
13. Edward P. Mulvey, *Highlights From Pathways to Desistance: A Longitudinal Study of Serious Adolescent Offenders* (Washington, DC: Office of Juvenile Justice and Delinquency Prevention, U.S. Department of Justice, 2011).
14. Peter Greenwood, *Changing Lives* (Chicago: University of Chicago Press, 2007).
15. Ibid.
16. Scott and Steinberg, *Rethinking Juvenile Justice.*
17. Lisa Aspinwall, Teneille Brown, and James Tabery, "The Double-Edged Sword: Does Biomechanism Increase or Decrease Judges' Sentencing of Psychopaths?" *Science* 337, no. 6096 (2012): 846–849; Deena S. Weisberg et al., "The Seductive Allure of Neuroscience Explanations," *Journal of Cognitive Neuroscience* 20, no. 3 (2008): 470–477.
18. Laurence Steinberg, "Should the Science of Adolescent Brain Development Inform Public Policy?" *Issues in Science and Technology* (Spring 2012): 67–78.
19. Eveline Crone and Ronald Dahl, "Understanding Adolescence as a Period of Social-Affective Engagement and Goal Flexibility," *Nature Reviews Neuroscience* 13 (2012): 636–650.
20. Lynn D. Selemon, "A Role for Synaptic Plasticity in the Adolescent Development of Executive Function," *Translational Psychiatry* 3, e238 (2013), doi:10.1038/tp.2013.7.
21. Jill L. Kays, Robin A. Hurley, and Katherine H. Taber, "The Dynamic Brain: Neuroplasticity and Mental Health," *Journal of Clinical Neuropsychiatry and Clinical Neuroscience* 24, no. 4 (2012): 118–124.
22. Benjamin J. Shannon et al., "Premotor Functional Connectivity Predicts Impulsivity In Juvenile Offenders," *Proceedings of the National Academy of Sciences of the United States of America* 108, no. 27 (2011): 11241–11245.
23. Howard N. Snyder and Melissa Sickmund, "Juvenile Offenders and Victims: 2006 National Report" (Office of Juvenile Justice and Delinquency Prevention, U.S. Department of Justice, Washington, DC, 2006).

24. See http://www.wsipp.wa.gov.
25. For example, Alison Evans Cuellar, Larkin McReynolds, and Gail Wasserman, "A Cure for Crime: Can Mental Health Treatment Diversion Reduce Crime Among Youth?" *Journal of Policy Analysis and Management* 25, no. 1 (2006): 197–214; Steven Patrick and Robert Marsh, "Juvenile Diversion: Results of a 3-Year Experimental Study," *Criminal Justice Policy Review* 16, no. 1 (2005): 59–73.
26. Jön Bernburg and Marvin Krohn, "Labeling, Life Chances, and Adult Crime: The Direct and Indirect Effects of Official Intervention in Adolescence on Crime in Early Adulthood," *Criminology* 41, no. 4 (2003): 1287–1318; Spencer De Li, "Legal Sanctions and Youths' Status Achievement: A Longitudinal Study," *Justice Quarterly* 16, no. 2 (1999): 377–401; Randi Hjalmarsson, "Criminal Justice Involvement and High School Completion," *Journal of Urban Economics* 63, no. 2 (2008): 613–630; Gary Sweeten, "Who Will Graduate? Disruption of High School Education by Arrest and Court Involvement," *Justice Quarterly* 23, no. 3 (2006): 462–480.
27. Scott and Steinberg, *Rethinking Juvenile Justice*.
28. John Roman and Jeffrey A. Butts, "The Economics of Juvenile Jurisdiction" (white paper, Urban Institute, Washington, DC, 2005).
29. Philip J. Cook and Jens Ludwig, "Economical Crime Control," in *Controlling Crime: Strategies and Tradeoffs*, ed. Philip J. Cook, Jens Ludwig, and Justin McCrary (Chicago: University of Chicago Press, 2011), 1–39.
30. For example, Elizabeth Drake, "Washington State Juvenile Court Funding: Applying Research in a Public Policy Setting" (report, Washington State Institute for Public Policy, Olympia, 2010).

Chapter 13

1. For details on the method we used to make poverty and income comparisons back to the 1960s and 1970s, see Arloc Sherman, *Official Poverty Measure Masks Gains Made Over the Last 50 Years* (Washington, DC: Center on Budget and Policy Priorities, 2013).
2. The U.S. Census Bureau provides an estimated dollar value for medical care. Although medical care is a crucial benefit for many, the Census Bureau, in its own recent alternative poverty measurement work, does not count medical benefits as income, and neither does this analysis. Many experts have concluded that medical benefits are too dissimilar to cash to treat as income in measuring poverty and regard medical coverage instead as a separate dimension of well-being. A 1995 panel of the National Academy of Sciences, for example, concluded that because medical needs and expenditures vary far more widely among the poor than do needs and expenditures for, say, food and shelter, counting them as cash can lead to some perverse results. The panel also noted that medical needs are not adequately represented in the current poverty line, so including medical benefits as income and comparing them to the current poverty line would not be consistent. Constance F. Citro and Robert T. Michael,

eds., *Measuring Poverty: A New Approach,* National Research Council Committee on National Statistics (Washington, DC: National Academy Press, 1995), 223–231. Following the panel's advice, the Census Bureau currently addresses medical budgeting in a number of its alternative poverty measures by subtracting a family's out-of-pocket medical expenditures from family resources. However, the data needed for this newer approach are not available back to the 1960s or 1970s.

3. The nine million figure also includes the offsetting effect of federal and state income and payroll taxes, which pushed some families *below* the poverty line. Note that these antipoverty estimates are understated because these benefits are under-counted in the Census Bureau data.

4. Eric Dearing refers to a version of this measure—cash income below half the poverty line—as "extreme poverty." See "The State of Research on Children and Families in Poverty: Past, Present, and Future Empirical Avenues of Promise," chap. 14 this volume.

5. Yonatan Ben-Shalom, Robert A. Moffitt, and John Karl Scholz "An Assessment of the Effectiveness of Anti-Poverty Programs in the United States" (NBER Working Paper 17042, National Bureau of Economic Research, Washington, DC, May 2011), Table 3. The study counts noncash benefits and taxes.

6. H. Luke Shaefer and Kathryn Edin, "Rising Extreme Poverty in the United States and the Response of Federal Means-Tested Transfer Programs" (Ann Arbor, MI: National Poverty Center, May 2013).

7. Anna Gassman-Pines, Hirokazu Yoshikawa, and Sandra Nay, "Can Money Buy You Love? Dynamic Employment Characteristics, the New Hope Project, and Entry into Marriage," in *Making It Work: Low-Wage Employment, Family Life, and Child Development,* ed. Hirokazu Yoshikawa et al. (New York: Russell Sage Foundation, 2006), 212; Lisa Gennetian and Cynthia Miller, *Effects on Children: Final Report on the Minnesota Family Investment Program* (New York: MDRC, 2000), 55–59.

8. Gassman-Pines, Yoshikawa, and Nay, "Can Money Buy You Love?" 209.

9. Cynthia Miller, Virginia Knox, Lisa A. Gennetian et al., *Reforming Welfare and Rewarding Work: Final Report on the Minnesota Family Investment Program* (New York: MDRC, 2000), 171–176.

10. For share in single-parent families, see LIS Cross-National Data Center, "Key Tables," June 13, 2013, http://www.lisdatacenter.org/wp-content/uploads/data-key-inequality-workbook.xlsx. Figures on poverty reduction are calculated from Markus Jäntti and Janet Gornick, "Child Poverty in Comparative Perspective: Assessing the Role of Family Structure and Parental Education and Employment" (Paper No. 570, LIS Cross-National Data Center, Luxembourg, September 2011), Table 4, which shows that poverty rates for children in single-mother families in the UK fall from 78.3 percent when government benefits are not counted to 32.6 percent when government benefits are counted; the comparable decline in the United States is from 62.9 percent to 50.5 percent.

11. Maria Cancian and Deborah Reed, "Changes in Family Structure, Childbearing, and Employment: Implications for the Level and Trend in Poverty" (paper, Institute for Research on Poverty, University of Wisconsin–Madison, April 2008), Table 3, http://gatton.uky.edu/Faculty/Ziliak/Cancian_Reed_2008_final.pdf; Lawrence Mishel, Josh Bivens, Elise Gould, and Heidi Shierholz, *The State of Working America,* 12th ed., Economic Policy Institute (Ithaca, NY: Cornell University Press, 2012), 440–444, http://stateofworkingamerica.org; Maria Cancian and Deborah Reed, "Family Structure, Childbearing, and Parental Employment: Implications for the Level and Trend in Poverty," in *Changing Poverty, Changing Policies,* ed. Maria Cancian and Sheldon Danziger (New York: Russell Sage Foundation, 2009), 109–111.

12. Dottie Rosenbaum, "The Relationship between SNAP and Work among Low-Income Households" (paper, Center on Budget and Policy Priorities, Washington, DC, 2013).

13. Ben-Shalom, Moffitt, and Scholz, "An Assessment of the Effectiveness of Anti-Poverty Programs in the United States," Table 2.

14. Jäntti and Gornick, "Child Poverty in Comparative Perspective."

15. Gordon Dahl and Lance Lochner, "The Impact of Family Income on Child Achievement: Evidence from the Earned Income Tax Credit," *American Economic Review* 102, no. 5 (2012): 1927–1956.

16. Raj Chetty, John N. Friedman, and Jonah Rockoff, "New Evidence on the Long-Term Impacts of Tax Credits" (Statistics of Income Paper Series, Internal Revenue Service, Washington, DC, November 2011).

17. Gordon L. Berlin, "Remarks at National Summit on America's Children" (MDRC, New York, May 22, 2007).

18. Hilary Hoynes, Diane Whitmore Schanzenbach, and Douglas Almond, "Long Run Impacts of Childhood Access to the Safety Net" (NBER Working Paper 18535, National Bureau of Economic Research, Cambridge, MA, 2012).

19. Leighton Ku and Matthew Broaddus, "Public and Private Insurance: Stacking up the Costs," *Health Affairs,* June 24, 2008, http://content.healthaffairs.org/content/27/4/w318.abstract. See also Teresa Coughlin, et al., "What Difference Does Medicaid Make? Assessing Cost Effectiveness, Access and Financial Protection under Medicaid for Low-Income Adults" (research report, Urban Institute, Washington, DC, May 2013).

20. Gene Falk, *The Temporary Assistance for Needy Families (TANF) Block Grant: A Primer on TANF Financing and Federal Requirements* (Washington, DC: Congressional Research Service, 2013), http://www.fas.org/sgp/crs/misc/RL32748.pdf.

21. Neil Ridley and Elizabeth Kenefick, "Research Shows the Effectiveness of Workforce Programs," Center for Law and Social Policy, 2011, http://www.clasp.org/admin/site/publications/files/workforce-effectiveness.pdf.

22. Harry J. Holzer, "Raising Job Quality and Skills for American Workers: Creating More-Effective Education and Workforce Development Systems in the States" (Hamilton Project Discussion Paper 2011-10, Brookings Institution, Washington, DC, November 2011).

23. Linda Giannarelli, Joyce Morton, and Laura Wheaton, "Estimating the Anti-Poverty Effects of Changes in Taxes and Benefits with the TRIM3 Microsimulation Model" (research report, Urban Institute, Washington, DC, 2007).

24. Although test score gains from average Head Start programs appear to diminish over time and a continued focus on improving Head Start quality is warranted, David Deming looks over a longer period and finds that children who participated in Head Start measured better than their siblings who did not on an index of young adult outcomes, including high school completion, being out of work and out of school, and poor health. For these long-term outcomes, Deming concludes that Head Start "closes one-third of the gap between children with median and bottom quartile family income." David Deming, "Early Childhood Intervention and Life-Cycle Skill Development: Evidence from Head Start," *American Economic Journal: Applied Economics*, 1, no. 3 (2009): 111–134.

25. Isabel Sawhill and Quentin Karpilow, "Strategies for Assisting Low-Income Families" (paper, Brookings Institution, Washington, DC, June 2013).

26. Center for Law and Social Policy, "Pell Grants Help Keep College Affordable for Millions of Americans," March 2013, http://www.clasp.org/admin/site/documents/files/Overall-Pell-one-pager-FINAL-03-15-13.pdf.

27. Bipartisan Policy Center Housing Commission, *Housing America's Future: New Directions for National Policy* (Washington, DC: Bipartisan Policy Center, 2013), 89.

28. See Robert G. Schwartz, "The Wheel Turns: Recreating a System of Justice for Juveniles," chap. 11 this volume; and Laurence Steinberg, "Using Scientific Research to Transform Juvenile Justice Policy and Practice: A Modest Success Story and Some Suggestions for the Next Four Decades," chap. 12 this volume.

29. Michael Leachman, Inimai M. Chettiar, and Benjamin Geare, "Improving Budget Analysis of State Criminal Justice Reforms: A Strategy for Better Outcomes and Saving Money" (paper, Center on Budget and Policy Priorities and American Civil Liberties Union, Washington, DC, January 2012).

Chapter 14

1. Ron Haskins and Isabel Sawhill, "The Next Generation of Antipoverty Policies: Introducing the Issue," *The Future of Children* 17, no. 2 (2007): 3–16.

2. United Nations Children's Fund (UNICEF), *Child Wellbeing in Rich Countries: A Comparative Overview*, April 2013, http://www.unicef-irc.org/publications/pdf/rc11_eng.pdf.

3. Sean Reardon, "The Widening Academic Achievement Gap between the Rich and the Poor: New Evidence and Possible Explanations," in *Whither Opportunity? Rising Inequality, Schools, and Children's Life Chances*, ed. Greg J. Duncan and Richard J. Murnane (New York: Russell Sage Foundation, 2012), 91–116; Arloc Sherman, Robert Greenstein, and Sharon Parrott, "Policies to Reduce Poverty: Supporting Family Income as an Investment in Children's Futures," chap. 13 this volume; Gopal K. Singh and Michael D. Kogan. "Widening Socioeconomic Disparities in US Child-

hood Mortality, 1969–2000," *American Journal of Public Health* 97, no. 9 (2007): 1658–1665.

4. Kathleen McCartney and Robert Rosenthal, "Effect Size, Practical Importance, and Social Policy for Children," *Child Development* 71, no. 1 (2000): 173–180; Jack P. Shonkoff, "Science, Policy, and Practice: Three Cultures in Search of a Shared Mission," ibid., 181–187.

5. Sherman, Greenstein, and Parrott, "Policies to Reduce Poverty."

6. Eric Dearing, "The Psychological Costs of Growing up Poor," in *Scientific Approaches to Understanding and Reducing Poverty*, ed. S. G. Kaler and O. M. Rennert, special issue, *Annals of the New York Academy of Sciences*, 1136 (2008): 324–332; Gary Evans, "The Environment of Childhood Poverty," *American Psychologist* 59, no. 2 (2004): 77–92.

7. Harry J. Holzer, Diane Whitmore Schanzenbach, Greg J. Duncan, and Jens Ludwig, "The Economic Costs of Childhood Poverty in the United States," *Journal of Children and Poverty* 14, no. 1 (2008): 41–61.

8. Ibid.

9. Evans, "The Environment of Childhood Poverty."

10. Ibid.

11. Kristal Chichlowska et al., "Life Course Socioeconomic Conditions and Metabolic Syndrome in Adults: The Atherosclerosis Risk in Communities (ARIC) Study," *Ann Epidemiol* 19, no. 12 (2009): 875–883; A. Danese and B. S. McEwen, "Adverse Childhood Experiences, Allostasis, Allostatic Load, and Age-Related Disease," *Physiological Behavior* 106, no. 1 (2012): 29–39.

12. Gary Evans and Michelle Schamberg, "Childhood Poverty, Chronic Stress, and Adult Working Memory," *Proceedings of the National Academy of Sciences of the United States of America* 106, no. 16 (2009): 6545–6549; Charles Nelson III and Margaret Sheridan, "Lessons from Neuroscience Research for Understanding Causal Links between Family and Neighborhood Characteristics and Educational Outcomes," in Duncan and Murnane, *Whither Opportunity?* 27–46.

13. Ann Locke, Jane Ginsborg, and Ian Peers, "Development and Disadvantage: Implications for the Early Years and Beyond," *International Journal of Language and Communication Disorders* 37, no. 1 (2002): 3–15; Gloria Simpson, Lisa Colpe, and Stanley Greenspan, "Measuring Functional Developmental Delay in Infants and Young Children: Prevalence Rates from the NHIS-D," *Pediatric and Perinatal Epidemiology* 17, no. 1 (2003): 68–80.

14. Neeraj Kaushal, Katherine Magnuson, and Jane Waldfogel, "How Is Family Income Related to Investments in Children's Learning," in Duncan and Murnane, *Whither Opportunity?* 187–206; Reardon, "The Widening Academic Achievement Gap."

15. B. Taylor, E. Dearing, and K. McCartney, "Incomes and Outcomes in Early Childhood," *Journal of Human Resources* 39, no. 4 (2004): 980–1007; Elizabeth Votruba-Drzal, "Economic Disparities in Middle Childhood Development: Does Income Matter?" *Developmental Psychology* 42, no. 6 (2006): 1154–1167.

16. Reardon, "The Widening Academic Achievement Gap."
17. Greg J. Duncan, W. Jean Yeung, Jeanne Brooks-Gunn, and Judith Smith, "How Much Does Childhood Poverty Affect the Life Chances of Children?" *American Sociological Review* 64 (June 1998): 406–423.
18. National Institute of Child Health and Human Development Early Child Care Research Network, "Duration and Developmental Timing of Poverty and Children's Cognitive and Social Development from Birth Through Third Grade," *Child Development* 76, no. 4 (2005): 795–810.
19. Ibid.
20. Erick Dearing and Beck A. Taylor, "Home Improvements: Within-Family Associations Between Income and the Quality of Children's Home Environments," *Journal of Applied Developmental Psychology* 28, nos. 5 & 6 (2007): 427–444; Evans, "The Environment of Childhood Poverty."
21. Katherine A. Magnuson, Marcia K. Meyers, Christopher J. Ruhm, and Jane Waldfogel, "Inequality in Preschool Education and School Readiness," *American Educational Research Journal* 41, no. 1 (2004): 115–157; Robert C. Pianta et al., "The Relation of Kindergarten Classroom Environment to Teacher, Family, and School Characteristics and Child Outcomes," *The Elementary School Journal* 102, no. 3 (2002): 225–238.
22. Eric Dearing et al., "Do Neighborhood and Home Contexts Help Explain Why Low-Income Children Miss Opportunities to Participate in Activities Outside of School?" *Developmental Psychology* 45, no. 6 (2009): 1545–1562.
23. Beck Taylor, Eric Dearing, and Kathleen McCartney, "Incomes and Outcomes in Early Childhood," *Journal of Human Resources* 39, no. 4 (2004): 980–1007; Votruba-Drzal, "Economic Disparities in Middle Childhood Development."
24. E. Jane Costello et al., "Psychiatric Disorders among American Indian and White Youth in Appalachia: The Great Smoky Mountains Study," *American Journal of Public Health* 87, no. 5 (1997): 827–832.
25. Susan Campbell et al., "Predictors and Sequelae of Trajectories of Physical Aggression in School-Age Boys and Girls," *Development and Psychopathology* 22, no. 1 (2010): 133–150.
26. Glen Elder Jr. and Avshalom Caspi, "Economic Stress in Lives: Developmental Perspectives," *Journal of Social Issues* 44, no. 4 (1988): 25–45.
27. K. N. Thompson et al., "Stress and HPA-Axis Functioning in Young People at Ultra High Risk for Psychosis," *Journal of Psychiatric Research* 41, no. 7 (2007): 561–569.
28. Gary W. Evans and Pilyoung Kim, "Childhood Poverty and Health: Cumulative Risk Exposure and Stress Dysregulation," *Psychological Science* 18, no. 11 (2007): 953–957; Jack P. Shonkoff, "A Healthy Start Before and After Birth: Applying the Biology of Adversity to Build the Capabilities of Caregivers," chap. 2 this volume.
29. Rand E. Conger et al., "Economic Pressure in African American Families: A Replication and Extension of the Family Stress Model," *Developmental Psychology* 38, no. 2 (2002): 179–193.

30. Jim Cummins, "Pedagogies for the Poor? Realigning Reading Instruction for Low-Income Students with Scientifically Based Reading Research," *Educational Researcher* 36, no. 9 (2007): 564–572; Robert C. Pianta et al., "The Relation of Kindergarten Classroom Environment to Teacher, Family, and School Characteristics and Child Outcomes," *The Elementary School Journal* 102, no. 3 (2002): 225–238.

31. Evans, "The Environment of Childhood Poverty."

32. Tama Leventhal and Jeanne Brooks-Gunn, "The Neighborhoods They Live in: The Effects of Neighborhood Residence on Child and Adolescent Outcomes," *Psychological Bulletin* 126, no. 2 (2000): 309–337.

33. Greg J. Duncan and Katherine Magnuson, "Off with Hollingshead: Socioeconomic Resources, Parenting, and Child Development," in *Socioeconomic Status, Parenting, and Child Development*, ed. Marc H. Bornstein and Robert H. Bradley (Mahwah, NJ: Lawrence Erlbaum, 2001), 10.

34. E. Jane Costello, Scott N. Compton, Gordon Keeler, and Adrian Angold, "Relationships Between Poverty and Psychopathology: A Natural Experiment," *Journal of the American Medical Association* 290, no. 15 (2003): 2023–2029; Eric Dearing, Kathleen McCartney, and Beck A. Taylor, "Within-Child Associations Between Family Income and Externalizing and Internalizing Problems," *Developmental Psychology* 42, no. 2 (2006): 237–252; Greg J. Duncan, Pamela A. Morris, and Chris Rodrigues, "Does Money Really Matter? Estimating Impacts of Family Income on Young Children's Achievement with Data from Random-Assignment Experiments," ibid., 47, no. 5 (2011): 1263–1279.

35. Deborah A. Phillips, "The Foundation for Child Development Young Scholars Program: A Review," paper presented at the Migration Policy Institute, Washington DC, February 7, 2013.

36. Donald J. Hernandez and Jeffrey S. Napierala, "Diverse Children: Race, Ethnicity, and Immigration in America's New Non-Majority Generation" (report, Disparities Among America's Children, no. 1, Foundation for Child Development, New York, 2013), http://fcd-us.org/sites/default/files/DiverseChildren%20-%20Full%20Report.pdf.

37. Donald J. Hernandez and Jeffrey S. Napierala, "Children in Immigrant Families: Essential to America's Future" (policy brief, Foundation for Child Development Child and Youth Well-Being Index, New York, 2013).

38. Ibid. I use the general term *immigrant children* to refer both to first-generation immigrants and to children of recent immigrants.

39. The paradox is generally most robustly evident among Asian and black immigrant groups but is also evident for Latin immigrants, particularly once controlling for family socioeconomic factors.

40. Robert Crosnoe and Ruth N. López Turley, "K–12 Educational Outcomes of Immigrant Youth," *The Future of Children* 21, no. 1 (2011): 129–152.

41. Ibid.

42. Ibid.; Hirokazu Yoshikawa, *Immigrants Raising Citizens: Undocumented Parents and Their Young Children* (New York: Russell Sage Foundation, 2011).

43. Hirokazu Yoshikawa et al., "Racial/Ethnic Differences in Effects of Welfare Policies on Early School Readiness and Later Achievement," *Applied Developmental Science* 14, no. 3 (2010): 137–153.

44. Participants who received education-first treatments were compared with control participants whose families received welfare benefits without education requirements and time limits according to Aid to Families with Dependent Children rules prior to 1996 welfare reforms.

45. C. Cybele Raver, Elizabeth T. Gershoff, and J. Lawrence Aber, "Testing Equivalence of Mediating Models of Income, Parenting, and School Readiness for White, Black, and Hispanic Children in a National Sample," *Child Development* 78, no. 1 (2007): 96–115.

46. Yoshikawa et al., "Racial/Ethnic Differences."

47. Mariana Chilton et al., "Food Insecurity and Risk of Poor Health among US-Born Children of Immigrants," *American Journal of Public Health* 99, no. 3 (2009): 556–562.

48. Ibid.

49. Tiffany Yip, Gilbert C. Gee, and David T. Takeuchi, "Racial Discrimination and Psychological Distress: The Impact of Ethnic Identity and Age among Immigrant and United States–Born Asian Adults," *Developmental Psychology* 44, no. 3 (2008): 787–800.

50. Lyn Y. Abramson, Martin E. Seligman, and John D. Teasdale, "Learned Helplessness in Humans: Critique and Reformulation," *Journal of Abnormal Pyschology* 87, no. 1 (1978): 49–74.

51. George J. Borjas, "Making It in America: Social Mobility in the Immigrant Population" *The Future of Children* 16, no. 2 (2006): 55–71.

52. Paolo Brunori, Francisco H. G. Ferreira, and Vito Peragine, "Inequality of Opportunity, Income Inequality and Economic Mobility: Some International Comparisons" (Policy Research Working Paper No. 6304, World Bank, New York, January, 2013); Stephen P. Jenkins and Philippe van Kerm, "Trends in Income Inequality, Pro-Poor Income Growth and Income Mobility," *Oxford Economics Papers* 58, no. 3 (2006): 531–548; Linda Levine, "The U.S. Income Distribution and Mobility: Trends and International Comparisons" (report, Congressional Research Service, November 2012); UNICEF, "Measuring Child Poverty: New League Tables in the World's Rich Countries" (Innocenti Report Card 10, UNICEF Innocenti Research Centre, Florence, Italy, 2012).

53. UNICEF, "Measuring Child Poverty."

54. Shonkoff, "A Healthy Start Before and After Birth."

55. Clancy Blair et al., "Salivary Cortisol Mediates Effects of Poverty and Parenting on Executive Functions in Early Childhood," *Child Development* 82, no. 6 (2011): 1970–1984.

56. Clancy Blair et al., "Cumulative Effects of Early Poverty on Cortisol in Young Children: Moderation by Autonomic Nervous System Activity," *Psychoneuroendocrinology* 38, no. 11 (2013), http://www.sciencedirect.com/science/article/pii/S0306453013002424.

57. Daniel Berry et al., "Child Care and Cortisol Across Early Childhood: Context Matters," *Developmental Psychology,* 2013, http://www.ncbi.nlm.nih.gov/pubmed/23772818; Blair et al., "Cumulative Effects."

58. Clancy Blair et al., "Maternal and Child Contributions to Cortisol Response to Emotional Arousal in Young Children from Low-Income, Rural Communities," *Developmental Psychology* 44, no. 4 (2008): 1095–1109.

59. Clancy Blair et al., "Salivary Cortisol Mediates Effects."

60. Thomas J. Dishion et al., "The Family Check-Up with High-Risk Indigent Families: Preventing Problem Behavior by Increasing Parents' Positive Behavior Support in Early Childhood," *Child Development* 79, no. 5 (2008):1395–1414; Susan H. Landry et al., "A Responsive Parenting Intervention: The Optimal Timing Across Early Childhood for Impacting Maternal Behaviors and Child Outcomes," *Developmental Psychology* 44, no. 5 (2008): 1335–1353.

61. Mary Dozier et al., "Effects of an Attachment-Based Intervention on the Cortisol Production of Infants and Toddlers in Foster Care," *Development and Psychopathology* 20, no. 3 (2008): 845–859.

62. Mary E. Walsh et al., "A New Model for Student Support in High-Poverty Urban Elementary Schools: Effects on Elementary and Middle School Academic Outcomes" (manuscript under review). http://www.bc.edu/schools/lsoe/cityconnects/.

63. Ibid.

64. Eric Dearing and Mary Walsh, "Can a Student Support Intervention Improve the Achievement of Immigrant Children in High-Poverty Elementary Schools?" (paper, Society for Research in Child Development, Seattle, April 19, 2013).

65. Reardon, "The Widening Academic Achievement Gap."

Acknowledgments

Marion Wright Edelman was the inspiration for this project. Our goal was ambitious—to produce a volume that would serve as a road map for child and family policy activists, just as the *Harvard Educational Review* special issue on the rights of children, which effectively launched the Children's Defense Fund, did more than forty years ago. As we edited the chapters, we were continuously inspired by the legacy and the continued power and relevance of the Children's Defense Fund. We are grateful to the entire team at the Children's Defense Fund, especially MaryLee Allen and Patti Hassler, for their wise counsel as we moved from book concept to final product.

Second, we acknowledge the distinguished slate of authors whose chapters offer important new directions in education practice, policy, and research. The result of their efforts is a compilation of singular voices united in their passion for child and family advocacy.

We also thank our colleagues and friends at the Harvard Education Publishing Group, especially Douglas Clayton and Christopher Leonesio. Their dedication to this project was evident in their astute editorial suggestions as well as their never-ending patience.

While editing this volume, we reflected often on the pioneering work of the prescient academics who inspired the field of child and family policy: Bettye Caldwell, Edmund Gordon, Jane Knitzer, Julius Richmond, Sandra Scarr, Sheldon White, and Edward Zigler.

Finally, we acknowledge the support of our partners—Bill Hagen, Stuart Freeman, and Mark Paskowsky—who understood that this project was a labor of love, even as we worked nights and weekends.

About the Editors

Kathleen McCartney is the president of Smith College and the former dean of the Harvard Graduate School of Education. She is a developmental psychologist who conducts research on the effects of early childhood education policy and practice, especially for low-income children. She has published more than150 research articles and edited several volumes, including *The Handbook of Early Childhood Development* (Blackwell, 2008). She is a fellow of the American Academy of Arts and Science, the National Academy of Education, and the American Psychological Society.

Hirokazu Yoshikawa is the Courtney Sale Ross University Professor of Globalization and Education at New York University. He conducts research on the effects of policies related to early childhood development, immigration, and poverty reduction on children in high-, middle-, and low-income countries. He is the author of *Immigrants Raising Citizens: Undocumented Parents and their Young Children* (Russell Sage, 2011). He currently serves as co-chair of the UN Sustainable Development Solutions Network workgroup on education; he also serves as a member of the presidentially appointed U.S. National Board for Education Sciences.

Laurie B. Forcier is senior academic projects manager at the Harvard Graduate School of Education. Previously, she was a research associate with the Program for Education and Equity Research in the Education Policy Center of the Urban Institute. She was also a member of the research team for the Congressional Commission for the Advancement of Women and Minorities in Science, Engineering and Technology Development, contributing to its 2000 publication *Land of Plenty: Diversity as America's Competitive Edge in Science, Engineering and Technology* and co-authoring a paper on math and science teacher recruitment for the National Commission on Mathematics and Science Teaching for the 21st Century.

About the Contributors

Eric Dearing is an associate professor in the Lynch School of Education at Boston College and a senior researcher at the Norwegian Center for Child Behavioral Development, University of Oslo. As a developmental psychologist, Dearing studies policy-relevant approaches to promoting the achievement and mental health of children growing up in poverty. In 2011 he received a Young Scholar Award from the Foundation for Child Development to examine the long-term achievement of young immigrant children who received a school-based intervention that connected students in high-poverty schools with enrichment services provided by community agencies. His research has also been funded by the National Institute of Child Health and Human Development, National Institute of Aging, National Science Foundation, Norwegian Research Council, and the Spencer Foundation.

Greg J. Duncan is Distinguished Professor in the School of Education at the University of California, Irvine. He was president of the Society for Research in Child Development between 2009 and 2011 and was elected to the National Academy of Sciences in 2010.

Marian Wright Edelman, president of the Children's Defense Fund, has been an advocate for disadvantaged Americans for her entire professional life. A graduate of Spelman College and Yale Law School, Edelman was the first black woman admitted to the Mississippi Bar, and she directed the NAACP Legal Defense and Educational Fund office in Jackson, MS. She has received more than a hundred honorary degrees and many awards, including the Albert Schweitzer Humanitarian Prize, the Heinz Award, a MacArthur Foundation Prize Fellowship, the Presidential Medal of Freedom (the nation's highest civilian award), and the Robert F. Kennedy Lifetime Achievement Award.

Robert Greenstein is the founder and president of the Center on Budget and Policy Priorities. Previously, he was administrator of the Food and Nutrition Service at the Department of Agriculture, where he directed the agency that operates the food stamp, school lunch, and other nutrition programs and helped design the Food

Stamp Act of 1977. He was awarded the MacArthur Fellowship in 1996, the Heinz Award for Public Policy in 2008, and the American Academy of Political and Social Sciences' Daniel Patrick Moynihan Prize in 2010.

Deborah Jewell-Sherman is the first woman Professor of Practice at the Harvard Graduate School of Education (HGSE). As superintendent of the Richmond (VA) Public Schools from 2002 to 2008, she led the district to exponential increases in student achievement. At HGSE she serves as director of the Urban Superintendents Program, as core faculty in the doctorate of Education Leadership (EdLD) program, and as principal investigator on a collaboration between HGSE and the University of Johannesburg, South Africa. Jewell-Sherman was named the 2009 Virginia Superintendent of the Year and is the 2011 Dr. Effie Jones Humanitarian Award Winner.

Joan Lombardi is the director of Early Opportunities, LLC, and a senior adviser to the Buffett Early Childhood Fund. She served as the first deputy assistant secretary and interagency liaison for early childhood development in the U.S. Department of Health and Human Services (2009–2011), as deputy assistant secretary for policy and external affairs in the Administration for Children and Families, and as the first commissioner of the Child Care Bureau, among other positions (1993–1998). She also served as the founding chair of the Birth to Five Policy Alliance (now the Alliance for Early Success), a group of organizations dedicated to shifting the odds for at-risk children ages 0–8.

Jal Mehta is an associate professor at the Harvard Graduate School of Education. His primary research interest is in understanding what it would take to create high-quality schooling at scale, with a particular interest in the professionalization of teaching. He is the author of *The Allure of Order: High Hopes, Dashed Expectations and the Troubled Quest to Remake American Schooling* (Oxford University Press, 2013) and the co-editor (with Robert B. Schwartz and Frederick M. Hess) of *The Futures of School Reform* (Harvard Education Press, 2012). He is currently working on two projects: *In Search of Deeper Learning*, a contemporary study of schools, systems, and nations that are seeking to produce ambitious instruction; and *The Chastened Dream*, a history of the effort to link social science with social policy to achieve social progress. Mehta received his PhD in sociology and social policy from Harvard University.

George Miller is a Democratic congressman from California who has served in the House since 1975. He was the founding chair of the Select Committee on Children, Youth and Families (1983–1992), chair of the Natural Resources Committee (1992–1994), and chair of the Education and Labor Committee (2007–2010). He now serves as the education committee's senior Democratic member. Miller has a long record of legislative accomplishments in the areas of early childhood education, elementary and secondary education, higher education, and nutritional assistance for low-income children and families.

Richard J. Murnane is the Thompson Professor of Education and Society at the Harvard Graduate School of Education and a research associate at the National Bureau of Economic Research. His research focuses on how computer-based technological change has affected skill demands in the U.S. economy, how increases in family income inequality in the United States have influenced educational opportunities for children from low-income families, and the consequences of policies aimed at improving education. Murnane is the co-editor (with Greg J. Duncan) of *Whither Opportunity? Rising Inequality, Schools, and Children's Life Chances* (Russell Sage, 2011) and the co-author (with Greg J. Duncan) of *Restoring Opportunity: The Crisis of Inequality and the Challenge for American Education* (Harvard Education Press and Russell Sage, 2014).

Sharon Parrott is the vice president for budget policy and economic opportunity at the Center on Budget and Policy Priorities. Her work focuses on federal fiscal issues and how budget decisions affect low- and moderate-income individuals and families. Previously, she was the counselor for human services for Secretary Kathleen Sebelius at the U.S. Department of Health and Human Services.

Sara Rosenbaum is the Harold and Jane Hirsh Professor of Health Law and Policy and founding chair of the Department of Health Policy, George Washington University School of Public Health and Health Services. She has emphasized public engagement as a core element of her professional life. Her career has focused on Medicaid, expanding health care access to medically underserved communities, civil rights in health care, and national health reform. Rosenbaum is the lead author of *Law and the American Health Care System,* 2nd ed. (Foundation Press, 2012), which provides an in-depth exploration of the interaction between law and the U.S. health care system. She is a member of the Institute of Medicine and a commissioner on the Medicaid and CHIP Payment and Access Commission (MACPAC), which advises Congress on federal Medicaid policy.

Robert B. Schwartz is Professor of Practice Emeritus in Educational Policy and Administration at the Harvard Graduate School of Education. He has filled a variety of roles in education, including high school teacher and principal, education policy adviser to Boston mayor Kevin White and Massachusetts governor Michael Dukakis, education program director at The Pew Charitable Trusts, and president of Achieve, Inc. He co-authored (with William C. Symonds and Ronald Ferguson) *Pathways to Prosperity: Meeting the Challenge of Preparing Young Americans for the 21st Century* (Harvard Graduate School of Education, 2011) and now co-leads the Pathways to Prosperity State Network.

Robert G. Schwartz co-founded Juvenile Law Center in 1975 and has been its executive director since 1982. Juvenile Law Center is a national public interest law firm that shapes and uses the law on behalf of adolescents in the child welfare and justice systems to promote fairness, prevent harm, ensure access to appropriate services, and create opportunities for success. In 2000, he co-edited (with Thomas Grisso) *Youth on Trial: A Developmental Perspective on Juvenile Justice* (University of Chicago Press, 2000).

Arloc Sherman is a senior researcher at the Center on Budget and Policy Priorities, where he focuses on family income trends, income support policies, and the causes and consequences of poverty. Previously he worked for the Children's Defense Fund, where he wrote the 1994 Robert F. Kennedy Book Award nominee *Wasting America's Future: The Children's Defense Fund Report on the Cost of Child Poverty* (Beacon Press, 1994).

Jack P. Shonkoff is the Julius B. Richmond FAMRI Professor of Child Health and Development at the Harvard Graduate School of Education and Harvard School of Public Health; professor of pediatrics at Harvard Medical School and Boston Children's Hospital; and director of the university-wide Center on the Developing Child at Harvard University. He chaired the National Academy of Sciences committee that produced the landmark 2000 report *From Neurons to Neighborhoods: The Science of Early Childhood Development*. In 2011, Shonkoff launched Frontiers of Innovation, a community of researchers, practitioners, policy makers, investors, and experts in systems change who are committed to driving science-based innovation that achieves breakthrough impacts on the development and health of young children experiencing adversity.

Laurence Steinberg is the Distinguished University Professor and Laura H. Carnell Professor of Psychology at Temple University. His research has focused on a variety of topics in the study of normative and atypical adolescent development, and he has written extensively on the implications of the science of adolescent development for social and legal policy. He directed the John D. and Catherine T. MacArthur Foundation Research Network on Adolescent and Juvenile Justice. Steinberg is a fellow of the American Psychological Association, the Association for Psychological Science, and the American Academy of Arts and Sciences.

Michael S. Wald is the Jackson Eli Reynolds Professor of Law Emeritus at Stanford University. In addition to his teaching and research on children and families, he has been actively involved in designing and implementing public policies and programs to help children. He acted as the reporter for the American Bar Association's Standards Regarding Child Abuse and Neglect, drafted major federal and state legislation related to child welfare, and served as director of the San Francisco Human Services Agency in 1996–1997 and as deputy general counsel of the U.S. Department of Health and Human Services from 1993 to 1995. He also was a member of the Carnegie Foundation Task Force on Meeting the Needs of Young Children and of the U.S. Advisory Committee on Child Abuse and Neglect.

Jane Waldfogel is the Compton Foundation Centennial Professor at Columbia University School of Social Work and a visiting professor at the Centre for Analysis of Social Exclusion at the London School of Economics. She received her PhD in public policy from the Kennedy School of Government at Harvard University and has written extensively on the impact of public policies on child and family well-being.

Jerry D. Weast, is founder and CEO of the Partnership for Deliberate Excellence, LLC, which provides educational consulting to a national clientele. He served as a school superintendent for thirty-five years. During his twelve-year tenure as superintendent of Montgomery County (MD) Public Schools the district achieved both the highest graduation rate among the nation's largest school districts for four consecutive years and the highest academic performance in its history as the non-English-speaking student population more than doubled and enrollment tipped toward low socioeconomic demographics. Weast is a 2012 recipient of awards from the American Educational Research Association and the Schott Foundation for Public Education. During his tenure as superintendent, Montgomery County Public Schools received the 2010 Malcolm Baldrige National Quality Award.

Partow Zomorrodian is a master's candidate in public health, specializing in health policy, in the Department of Health Policy and Management at the University of California, Los Angeles, Fielding School of Public Health. She completed her undergraduate career at the University of California, Berkeley, where she earned a BA degree in public health and a minor in public policy.

Index